The Political Economy of Protest and Patience

THE POLITICAL ECONOMY OF PROTEST AND PATIENCE

East European and Latin American Transformations Compared

Béla Greskovits

Central European University Press

Published by

Central European University Press
Október 6. utca 12.
H–1051 Budapest
Hungary

© 1998 by Béla Greskovits

Distributed by
Plymbridge Distributors Ltd., Estover Road, Plymouth PL6 7PZ, United Kingdom
Distributed in the United States by
Cornell University Press Services, 750 Cascadilla Street, Ithaca, New York
14851-0250, USA

ISBN 963-9116-14-9 Cloth
ISBN 963-9116-13-0 Paperback

Library of Congress Cataloging in Publication Data
A CIP catalog record for this book is available from the Library of Congress

Printed in Hungary by Akaprint, Budapest

To Halina

Contents

Preface

Despite gloomy predictions, democracy and the market economy seem to be taking root throughout Eastern Europe—and also despite the background of a recession deeper and longer than the Great Depression of the 1930s. How was this possible? Why did Eastern Europeans protest less about the brutal social consequences of systemic change than the people of Latin America had a decade earlier? Why has a regionwide authoritarian or populist turnabout not occurred? Why has democracy in these countries proved to be crisis proof? And in what ways has economic crisis impacted the politics of the region? These are the major questions on which this book focuses. I hope to contribute to widening the horizon of East European transformation studies by drawing upon Latin American comparisons, and vice versa. I also hope to offer interesting reading for instructors and students of comparative political economy wishing to explore the East European experience, as well as for journalists writing on the region.

It took me four years to write this book. From 1993 to 1996 I taught in the Department of Political Science of the Central European University in Budapest; in 1997 I was in the Sociology Department of the CEU in Warsaw. In Budapest I contributed to a departmental research project titled "Transition to What?" Our purpose was the proper conceptualization of the political and economic system that has been emerging in East Central Europe. Generous funding for this project has been provided by the founder of the Central European University, Mr. George Soros.

It was mainly due to the intellectually stimulating atmosphere of the Political Science Department, as well as the interest and assistance of my colleagues, that I was able to conduct my research, raising my questions and gradually developing my answers. Specifically, without the challenge of weekly department seminars where I could present early drafts of various chapters and learn from my colleagues' own findings, writing this book would have been impossible. For their significant intellectual input I am indebted to my colleagues: Andrew Arató, Zoltán Balázs, András Bozóki, András Bragyova, András Bródy, László Bruszt, Iván Csaba, László Csontos, Nenad Dimitrijevic, Zsolt Enyedi, Attila Fölsz, Stefano Guzzini, János Kis, Mihály Laki, Anna Leander, Tamás Meszerics, István Rév, Tamás Rudas, Judit Sándor, Miklós Sükösd, and Gábor Tóka. Important technical assistance came from Gyöngyi Petrák and István

Gergics. In the Sociology Department of the CEU in Warsaw, my efforts to finish the book were supported by Edmund Mokrzycki. Brenda Leahy, my colleague in the department, helped me to correct the language of the English version.

I am also thankful to many Hungarian and foreign social scientists for their useful comments and criticisms on various draft versions of parts of the book. In Hungary such comments were offered by Mária Csanádi, János Köllő, János Kornai, András Kovács, András Köves, Kamilla Lányi, Iván Major, Péter Mihályi, András Nagy, Gábor Oblath, Éva Palócz, Péter Pete, Tamás Réti, Márton Tardos, Ádám Török, Péter Vince, and Éva Voszka.

I am indebted for comments and criticisms in response to various earlier presentations of my views to the following foreign scholars: Leszek Balcerowicz, Margarita Balmaceda, Valerie Bunce, Michel Dobry, Grzegorz Ekiert, Michal Federowicz, Carol Graham, Robert Kaufman, Jan Kubik, Bronislaw Misztal, Edmund Mokrzycki, Joan Nelson, Guillermo O'Donnell, David Ost, Jonas Pontusson, Andrzej Rychard, Hector Schamis, Alexander Smolar, David Stark, Sydney Tarrow, Norman Uphoff, and Lawrence Whitehead. However, all the usual caveats apply.

List of Tables

List of Abbreviations

AFEOSZ	National Federation of General Consumption Cooperatives
BDSZ	Union of Mine Workers
CMEA	Council for Mutual Economic Assistance
CRI	Council for the Reconciliation of Interests
EC	European Community
ÉSZT	Rally of Trade Unions for Intellectual Workers
EU	European Union
HWC	Hungarian Way Circles Movement
IFIs	International Financial Institutions
IMF	International Monetary Fund
IPOSZ	National Federation of Hungarian Industrial Associations—Hungarian Chamber of Artisans
ISI	Import-Substitution Industrialization
KISOSZ	National Organization of Petty Traders
LAÉT	Association of People Living below the Poverty Line
LDCs	Less Developed Countries
LIGA	Democratic League of Independent Trade Unions
MAOSZ	National Federation of Employers
MDF	Hungarian Democratic Forum
MGYOSZ	National Alliance of Hungarian Industrialists
MoP	Ministry of Privatization
MOSZ	National Alliance of Agricultural Producers and Cooperatives
MSZOSZ	National Federation of Hungarian Trade Unions
MSZP	Hungarian Socialist Party
NCRI	National Council for the Reconciliation of Interests
OECD	Organization for Economic Cooperation and Development
POFOSZ	National Alliance of Political Prisoners
PRI	Partido Revolucionario Institucional
SHP	Smallholders Party
SLD	Alliance of the Democratic Left
SOEs	State-Owned Enterprises
SZDSZ	Alliance of Free Democrats
SZEF	Reconciliation Forum of Trade Unions

SZOT	Communist Labor Federation
VAT	Value Added Tax
VOSZ	National Federation of Entrepreneurs

Chapter 1
Introduction: Good-bye Breakdown Prophecies, Hello Poor Democracies

The gloomy prophecies of massive political and economic breakdown in Eastern Europe following the breakup of the Soviet Union have not materialized. Despite a deep and long economic recession, we have not observed the violent and turbulent political life characterizing a number of Third World transformations. How was this possible? Why did Central and Eastern Europeans protest less about the brutal social conditions of systemic change than the people of Latin America had a decade earlier? How did it happen that, as a rule, less disruptive forms of protest emerged as dominant social responses to economic grievances? Why has the much-feared regionwide authoritarian or populist turnabout not occurred? Why has democracy in these countries proved to be crisis proof? What effect has economic crisis had on the politics of the region? These are the questions that motivated this book: both the failed predictions, and the realities of the postcommunist transformation.[1]

Failed Predictions

By now, analysts share almost a tradition of poor economic and political forecasts on Eastern European development. Most experts did not anticipate that communism would collapse so fast. Galbraith's sharp criticism can hardly be disputed: "The greatest economic failure of our time, needless perhaps to say, was in not foreseeing the recent revolutionary changes in Central Europe and the Soviet Union" (Galbraith 1991, quoted by Wojtyna 1992, 158). Indeed, Galbraith himself did not avoid this failure (Aslund 1991, 31).

Central planning and state ownership, now generally held responsible for the economic collapse of communism, were not always in ill repute in the West. Even analysts for the international financial institutions seemed to grant the system a chance for survival almost to its end. They attributed its relative success to the capability of controlling all resources through central planning (Walters 1992).

The failure of economists to foresee the systemic collapse was soon followed by a second failure. This time they failed to predict the dramatic scale of economic decline associated with transformation. For mainly theoretical reasons, they expected that recovery would be quicker. Nor have other social scientists performed much better in foreseeing the political dynamics of the transformation process.

Following the short-lived euphoria of the breakthrough years, pessimism predominated: "Irony of the ironies, it may be the earlier literature by American academics on the 'breakdown of democracy' in Latin America rather than the recent literature on the 'transition to democracy' that speaks most directly to the situation in Eastern Europe" (Jowitt 1992, 220). Kenneth Jowitt is but one of many theorists who expressed doubts concerning the feasibility of Eastern democratization. "Irony of the ironies" indeed: scenarios of destabilization or breakdown under postcommunism have become more profoundly elaborated than those of the collapse of communism ever were. At least three "schools" of pessimism can be identified.

Many have pointed out that communism failed to lay the foundations for democracy. Thus the *missing preconditions* of democracy—the absence of institutionalized political parties, professional political leaders, a responsible elite, an effective state apparatus, an organized civil society, a developed middle class, and a tradition of entrepreneurship, to mention only some items from a long list—were seen as obstacles to democratic consolidation and stable politics in countries in the process of transformation.

Other scholars, in turn, blame communism less for its failure to create the proper conditions than for leaving *a legacy inimical to democratic stability.* Herd behavior, apathetic toleration of authoritarian or unlawful behavior, fear of freedom, and other features characterize the totalitarian person, while egalitarianism and paternalist expectations invoke the moral economy of communism (Jowitt 1992, Offe 1993, Crawford and Lijphart 1995).

While it is easy to argue that many ingredients of fully developed Western-type democracies have been in short supply, and the legacy of Soviet-style communism is not advantageous, this is not enough to prove that democracy cannot take root in the East in any form. Methodologically, one should beware of repeating the erroneous approach so sharply criticized by Alexander Gerschenkron in a different context. As he put it, those who once—wrongly—conceptualized the divergence of nineteenth-century continental economies from that of

Britain because they lacked the prerequisites for modern industrialization, necessarily overlooked the institutional vehicles of the continental industrial revolution: the banks, which provided long-term investment finance, and the state (Gerschenkron 1962).

In seeking to understand democratic development we also have to consider Guillermo O'Donnell's warning about characterizing polities by "describing their political and economic misadventures" and indicating "which attributes—representativeness, institutionalization and the like—these countries do not have" because "the teleological characterization of emergent democracies according to the absence of certain attributes hinders conceptualization of the differences among emergent democracies" (O'Donnell 1993, 1356).

Finally, the argument most frequently used in the breakdown literature concerns the alleged *incompatibility* of simultaneous economic and political transformation (Elster 1993). It is this type of argument and its assessment to which I now turn.[2] Advocates of the incompatibility claim commonly referred either to the finding that economic crises in the past often had threatened democratic stability or to the conflicting logic of participatory political and exclusionary economic reforms.

While Adam Przeworski mainly worried about "inevitable authoritarian temptations," the waning acceptance of democracy by "financially bankrupt governments," and frustrated reform-elite (Przeworski 1991, 189–90), David Ost expected the danger of new dictatorship to come from below, "those millions of people, marginalized by the wager on the elite, who become receptive to demagogues" (Ost 1992, 49). Ellen Commisso, Steven Dubb, and Judy McTigue concluded, in turn, that it was rather the disruptive behavior of the propertied classes that could be the key barrier to economic restructuring and political stability (Commisso, Dubb and McTigue 1992, 27–28).

As to the frightful outcome, observers expressed worries about "the escalation and intensification of collective protest" (Ekiert 1993, 31), "outbursts of anomic movements, strikes and mass manifestations" that "can sweep away the whole politics" (Ágh 1991, 119), and the more gradual, but no less dangerous, erosion of democratic support (Przeworski 1991, 190), manifesting itself in waning support for parties, governments, institutions, and the regime. Moreover, deprivation originating in the economic crisis and reforms has not infrequently been mentioned as the ultimate cause of "a great upsurge across Central and Eastern Europe of nationalism and ethnic violence, racism and xenophobia" (Walton and Seddon 1994, 327; Ost 1995, 178). Related to such worries, a group of analysts warned of the possible mobilization "of political forces of a reactionary, populist, authoritarian, and chauvinist kind" (Offe 1993, 660), while others foresaw the rise of regimes like "Franco's Spain or the Greece of the colonels, Perón's Argentina or Chile under Pinochet" (Lomax 1993, 5), the "populist scenario" (Hausner 1992, 129), "populist authoritarianism" (Ost 1995, 50), the "dictatorship of intellectual elite" (Lomax 1993, 9), or "authoritarian renewal" in a reform dictatorship of "tyrannical majorities" (Ágh 1994, 11).

Crisis without Breakdown

The gloomy body of theorizing that I have just described, which I call the postcommunist breakdown-of-democracy literature, has been challenged by regional political trends running counter to many of its predictions. Against the background of a transformational recession (a term coined by Kornai [1993]) deeper and longer than the Great Depression had been in Eastern Europe, and in the context of sweeping neoliberal reforms, none of the predicted catastrophic political outcomes have so far materialized in the East. Protests against the dire economic conditions have been mostly sporadic, nonviolent, or insignificant. Although governments have used populist gestures or rhetoric occasionally, there was no single populist authoritarian takeover or populist economic episode in the region. Moreover, by now even the greatest evil, the transformational recession itself, appears to be waning. Except in the post-Soviet republics, growth has begun to resume (Murrell 1996).

Certainly, Eastern democracies may still get into trouble in the future. Should this occur, however, the explanation would not be the transformational recession or the initial, brutal shock of economic transformation. Thus it now seems justified to write in the past tense: the breakdown literature has failed. Instead of breaking down, the new regimes have continued the longest regionwide experience with democracy in the East not only of the postwar period but probably of the entire twentieth century.

How could this happen? Why is it that the actual political experience of transformation under economic stress appears to belie a wide variety of pessimistic expectations? Two questions are, in fact, hidden in this one: we may ask either about the quality of theories, or about the mechanisms and nature of the emerging new system under postcommunism. While the first approach implies a criticism of the breakdown literature, the second points to the necessity of an in-depth inquiry into the possible factors contributing to the durability and survival of new democracies. What follows first is my critical assessment of the postcommunist breakdown-of-democracy literature.

I present two possible explanations for the breakdown prophets' failure to credit the East's chances for democracy. One is that the prediction failures stem from the wrong choice of analogies. The second is that questionable theoretical perspectives underlie the pessimistic prophecies. To some extent, I also consider a third explanation offered by Valerie Bunce, that "predictions are only as reliable as the base upon which the prediction is predicated. The base, in this case, however, is a highly unstructured situation" (Bunce 1993, 42). However, while the unusual, chaotic, and "bizarre time" may explain why so many predictions failed, it leaves us without an answer to the question: Why were they mostly negative?

The Third World Analogy

Attempts to use other regions' experience as an analogy, a point of reference, or at least a negative contrast are certainly not uncommon to social science (Bunce 1993, 39). But how much is the Third World, or more specifically Latin America, a proper analogy if our aim is to understand the emergence of a market society under postcommunism?

In fact, the issue of comparability has been widely debated, and there is a wide array of conflicting views of its possibilities and limits.[3] Some political scientists have argued that the analogy is misplaced because "State socialism was different along virtually every dimension that economists, sociologists and political scientists recognize as important" (Bunce 1995, 119). Walton and Seddon expressed the opposite viewpoint—similarity along virtually every dimension: "By the end of the 1980s, profound changes, both political and economic, were taking place which brought about the collapse of state socialism and the redefinition of Central and Eastern Europe as part—even if a distinctive part—of 'the developing world'" (Walton and Seddon 1994, 289). Equally conflicting views on how relevant the less developed countries' experience is to Eastern Europe are sometimes raised in the discourse of economists.

In any case, the experiences of the Third World and especially of Latin America have not infrequently served as a basis for pessimistic prophecies about the new East European democracies. Analysts sometimes pointed to the political turbulence and violence triggered by economic recession and neoliberal reforms in the 1980s and 1990s. Similarly, apprehensions about authoritarianism or populism have been partially buttressed by Latin American examples. Przeworski's famous and controversial statement "The East has become the South" was based partly on the assumption that the differences were negligible: Poland could be put in the place of Argentina, Hungary in the place of Uruguay (Przeworski 1991, 191).

Thus, what happened in the South—the chaotic, turbulent, and violent transition to "poor capitalism" and enduring political instability rooted in the economic crisis and precipitated by its therapies—may also be repeated in the East. Similar assumptions and comparisons may have led Walton and Seddon to state "Consequently, we feel able to analyse popular responses to economic reform in Central and Eastern Europe in broadly the same terms as we analyse them elsewhere in the developing world" (Walton and Seddon 1994, 289–90).

Nevertheless, as I have noted, with respect to mass popular protest and uprising against neoliberal reforms, there was not much to be analyzed "in the same terms" in the East. From this point of view the direct application of the Third World or Latin American analogy turns out to be a failure. Democracy appeared to be crisis proof under postcommunism.

However surprising, this is not the first time in history that this has happened. "Irony of the ironies," the most recent political example to belie the theorists' pessimism is Latin America itself in the 1980s. While the region's "worst economic crisis since the Great Depression" similarly "provoked regional specialists to paint a dismal picture of the future of Latin American democracy," it is a fact that despite passionate protests and recurring riots against International Monetary Fund (IMF)–imposed austerity measures, Latin America "underwent a far-reaching process of political transformation that resulted in the largest and most extended series of competitive elections in its entire history" (Remmer 1991, 778–79). No new democracy broke down during the 1980s in Latin America.

Why did social science not seize on this kind of Latin American analogy? Why is it that the negative forecasts were soon repeated, only to fail again in the East European case? An explanation may be that the theoretical perspectives underlying the prophecies are questionable. In fact, a closer look at the foundation of the failed predictions reveals some deficiencies and an ideological bias.

All Bad Things Go Together?

To begin with ideology, let us recall an analogous story from Latin America: the decline of development economics in the 1960s. In Albert Hirschman's presentation, its proponents cultivated the discipline "not as narrow specialists, but impelled by the vision of a better world. As liberals, most of them presumed that 'all good things go together' and took it for granted that if only a good job could be done in raising the national income of the countries concerned, a number of beneficial effects would follow in the social, political, and cultural realms." However, by the 1960s, confounded by the fact that economic development had entailed a turn to abhorrent dictatorships, the economists reversed the maxim "all good things go together." "Now that political developments had taken a resoundingly wrong turn, one had to prove that the economic story was similarly unattractive" (Hirschman 1981, 20–22). Led by political frustration, development economists became tough critics of the strategies they had once so enthusiastically promoted.

The pessimism of many analysts in the 1980s and 1990s might stem from the opposite starting point of the same logic. With respect to post-communism, in contrast to the case of the development economists, it was certainly not the political but the economic transformation that might have frustrated socially minded theorists of transition. Primarily, I assume, it was disappointment with the early, brutal consequences, such as social dislocation and deterioration of the standard of living, and mistrust of the regnant neoliberal strategy that have spread pessimism regarding the prospects of the generally favored political outcome: democratic stabilization. Many scholars seem to share the view succinctly formulated by David Ost that "the danger to political liberalism comes from the reliance on economic liberalism" (Ost 1995, 178). In other words, many breakdown prophecies reflect nothing but a bias against neoliberal strategy: a skepticism regarding the positive social and political impact of neoliberalism.

Clearly, the important issue is not whether the values justifying the mistrust are to be shared or not. The question is, rather, whether a biased approach can adequately grasp the realities of Eastern transformation. I seriously doubt that it can. My doubts rest on the observation that the ideological bias of the transition theorists further manifests itself in a normative and activist approach, which I call adviserism, rather than an analytical one.

It is striking how often recent political-science analyses produce not just political- but economic-policy conclusions, recommendations, or implications for action. Presuming that dark political scenarios may be avoided "if only a good job is done" in imbuing neoliberal economic blueprints with social sensitivity, political scientists and sociologists appear to have elaborated a comprehensive set of economic conditions for democratic stabilization. The list includes adequate welfare provision, less haste and more speed in economic transformation, various tactics for sequencing reforms and compensating the losers, involving employee organizations in market restructuring, forms of employee ownership, and neocorporatist strategies.[4] The conditions look almost like a social democratic counterpart to IMF and World Bank stipulations, except that the transition theorists do not employ financial "carrots and sticks" to enforce their prescriptions. Certainly some of their recommendations, such as the provision of a social safety net or the sequencing of reforms, are also part of the mainstream reform agenda, but with a different manifestation. But at this point, as I mention advisers and conditionality, it is fair to point out that the above group of socially minded theorists has not been the only source of negative prophecies. Sometimes, though less frequently, such forecasts have been made by analysts who at least could be charged with having reservations about neoliberalism, such as the foreign advisers to East European reform strategists.

Anders Aslund, an adviser to Yegor Gaidar, for example, wrote, "The experiences of Latin American countries with their largely state owned industries suggest an imminent danger of populist authoritarian dictatorship with chronic economic imbalances, if privatisation does not proceed fast enough" (Aslund 1991, 19). Similarly, Jeffrey Sachs and David Lipton argue that if the economic-reform programs fail, "the meagre living conditions in Eastern Europe will fall further, which could in turn provoke serious social conflict and even a breakdown of the new democratic institutions" (Sachs and Lipton 1990, 48–49). Sachs and Lipton suggest rapid and decisive government action in order to avoid negative economic and political outcomes. Clearly, neoliberals, just like their leftist opponents, remind us from time to time of the threat of large-scale political failure. But what appeared as the problem for the latter was the *solution* for the former: rapid and radical implementation of the neoliberal reform strategy.

Hence, it does not seem too much of an exaggeration to conclude that the postcommunist breakdown-of-democracy literature might have originated to a large extent in debates on economics rather than politics. Representatives of rival views of postcommunist market society kept frightening each other and their audience with (equally false) political arguments, while the autonomy of politics was barely considered by any of them.

It is fair to emphasize that the neoliberals' breakdown prophecies turned out to be just as false as those of their opponents. Firstly, populist authoritarian dictatorship has not materialized in the nations that were quickest to privatize, Russia and the Czech Republic, or in Slovakia, which has proceeded more slowly. One may wonder, however, which democracy appears to be more stable: the Slovakian or the Russian one. The "democratic rights" index, based on a widely cited 1994 survey of political conditions, stood at 75 in the case of Slovakia but only at 58 in the case of Russia (Murrell 1996, 28). While the Russian and the Slovakian political systems might each have serious shortcomings, clearly there is a plethora of explanatory variables for them other than just the pace of privatization. Secondly, Aslund and other advocates of rapid privatization failed to consider the possibility that public firms might efficiently adapt to a new market environment. However, this was not infrequently what happened (Brada 1996, 79–80). Thirdly, where there appears to be a relationship between regime type and the pace of privatization in the East, it is the inverse of Aslund's suggestion. Belarus and Uzbekistan more or less kept the authoritarian features and elite of their past intact, and did not privatize. Neither did the overall pace and degree of reforms prove to be a strong indicator for political development. While radical reforms did not result in democratic breakdown, as expected by the opponents of the neoliberals, neither did gradual reforms as prophesied by the latter.

Coming back to socially minded adviserism, it is not my aim to point out that most advice was offered when legislative or executive efforts in the proposed direction were already underway. Nor is my intention to reject the values underlying the strong interest in the social dimensions of transformation. What I disagree with, rather, is the exclusive political significance attributed to the social-welfare component and its perceived role as a direct precondition or guarantee of democratic survival. New democracies in the East (as in the 1980s in the South) have survived even serious social disruption. This point, however, seems to have been missed by all breakdown prophets, socially minded and neoliberal alike. Hence, much of my criticism is directed against both groups' views. Specifically, I argue that this body of postcommunist transformation literature has doubtful theoretical underpinnings: economic determinism, universalism, globalism, and teleology.

Many transition theorists—political scientists, sociologists, and economists alike—seem to believe that "The durability of the new democracies will depend . . . to a large extent on their economic performance" (Przeworski 1991, 189). The intriguing question, however, at least for political scientists, should be upon what does democracy depend besides economic performance, and to what extent? This is exactly the problem that, in the specific Eastern context, deserves much more attention. More weight, therefore, should be given to alternative theoretical perspectives, such as Remmer's suggestion "that in the less politically stable regions of the world, 'democratic goods' may factor heavily into the calculus" of citizens (1991, 779).

The field where conventional or innovative political science explanations would seem legitimate is further narrowed by the apparent universalism inherent in economic-determinist reasoning. In the East Europeanist's transition schema there is a tendency to attribute too many aspects of the Eastern systemic cataclysm simply to economic malaise: the Czechoslovakian velvet divorce, the breakdown of Yugoslavia, nationalism, ethnic violence, racism, and xenophobia (Walton and Seddon 1994, 327). Finally, it is not infrequently said that everything with which East European politics is allegedly plagued is nothing but the local manifestation of globality: global political protest against global economic adjustment (Walton and Seddon 1994, 290).

Furthermore, breakdown theorists arrived at extreme conclusions partly, I assume, because they conceptualized postcommunism "by where it is heading" (Bunce 1993, 36). Postcommunism was perceived as a development toward the dual ideals of representative, institutionalized, consolidated democracy with strong civil and social components and of full-fledged, mature market economy with social "compromises," as many theorists seem to define them. It is probably this blueprint for transition that makes its designers conceptually closed and mistrustful of anything less than the targeted optimum balance between the political and the economic realms. Each divergence that causes the emerging system to fall short of the expected result is soon interpreted as a major source of systemic imbalance. Any imbalance, in turn, is seen as a source of catastrophic political or economic outcomes. My own conclusion is that an analytical approach based on the above questionable principles might in itself hinder reliable perception of the interaction between economy and politics, and similarly impede predictions of the fate of democracy and an adequate conceptualization of the emerging types of democracy.

Analytic Starting Points

The foregoing criticism clearly indicates that my aim is to break with direct economic determinist, universalist, globalist, and teleological assumptions. Only this break will allow for a proper understanding of the political impact of hard times under postcommunism.

This is not to say that economic or, more to the point, social conditions do not matter. They are of crucial importance, but not alone and not directly. Without considering a multitude of structural, institutional, cultural, and contextual factors that mitigate or limit their impact upon politics, it is impossible to evaluate their real role and significance. The now dominant view that politics is best approached through the economy does not seem to help in understanding how democracies could survive even during such a difficult time as the postcommunist transformational recession.[5]

Also, in criticizing globalist explanations, I do not mean to minimize the importance of globalization and international factors in the transformational context. To the contrary, I think these aspects are extremely important. What I am dissatisfied with rather is that the global view in its recent presentation overlooks important regional variations, exactly the ones with which I am concerned.

Finally, Michel Dobry suggests a useful methodological trick to side-step teleology: "[W]hen we think about transitions . . . the only thing to do is to try to forget, for a moment, by methodological decision . . . the result of a transition. It is not easy because the result . . . could have a very strong effect on the life of many people, on the course of the events, on history. But the strong influence . . . occurs mainly when this result *has happened"* (Dobry 1992, 30).

I have tried to adopt a corresponding approach throughout this book when asking about the nature of the system taking root under postcommunism. What we can observe, clearly, is a rather peaceful coexistence of incomplete democracies with imperfect market economies. What does it mean exactly in systemic terms? How long will it prevail? A conceptualization of the origins, mechanisms, characteristics, and perspectives of this *low-level equilibrium* implies further inquiry into the particular ways—other than by precipitating systemic collapse—in which economic crisis might have influenced politics in postcommunist East Europe. This question, however, leads me back to the Latin American analogy.

To find an adequate answer to it, transition theory has a great deal to learn from two new streams of research on Latin American political economy: one on the political impact of the economic crisis in Latin America of the 1980s, and the other on the emerging subspecies of democracy, that is, poor democracies.

The conclusion of the first body of this literature is that while a decade of deep recession in Latin America resulted in electoral instability, it did not lead either to a growth of political extremism or the breakdown of democracies (Remmer 1991, 794–95). Recent evidence on Eastern elections and political parties shows similar findings (Tóka 1995).

Equally important in the postcommunist context is the conceptual message of a second group of Latin Americanists. It is much less the mere existence or durability of democracy than some of its crucial qualitative aspects—its representativeness, liberal component, and participatory features—that are left with the mark of economic crisis and poverty. Democracies imprinted by economic stress and poverty have been conceptualized as "delegative" or "dual" democracies (O'Donnell 1992, Acuña and Smith 1994). What is most instructive in these approaches is that rather than be (mis)led by overly pessimistic or optimistic expectations deriving from teleological ideals, they indicate a direct conceptualization of the enduring low-level equilibrium between the economic and the political conditions in the Latin American context.

All the above naturally suggests that I rely heavily upon the Latin American analogy in my book. The fact that it led to failed predictions or exaggerated generalizations while serving the breakdown literature does not mean that it is useless per se. Rather, the problem was its improper application, as expected similarities turned out to be differences and actual similarities were overlooked. The possibilities for learning from comparisons with Latin American and other Southern cases are far from exhausted.

I am aware that there are fundamental contrasts between Southern and Eastern transformations. Eastern European countries lacked market economies, for instance, while the Latin American countries had them, even if in distorted form. Latin America also probably had more experience with democratic institutions. Further, there are differences between the Latin American authoritarian and the East European totalitarian legacy, in the "mode of transition" and its international context, and in the fact that democratization in the East has often gone hand in hand with nation and state building, while in Latin America and elsewhere in the South, this was hardly the case (Bunce 1995; Nelson 1994, 4). Later, I test the explanatory power of many other significant differences in the transformation processes in the two regions. However, I disagree with Bunce's suggestion that the best thing social scientists can do is not to "engage in comparisons between east and south" but compare instead "all or some of the 27 eastern European cases with each other" (Bunce 1995, 121). First, a reliable determination even of incomparability, paradoxically, requires in-depth comparison. Second, I think there are a number of important similarities between the economic pathways of Latin America and East Europe.

Both regions shared a common development strategy, albeit with important variations. As a consequence, both were much more industrialized than other non-OECD countries (excluding the Southeast Asian tigers). To put it simply, unlike other less developed regions, each had a domestic industry. But while being relatively industrialized, both regions shared to some extent similar shortcomings and rigidities in their economic structure. For example, their export capacities were limited, they were heavily dependent upon imports, and their economies were insufficiently diversified and competitive in world markets. Both regions were hard hit by the debt crisis and the structural transformation of the world economy. Both regions, although in part for different reasons, tried to delay structural adjustment to the changed economic conditions. Adjustment in the South and transformation in the East have had to advance under dramatically changed and harsh conditions in the world financial and capital markets. The strategy of both the Southern structural adjustment and the Eastern economic transformation has been heavily impacted by the ruling neoliberal development paradigm. Crisis, stabilization, and structural transformation in both the South and the East caused severe social dislocation and declining standards of living. Moreover, there are similarities in the politico-bureaucratic environment of implementing neoliberal transformations in the South and the East. However, similar strategies pursued in different structural, institutional, and cultural contexts led to differing social responses in the South and the East. The political dynamics of economic change also differed between the two regions. Even in this latter respect, however, as I shall show, we may find a few features that the two regions have in common.

Thus for me, the real question is not whether to use the Southern analogy but how to use it properly. Lawrence Graham wisely advises avoiding any extremes in this respect. Instead of looking for total similarities, Graham suggests asking "what aspects are common and which differ, and to begin to establish why this is so . . . in the current series of market reforms and in the current attempt to build democratic regimes, is there anything to be learned from the Latin American cases?" (L. Graham 1992, 51). This is the perspective I adopt in the following discussion.

Clearly, my main focus is Eastern Europe. What I hope to gain from Southern analogies is mainly to know more about postcommunism. In many instances the gain is nothing but the realization that something that was thought to be a specifically postcommunist phenomenon is not. I expect the opposite type of realization as well, that processes or outcomes assumed to be generally valid are, in fact, bound to particular historical, structural, and institutional conditions. As the failed breakdown prophecies show us, such knowledge is neither necessarily at hand nor entirely useless. In other instances, the Southern experience may raise questions or signal trends and tendencies that can be important for Eastern Europe in the future.

My discussion will address issues that have proved important in the context of postcommunism. These include the choice of the neoliberal transformation scenario; the bureaucratic and political conditions of its initiation and implementation; the forms and significance of external influence on the transformation, and the question of national autonomy; social response to the crisis and the economic reforms; populism in politics and the economy; government strategies to overcome opposition to reforms; and the qualitative characteristics of the emerging political regimes. In each case, I review and assess some of the relevant (whether similar or divergent) Southern experience and look for explanations.

Thus, the concrete issues both provide the axes of comparison and preselect the cases compared. This has several implications. First, it implies some uncertainty with regard to the cases to be chosen for analysis. By "postcommunist countries," "Eastern Europe," or simply "the East," I mainly mean the East Central European countries—Hungary, Poland, Czechoslovakia (and the Czech and Slovak Republics). At the same time, I think many of my observations are not refuted by the experiences of other countries in the broader East European region; they may be valid, for example, for Slovenia and Romania as well. However, I exclude the war-torn post-Soviet and post-Yugoslav republics. A few of the latter did not implement neoliberal reforms but have had very unstable and violent politics, with many elements of authoritarian leadership—not because their populations rebelled against economic hardship or the transformation strategy, but for ethnic and national reasons that are not addressed in this book.

While the East European stories are thus set in a more or less standard way, this is much less the case for the Southern examples. By the South I mostly mean those Latin American countries that initiated and implemented neoliberal stabilization programs and structural reforms in the last decades, although I also refer to examples from other Third World neoliberal reformer countries. I was fortunate in having access to the impressive literature that has accumulated in an emerging segment of political science and political economy, which contains valuable insights into the political environments of Third World reforms in the decades of the 1970s, 1980s, and 1990s. It was primarily these case studies that provided me with the (secondary) sources of evidence to contrast with the postcommunist cases. I learned much from the South/East comparative efforts as well.

However, the Southern examples vary, to some extent, with the axis of comparison, and in all cases with the sources I had. Thus, when I want to explain regional variations in social response to crises and reforms, I compare "rebellious" Latin American countries with "patient" East European ones based on the (correct) assumption that certain types of protest occurred more frequently in the former region as a whole than in the latter. Likewise, when I try to understand the reasons for the absence of populist takeovers in the East, the contrast is provided by Latin American countries with an experience with populism. Clearly, the feasibility and usefulness of such comparisons depend heavily upon the question being asked.

More important is that what I am capable of presenting is neither a broad and encompassing comparison of regions (Latin America versus Eastern Europe) nor a rigorous comparison of selected country cases. Instead, the book assesses selected problems of postcommunist transformation in contrast to selected Southern, mostly Latin American, evidence. In other words, the comparison rests on "stylized" facts that are considered to be important by the author.

Hence most of my observations are of a tentative and hypothetical nature and are aimed much more at signaling possible new perspectives of analysis and areas of comparison than at providing credible political assessment and forecasts. But if my arguments contribute to challenging false generalizations and misplaced predictions, I shall not be bothered by the multitude of problems left unsolved for the time being.

Main Questions and Structure of the Book

In Chapter 2, drawing on the Latin American experience, I explore why economic neoliberalism has won in East Europe. More specifically, I seek to explain why and how the neoliberal strategy outcompeted all alternative transformation scenarios under postcommunism. Through a brief comparison of the characteristics and results of the two regions' developmental pathways, I highlight some important common conditions making them equally exposed and receptive to neoliberal economic ideas and strategies. I also identify differences that may be helpful in explaining variations in the neoliberal scenario.

Chapter 3 is a comparative analysis of the politico-bureaucratic environment of neoliberalism's institutionalization. Specifically, I assess to what extent the East European cases exhibit a syndrome, described by many analysts in the context of Third World neoliberal transformations, that I term the loneliness of the economic reformer. Metaphorically, it denotes a politico-bureaucratic situation whereby top domestic policy-makers, allied with their foreign advisers or supervisors, and equally committed to a specific version of market-oriented policy, acquire discretionary influence and power in initiating and implementing sweeping economic adjustments and transformations. "Lonely" reformers have both the privilege and the responsibility of acting alone, beyond any political or societal control, in a sort of political vacuum.

In Chapter 4 I assess the importance and role of external influence in postcommunist transformations. I do not attempt to cover the entire complexity of foreign influence but concentrate on one element, the function of foreign policy advisers. Specifically, I am interested in comparing the roles of two influential cohorts of economic policy makers—local reformist teams and foreign experts—in the implementation of the neoliberal prescriptions. Was foreign technical assistance merely an important source of new technologies and institutions of economic policy making? I argue that the significance of foreign intellectual input varied according to country characteristics (size, importance, and level of academic and bureaucratic integration into worldwide networks) and policy area: in negotiations concerning aid and debt relief, and in privatization, foreign assistance was more present—and significant—than in those concerning stabilization or trade reforms. I also point out the international and domestic political significance of the roles played by foreign advisers.

In Chapter 5 I ask why, in spite of economic hardship, political life in the transformation period has exhibited, so far, less instability and violence in Eastern Europe than the politics of adjustment in many Latin American countries. Why has the transition continued to be relatively free of disruptive political unrest? I compare the intensity and typical forms of social responses to neoliberal reforms in the South and the East, and conclude that the difference is mainly explained by the fact that, in combination with the effects of the transformational recession, many structural, institutional, and cultural legacies of communism have a demobilizing impact on contentious collective action. Thus, East Europeans' most frequent response to economic hardship is not to engage in strikes, riots, mass demonstrations, and violence, but to shift to the informal economy or use the protest vote.

Chapter 6 explores why it is that, against many analysts' expectations and unlike in Latin America, populism has remained on the sidelines in Eastern Europe if in the early transformation period much of the political spectrum had a chance at coming to power. Why have populist macroeconomic policies, an effective means for direct political mass mobilization, been avoided? I conclude that the grave macroeconomic situation, crucial early political choices, and varying degrees of external influence led to a general subordination of politics to economic conditions in the East European transformations, in the process excluding populist expansionary, protectionist, and redistributive policies and their advocates from the circle of presentable alternatives.

Chapter 7 examines the rhetoric, ideology, and economic strategy of recent Hungarian populist parties and movements. In comparing Hungarian populist manifestos with the ideas of major Latin American populist movements, I found merely rhetorical and ideological resemblances. Despite partly similar arguments and expressions, however, Hungarian populists do not share the economic ideas of New World mass movements. I found the opposite when I compared Hungarian populism with other Hungarian parties' programs. When populists attack their socialist and liberal opponents, their rhetoric is typically permeated with prewar extremist, chauvinist, and racist terminology, and their ideological stance could not be more different. Paradoxically, however, there are striking similarities between the populist and the liberal (or the postcommunist socialist) economic transformation project. Hungarian populists' economic transformation strategies depart much less from the mainstream than their rhetoric would indicate.

In Chapter 8 I elaborate an analytic framework to understand a specific strategy frequently used by both Southern and Eastern governments in order to overcome opposition to economic reforms; that is, compensation. I address questions such as: What is compensation? Who is (or should be) compensated? How are they compensated while politically engineered adjustment occurs? I also assess and compare justifications for compensating specific economic, political, and social groups affected by the reforms, including the poor, the working classes, and specific business groups, winners and losers. In addition, I address the role and significance of various political and economic interest organizations in issues of compensation.

Chapter 9 complements Chapter 8 by presenting a study of a case where compensation was provided. I examine the Hungarian Social Pact of 1992, including the political conflicts preceding and following it. By observing how democratic agents struggle and compete in the global context of the political institutional system, the case study also illuminates the type of democracy currently emerging in Hungary, and so contributes to its conceptualization. Hungarian democracy appears to have stabilized at a remarkable speed—however, not least at the cost of some of its qualitative features such as a participatory character and liberal elements. In this it resembles, to some extent, the "dual democracies" described in Latin America.

Finally, in Chapter 10 I present my conclusions and predictions. I recall my main findings regarding the systemic legacies, the structural, institutional, and contextual features that have made East European democracies crisis proof and enduring—though incomplete—and have thus paved the way for the emergence of a "low-level equilibrium" between the economic and the political spheres. Low-level equilibrium briefly means that democracy and market economy could be simultaneously introduced only because neither has been fully implemented. Democracy could only stabilize at the cost of some of its qualitative aspects due to the economic crisis and economic transformation. Economic transformation, in turn, has remained feasible only at the cost of its speed and radicalism, and its many imperfections are due not least to the democratic framework of the change. The economic and political systems reached an equilibrium, but at a lower level than in developed Western market democracies. My hypothesis is that this low-level equilibrium will remain characteristic of most East European political economies for the foreseeable future.

Chapter 2
Crises and Neoliberal Transformations in the 1980s and 1990s

In this chapter I draw on the Latin American experience to understand why economic neoliberalism has won in East Europe. More specifically, I discuss why and how the neoliberal strategy has been able to outcompete all alternative transformation scenarios under postcommunism. Through a brief comparison of the characteristics and results of the two regions' developmental pathways, I highlight some important common conditions making them equally exposed and receptive to neoliberal economic ideas and strategies. I shall also identify differences that may help in explaining variations in the neoliberal scenario.

Why Has the Neoliberal Strategy Won?

In early 1990, David Lipton and Jeffrey Sachs characterized the political decision of the leaders of Eastern Europe's revolutions of 1989 as a "return to Europe" involving the creation of multiparty parliamentary democracies and market economies with large private sectors. Lipton and Sachs also stressed that choosing among the variants of the Western European economic model ought to be preceded by putting in place a "common core" of market institutions (Lipton and Sachs 1990, 1–2). While it does not seem feasible to create "core" market institutions without first opting for one of their particular manifestations, the real message could be that East Europeans had to keep their transformation plans within a consensus on what constitutes the "core" of a market economy and how to create it. In this respect, Lipton and Sachs found more consensus in Eastern Europe than in the Third World, especially Latin America.

My aim here is to understand how and why Eastern Europe arrived at this consensus. Indeed, how could a consensus on policy reform be reached so rapidly in the first place? More specifically, I want to understand why economic neoliberalism has won in Eastern Europe. Why and how was the neoliberal strategy able to outcompete all alternative transformation scenarios under postcommunism?

In answering such questions, I believe it is helpful to turn to the Third World experience. To accept this as an appropriate and useful analogy in the current context, we should keep in mind that by the time communism collapsed, neoliberalism had become by far the most influential policy paradigm throughout the world, if not the only one. It was also in 1990 that John Williamson formulated "What Washington Means by Policy Reform," in which he described "the conventional wisdom of the day among the economically influential bits of Washington"–Congress, senior members of the administration, the international financial institutions, the economic agencies of the U.S. government, the Federal Reserve Board, and the think tanks (Williamson 1990; Williamson 1993, 1329). Commenting on the Washington consensus, Stanley Fischer concluded, "the key fact is, that there are no longer two major competing economic development paradigms: participants in the development debate now speak the same language," the language of the market-oriented paradigm (Fischer 1990, 25).

What Is the Neoliberal Strategy?

I use the terms "neoliberal strategy," "neoliberal scenario," or simply "neoliberalism" in accordance with Alejandro Foxley's definition. They denote a combination of short-term neoclassical economic-stabilization measures—tight fiscal and monetary measures and exchange-rate policies, implying in most cases devaluation, with medium- and long-term structural reforms aimed at decreasing the role of the state and increasing the role of the market in the economy. Such structural reforms include trade liberalization, deregulation, and privatization (Foxley 1983).

Equally, my interpretation builds on the more detailed prescriptions of the "Washington consensus" on policy reform. John Williamson has described it as "the outcome of world-wide intellectual trends to which Latin America contributed (principally through the work of Hernando de Soto) and which have had their most dramatic manifestation in Eastern Europe" (Williamson 1993, 1329). In his critical article, Luis Carlos Bresser Pereira took note of the scholarly sources of the consensus, and assumed that it was shared by the ministries of finance of the G-7 countries and the presidents of the twenty most important commercial banks (Bresser Pereira 1993, 19). This policy package consists of the following set of prescriptions and instruments.

1.   Fiscal discipline has to be restored.
2.   Government subsidies need to be cut, although education and health care should be priorities for public expenditures.

3. Tax reform is necessary and should be aimed at broadening the tax base and moderating the marginal tax rates.
4. Interest rates have to be determined by the market, and real interest rates must be positive.
5. Exchange rates have to be determined by the market as well.
6. There is a need for liberalized, export-oriented trade regimes, while liberalization of foreign financial flows is not required.
7. Restrictions on foreign direct investment should be abolished.
8. State-owned firms have to be privatized.
9. Economic activities are to be deregulated.
10. Property rights are to be protected and secure.

The application of the neoliberal strategy throughout the Third World, and especially Latin America, preceded its canonization in the Washington consensus. The stabilization package has been applied as a means of overcoming macroeconomic and external imbalances for many decades. However, in the mid-1980s, when the debt crisis struck the Third World and serious inflationary or foreign-exchange crises became everyday phenomena, practically every developing country implemented one or more neoclassical stabilization programs. Only a few countries—Argentina, Brazil, and Peru—implemented heterodox stabilization programs that did not rely primarily on demand restraint (Nelson 1990, 9). Moreover, by the mid-eighties, more and more developing countries adopted medium- and long-term structural adjustment programs that were neoliberal according to the above criteria. Such measures included flexible exchange-rate arrangements, increased real interest rates, export incentives, rationalization of public-sector investment programs, tightened revenue collection, subsidy cuts for public services and publicly distributed goods, trade liberalization, tax reforms, privatization of state enterprises, and cuts in public-sector employment (World Bank 1988, quoted by Nelson 1990, 9).

For many developing countries, especially in Latin America, these structural reforms meant a sharp break with their earlier development pattern, namely, import-substitution industrialization. The strategy shift affected the interests of major social groups in a negative way, and they made their interests heard. But by the late 1980s and early 1990s, the battles over policy and the preferred society seem to have been lost by the opponents of the neoliberal strategy. Even Barbara Stallings, who believes it is too early to declare the neoliberal policies victorious, stresses that "the change in direction is greater than any time since the 1930s" (Stallings 1992, 76). Neoliberal structural reforms continued at an even faster pace at the end of the 1980s and into the 1990s throughout the Third World. The worldwide strategy shift materialized along with the increasing involvement of international financial institutions (IFIs), mainly the IMF and the World Bank, both in the number of programs approved and the extent of financial support (Stallings 1992, 70, 78).

And what about Eastern Europe in the 1990s? Between January 1990 and April 1995, and out of twenty-six postcommunist countries, twenty-five made one or more attempts at fiscal and monetary stabilization (six countries implemented several programs) and introduced market-oriented (flexible or fixed) exchange-rate regimes (Fischer, Sahay, and Végh 1996, 50). Most stabilization programs were heterodox in the sense that they included income policies and various forms of state control over wage increases (for example, progressive or prohibitive taxes or levies).

East European nations rapidly liberalized their internal markets, foreign trade, and the process of starting new private businesses. Using the three measures of economic freedom—freedom of domestic market, foreign trade, and the conditions for private business—developed by De Melo, Denizer, and Gelb (1995), the median East European country has advanced from 3 to 70. A score of zero on this scale would indicate a centrally planned economy, and 100 would designate a typical OECD nation (Murrell 1996, 31). In 1994 the median score for economic freedom was above the mean in all East Central European countries: it was 90 in the Czech Republic, and 87 in Hungary, Poland, and Slovakia; and, as is well known, the Czech Republic, Hungary, and Poland became members of the OECD in 1996. "Taken as a whole," Peter Murrell concluded, "this is the most dramatic episode of economic liberalization in economic history" (Murrell 1996, 31).

Although individual cases vary, most East European countries rapidly increased the contribution of the private sector to gross domestic product (GDP). According to estimates at the end of 1994, this share was 75–80 percent in the Czech Republic, 55 percent in both Poland and Hungary, and 40 percent in the Slovak Republic. Romania's private sector had 35 percent of GDP, Bulgaria's 24 percent, Croatia's 40 percent, and Slovenia's 40 percent, while half of Russia's GDP came from the private sector (Brada 1996, 77).

We witness in the postcommunist world a process similar to what has occurred in the Third World, especially Latin America: a landslide victory of the neoliberal project. How and why could this happen? And why did it occur at such an unprecedented speed in Eastern Europe?

Social Learning and External Pressure

There are two widespread explanations for the worldwide rush to neoliberalism, "as if it were the Holy Grail of economic development."[1] According to the first, the shift is an example of social learning (Kahler 1990, 31). In this view neoliberalism won mainly because it proved superior to its rivals, and governments finally came to accept it. Keynesian policies, or development economics, were assumed to produce catastrophic results in the Third World and elsewhere. Essentially the same argument was raised in the East European context regarding Stalinist planning and market socialism, the alternatives specific to the region. It has frequently been stated that socialism necessarily led to economic collapse, both in its Stalinist and reformed versions (Kornai 1990, 1992a; Sachs 1990). It took a long time, so the argument goes, for economic professionals and citizens to learn that socialism was unreformable. However, when the existing system broke down, it was natural for them to turn to the correct strategy.

The second view, however, attributes the triumph of orthodox prescriptions in the Third World to the external pressure of the rich and developed Western countries (Kahler 1990, 33). This explanation, too, had been adopted in the East European context. As some analysts argue, "Radical market-oriented policies are urged on Eastern Europe as they have been urged on Latin America" (Ost 1992, 48; see also George 1992).

I regard the actual transformation of radical neoliberal ideas into economic policies and institutions to be much more complex both in the South and the East than the above explanations indicate. To understand this, even a broad comparison of the characteristics and results of the two regions' earlier development paths may highlight some important common conditions making them equally exposed and receptive to neoliberal economic strategies in the 1980s and 1990s. Conversely, observed differences may be helpful in identifying variations in the expansion of the neoliberal scenario.

Development Paths and Results Compared

Crises and the ultimate breakthrough of neoliberal reforms in the South in the 1980s and the East in the 1990s have, to some extent, common origins. In the 1970s and 1980s many Latin American and East

European countries accumulated huge foreign debts at a time when repayment was becoming increasingly difficult under adversely changing world market conditions.

Due to erroneous interpretations of the situation, fears of the political consequences, and easy access to unconditional new financing that continued until the early 1980s, adjustment in most Latin American countries was postponed until problems became acute. Adjustment came even more belatedly in the late 1980s and early 1990s in Eastern Europe, where debt-induced measures happened to coincide with stabilization efforts and the much broader economic policies of systemic transformation, thereby increasing the stress on society in the debtor countries. Both indebtedness and the failure to adjust in a timely manner to pressures exerted by the structural transformations of the world economy in the 1970s and 1980s originated partly in the common development strategy shared by both regions, that is, import-substitution industrialization (ISI). (See Fishlow 1986 and Hirschman 1968 on ISI in Latin America.)

Thus the 1970s, a decade of easy and cheap credit, found many Southern countries busy shifting to the later, more capital-intensive stages of ISI, involving construction of various debt-financed "big projects" (Frieden 1988). A similar process materialized in the East in the centrally coordinated, large development programs of the 1970s. In Hungary such programs focused on developing the bauxite and aluminum industry, bus manufacturing, and the petrochemical industry.[2] The Brezhnev era in the Soviet Union was characterized by a last ambitious effort to centrally plan and implement large investment projects. These targeted both the military-industrial complex and other industries, and utilized cheap energy and cheap labor. Poland's government invested massively in new steel mills and shipyards and, fearing societal unrest, supported consumption as well. Both Kádár's Hungary and Gierek's Poland were borrowing heavily from international financial markets. Czechoslovakia, however, was different. Either for the now frequently recalled Czech tradition of caution about internal and external macroeconomic balance, or because the country's fundamentalist communist leaders might have opposed any close involvement with the international financial community, Czechoslovakia's central development programs were undertaken without reliance on Western loans.

The fact that both the Latin American and East European nations were relatively developed and industrialized middle-income countries helps to explain why they became major borrowers. The developed West underwent a serious recession at that time, while the poor agrarian countries of Africa (and partly of Asia and Latin America) also did not demand the available huge loans.

However, there were a number of important aspects in which ISI differed between Eastern Europe and Latin America. First, the import-substitution strategy under communism was pursued in the framework of the Council for Mutual Economic Assistance (CMEA), and aimed at autarky and forced industrialization more on the regional than the national level. It effectively meant that the smaller communist countries' industrial-development efforts became subordinated to their strategic orientation toward the Soviet Union and the huge, insatiable demand of the latter characterized by rather low requirements in terms of quality and innovation (Greskovits 1986). The resulting problems were exacerbated by the nonmarket principles and institutional arrangements under which trade was conducted within CMEA, which created an unprecedented degree of insulation from world markets.

Another important difference was that while in Latin America the involvement of the state, and specifically of public firms, in ISI varied across nations, in Eastern Europe the state had a monopolistic role in every country. A third difference is related to intellectual climate. While ISI in Latin America reflected the scholarly and ideological innovations of that region, the central-development programs in the East lacked a comparable character. They mirrored the regionwide revival of Stalinist planning rather than what was probably the only intellectual innovation in economic policy under communism, market socialism. The majority of market-socialist thinkers strongly opposed and criticized their countries' central-development programs (Nagy 1989).

Competing Ideologies of Development

Beginning in the 1950s, the theoretical perspective underlying the Latin American development strategy was development economics. As characterized in Albert Hirschman's seminal essay, development economics focused on problems of the belated industrialization of the Third World and especially of Latin America. Its advocates asserted that economic relations among developed and developing countries offered mutual benefits, and rejected the claim that the problems of underdevelopment could be addressed with the same analytic and policy tools applied to the economic problems of the developed West (Hirschman 1981, 3). Let me review the main points of the ideological controversy.

First, orthodox economists suggested the continuation of an export-oriented strategy based, for Latin America, on primary products of agriculture and mining. However, by the late 1940s and the early 1950s, Latin American economic and political strategists, along with their supporters in Western social science, had become convinced that such a strategy would only preserve the region's dependence on volatile world markets dominated by the demand of their developed trade partners.

In the 1950s, as pointed out in the famous "manifesto" of Raúl Prebisch, one of the most famous Latin American development economists, who later became the secretary-general of the United Nations Conference on Trade and Development, "Industrialization has become the most important means of expansion" (quoted by Hirschman 1968, 2). Development economics, at odds with neoclassical orthodoxy, became the major theoretical perspective underlying import-substitution industrialization in Latin America. In the 1950s and 1960s, development economists continued to propose state-led strategies for economic development. While ISI originally worked mainly through overvalued exchange rates and high tariffs that combined with quantitative restrictions in order to keep domestic markets safe for import-substitution products, by the 1950s, in particular in Latin America, it became the official development strategy. This strategy used a multitude of devices and institutions of state intervention, such as credit and fiscal-policy schemes, pressures on foreign importing firms to set up manufacturing operations, and the creation of state-owned industries and development corporations or banks in support of industrial development. State action, in the development economists' view, had to overcome structural impediments and, indeed, structurally based opposition to such strategies (Hirschman 1968, 5, 18–19).

Second, orthodox economists continued to suggest traditional remedies for macroeconomic imbalance, namely, deflation. Policies of demand contraction would allow market forces to provide the needed self-correction while unemployment would force down labor costs, allowing prices to fall to the level of demand, which in turn would help the business cycle to start upward (Drake 1989). Development economists, however, thought that this approach would not work under the specific structural conditions of Latin American economies. Faced with recurring balance-of-payments and inflationary crises in the region, the structuralist school of development economics elaborated alternatives to the neoclassical therapy, also propagated by the IMF. These approaches emphasized "supply-side rigidities and bottlenecks as sources of inflation" such as the inelasticity of cash-crop production, or the failure of foreign currency–earning export sectors to adjust to changes in demand, or the immobility of production factors, or defective functioning of the price system (Kahler 1990, 35–36; Jameson 1985). In order to relieve structural bottlenecks, structuralists usually recommended far-reaching state-led reforms, specifically land reform and programs of import substitution and export diversification.

Hence short-term stabilization prescriptions and structural reforms were the two most important battle lines where the neoclassical orthodoxy and its intellectual rivals in Latin America conflicted. Initially, the conflict was asymmetrical, however. While structuralists actually had no short-term policy recommendations for crisis situations, the proponents of orthodoxy, concentrated in the international financial organizations, initially had no solution for the structural problems prevalent in development economics. This asymmetry prevailed during the 1950s and 1960s.

On one hand, whenever the inherent tensions of the import-substitution development strategy erupted in an inflationary or an external balance crisis in one or another country, its government called the IMF for assistance (and, of course, for financial support for the prescribed therapy). On the other hand, as far as the policies of structural change are concerned, the international financial organizations and their advisers were on the sidelines until the 1980s in Latin America.

Two new developments in the 1960s and 1970s changed the balance in favor of neoliberalism. These were the turn to authoritarianism in Latin America and the intellectual "rearmament" of neoclassical economics. As to the first, the discipline promoted by development economists was heavily stigmatized by the fact that, in the 1960s, their prescriptions for late-late industrialization were being implemented by abhorrent dictatorships in Latin America. Many development economists either turned silent or retreated in order to improve matters in specific areas, such as poverty alleviation (Hirschman 1981, 20–21).

At the same time, however, neoliberalism became intellectually stronger. It embraced scholarly developments in various fields such as the new criticism of the import-substitution model, which culminated in the discovery of the notion of effective protection rate by Little, Scitovsky, and Scott (1970) and Balassa et al. (1971); the strongly anti-statist public-choice literature; the concept of rent seeking and directly unproductive profit seeking; and, finally, the new findings on the costs of persistent high levels of inflation in the context of the developed economies (Kahler 1990, 41).

As a consequence, by the early 1970s orthodox neoliberals could become structuralists in the sense that they were able to incorporate their structuralist rivals' views into their own theories. They came to accept that the source of economic ills lay deeper than earlier thought, but for them "bottlenecks or social impasses that produced inflation and balance-of-payments crises would be alleviated not by additional government intervention but by radically reducing the role of government" (Kahler 1990, 39–40).

This, in brief, is the history of the worldwide intellectual victory of the neoliberal strategy prior to the collapse of communism. Neoliberals intellectually outcompeted their rivals in the Third World by providing a synthesis in the form of a universal package that combined short-, medium-, and long-term development prescriptions. Unlike the development economists and structuralists, the neoliberals had short-term measures aimed at containing inflation and balance-of-payments difficulties, which by the early 1970s became supplemented with structural reform recommendations running counter to those of their opponents.

However, a long time passed before this victory would become institutionalized (Kahler 1989, 1992; Stallings 1992). While development economics collapsed in the 1960s, the intellectually victorious neoliberal structuralism was only rarely implemented until the mid-1980s. Undoubtedly, during the 1970s the new neoliberal program strengthened its institutional roots in the worldwide centers of economics and policy education, the domestic financial bureaucracies of Third World countries, and the policy conditionality attached to the loans of the IMF and the World Bank. But its real breakthrough in the Third World did not occur until borrowers had access to easy and unconditional sources of finance, the commercial banks. In this sense the gradually increasing power of the neoliberal paradigm paralleled the growing significance of its institutional bulwarks, the IFIs, as lenders of last resort. Neoliberal structuralist prescriptions were not implemented in Latin America until they became the official therapy prescribed by the international financial community. Such therapies could be prescribed and had to be followed only when it became obvious that industrialization along the earlier lines, irrespective of its political environment, was unable to create an adequate economic base for debt service.

Institutionally, this happened after 1982, when commercial banks, shocked by their exposure to their "bad" loans, practically ceased lending. Instead, they joined the newly formed creditors' cartel managed by the IMF and the World Bank. This cartel united all important creditors, including the governments of major developed countries and the multi-national corporations, and prescribed for its clients—by that time the entire Third World—neoliberal structural reforms as conditions of life-saving new credits. The complex neoliberal package first became institutionalized internationally in the conditionality attached to the available but increasingly scarce credits.

This was the worldwide intellectual climate shortly before the collapse of communism. The events of 1989 and 1990 in Eastern Europe reinforced the process I have described, as the only remaining alternative to the neoliberal development scenario spectacularly disappeared from the scene.

Neoliberalism's Eastern Rivals: Market-Socialist Reformers

Those who take the power of ideas seriously would explain the East Europeans' rush to economic neoliberalism first in terms of neoliberalism's victory in the battlefield of economic ideas. There are indications, however, that it was initially far from clear that neoliberalism would triumph in the East. Western advisers, for instance, repeatedly warned East Europeans "to reject any lingering ideas about a 'third way' such as a 'chimerical market socialism' based on public ownership or worker self-management" (Sachs 1990, 19). That ideas of a "third way" were present in the breakthrough years seems also confirmed by leading East European reformers like Václav Klaus, Tomás Jezek, or Leszek Balcerowicz, who commented critically about "dreamers about a third way" (Klaus and Jezek 1991, 31), "perestroika men" (Klaus 1992, 13), or "'third way' elements in the Solidarity tradition" (Balcerowicz 1995, 303).

Clearly, neoliberalism's first step in Eastern Europe was to win the battle against rival ideologies. A serious challenge from the West did not appear, although Klaus complained of the British Keynesian economists who allegedly pressed him to introduce expansionary measures (Klaus 1992, 20). In a similar vein, Aslund criticizes John Kenneth Galbraith for harboring "social democratic nostalgia as well as lacking insights into socialist economies and the current state of Southeast and Central Europe" because of Galbraith's resistance to quick privatization (Aslund 1991, 23). Balcerowicz also criticizes structuralist and Keynesian economists and proponents of dependency theories (Balcerowicz 1995, 252, 256).

However, the most competitive rival views in East Central Europe were not the old-fashioned, rigid beliefs in state ownership and central planning or other streams of Marxist fundamentalism, but those of earlier reformers of the socialist system. While views of the former kind were constrained to so tiny a group of intellectuals that they were rightly termed "endangered species" (Klaus and Jezek 1991, 31), the latter were not.

In my view, the neoliberals' ideological battle against representatives of market socialism assumed the character of a debate between "utopias" and "pathologies"; that is, intellectual support for the neoliberal utopia was mobilized through the suggestion that the only alternative was pathology (Commisso, Dubb, and McTigue 1992). This, in turn, involved linking with the term "market socialism" various negative connotations originally associated with very different East European reform traditions. As a result, market socialism turned into a pejorative catchword. The pathological interpretation of market socialism simultaneously drew from several distinct sources.

First, neoliberals charged market-socialist reformers with harboring unrealistic beliefs in the possibility of a mixed economy, a combination of plan and market. This view had characterized the Czechoslovakian, Hungarian, Polish, Yugoslavian, and Soviet reform traditions of the 1960s, but was hardly a strong element during the Polish or Soviet perestroika reforms of the late 1980s. Sometimes, as in Klaus's and Jezek's accounts, the pathology included the charge that the early reformers were not merely unrealistic but actually deeply statist in their beliefs, just like their Stalinist opponents. In addition, reference was made to the reformers' Marxist ideological roots and convictions and their spiritual kinship with "such Western authors as J. K. Galbraith, D. Bell, and even J. M. Keynes and similar interventionists" (Klaus and Jezek 1991, 31).

In sharp contrast to the view that socialist reformers were essentially statist central planners, a second criticism pointed to their irresponsibility in carelessly abandoning state control over the economy. They were blamed for "half-hearted" or "bungled reforms of the 1980s" that had brought hyperinflation and catastrophic external imbalances (Blanchard et al. 1991, 2). Sachs, however, adapted the argument on the "bungled reforms" of the 1980s to a criticism of reform attempts under communism in general, saying that the countries with the "most market-oriented reforms—Hungary, Poland, and Yugoslavia" are "now suffering the greatest economic imbalance" (Sachs 1990, 19; see also Klaus 1992, 12).

The problem with the above assemblage of arguments is that the "perestroika men" behind the "bungled reforms" of the 1980s were not the early believers in a socialist market economy, such as Ota Sik, Wlodzimierz Brus, Márton Tardos, or Nikolai Petrakov. At best, these groups represent two *different* views of socialist market reforms. At worst, the catastrophic price liberalization and hurried decentralization of the late eighties in Poland and the Soviet Union were not market-socialist reforms as defined by earlier Hungarian, Czechoslovakian, or Yugoslavian traditions. However, even if the perestroika men and the proponents of a socialist market economy were ideological kin, they could not be obsessed with maintaining central planning at the cost of the market and, at the same time, irresponsibly destroying central planning, as various critics have charged.

Third, Klaus and Jezek accused their opponents of "unrestrained reform romanticism," "ambitious constructivist solutions," and of arguing for "positive and complex blueprints" (Klaus and Jezek 1991, 37–38). Ironically, this criticism is very much in line with the usual objections against the neoliberals, including Klaus for his voucher mass-privatization scheme. The charge of market socialists' statism also reappears, in a detailed and modernized version, based on the types of arguments raised in the U.S. debate on industrial policy by the opponents of state intervention (Klaus 1992, 12).

If nothing else, the vehement attempts of neoliberalism to depict the alternative as pathological indicate that it was primarily the ideas of market socialism and a mixed economy against which neoliberalism had to prevail. However, as we know from Gourevitch, "Good ideas do not always win. Many interesting and powerful theoretical constructs have been developed, be it economics or other domains, which have had little impact on policy. To become policy, ideas must link up with politics—the mobilization of consent for policy. Politics involves power. Even a good idea cannot become policy if it meets certain kinds of opposition, and a bad idea can become policy if it is able to obtain support" (Gourevitch 1989, 87–88).

In fact, neoliberalism's rivalry with market socialism was far from a solely ideological conflict; it also had strong administrative-bureaucratic and political aspects. Indeed, I believe it was for bureaucratic and political rather than strictly intellectual reasons that neoliberals attacked the socialist reformers with much more vehemence than they criticized the

Stalinist hard-liners. While the latter could not challenge the neoliberals' power aspirations, the former could, either because, both at home and abroad, they were less discredited in general, or because former socialist "liberals" were, for their part, just becoming "genuine liberals" (Kovács 1994, 22). In both cases, it was not their distance but rather their closeness to the neoliberals that made them formidable rivals and provoked the passionate rhetoric of pathology in the political-ideological discourse. Unlike the hard-liners, the believers in a mixed economy had not ruined their reputations in the breakthrough years. On the contrary, especially in countries with socialist reform traditions, they remained serious rivals to neoliberals and occupied important bureaucratic and political positions. In Hungary the socialist reformist technocracy never could be effectively challenged by neoliberal rivals, either domestic or foreign. Instead, the neoliberal "breakthrough" took place as an intellectual and bureaucratic evolutionary process. It included a few far-from-spectacular changes of worldview and personnel in the headquarters of economic policy making—the Ministry of Finance and the Central Bank. This produced a temporary advance of the lower echelons of the bureaucratic body along with the co-optation of a handful of liberal reform economists. Otherwise, from its start to recent days, the neoliberal strategy in Hungary has been implemented by economists and technocrats who were originally reform socialists, and by the largely intact bureaucratic corps, which, notwithstanding the systemic change, had more or less prepared strategy blueprints for each incoming government.[3]

The ideological battles between market socialists and neoliberals have been less pronounced in Hungary than elsewhere, although some have occurred. One group of the earlier generation of reform socialist economists outside the bureaucracy became increasingly critical of neoliberal solutions and expressed its worries in passionate petitions, alternative strategy recommendations, and serious critical publications. Moreover, the implemented strategy has been frequently criticized by sociologists.[4] It is not surprising, however, that while the successive governments represented very different ideological beliefs, the gradualist neoliberal path that began in the 1980s or even earlier has been followed with only minor modifications.

This latter observation also seems to hold true for Poland. The "post-communist liberals" of that country appear to resemble their Hungarian fellows in their successful transition to "genuine liberals," no matter which government they served. In my formulation, for neoliberals in power this would imply not less, but more political conflict with rivals who are similarly eligible—and probably as well prepared professional-ly—to carry out the neoliberal scenario, as they actually have done it since 1993. Therefore, I believe the extraordinary conditions at the beginning—the pervasive shortages, hyperinflation, and external imbal-ance, and the distinctive big-bang approach—*helped* the reformers led by Balcerowicz to triumph over the majority of like-minded, but probably more moderate (or less resolute) Polish economists, including some of the country's reform socialists. Less difficult times would probably have facilitated the transformation of liberal socialists into executors of the neoliberal strategy, as in Hungary.[5]

From this viewpoint Czechoslovakia, which had market socialist tra-ditions but where such reforms were frozen for two decades, and which did not inherit extreme macroeconomic imbalances from the outgoing regime, presents an especially interesting case. Klaus's attacks against Czechoslovakia's market socialists and perestroika men are more pas-sionate than similar disputes either in Poland or in Hungary. Why? I believe one factor at work, again, is ideological proximity, a shared his-tory of criticism of central planning. As Klaus commented, "The pere-stroika men seemed to play together with us in the past when we all crit-icized the irrationalities of the old system but when we started to build the new system they became the main opponents of our approach. Our rivals do not want a genuine market" (Klaus 1992, 12).

To face "irresponsible arguments" from the market socialists seems to have become a painful everyday reality for Klaus, who, in assuming the position of minister of finance on December 10, 1989, became subordi-nate to two (as he called them) revisionist "old boys." One of them, Valtr Komárek, became first deputy prime minister; as "acting overlord" of the economy, he was actually Finance Minister Klaus's boss. Another reform socialist, Vladimir Dlouhy, also a deputy prime minister, headed the State Planning Commission. Prior to the collapse of communism in Czechoslovakia and their appointments to the government, these three men had been colleagues in the Institute of Economic Forecasting head-ed by Komárek. After the changes they may have brought their old ide-ological and professional disputes to the highest politico-bureaucratic arena.

The major conflict of neoliberalism with its rivals in countries with less or no reform-socialist tradition seems to be of a different kind. As is well known, the most formidable challengers of Yeltsin's neoliberal reforms were not the Russian reform socialists, although they raised objections to them. Both Nikolai Petrakov and Oleg Bogomolov, for example, criticized radicalism and urged the "more evolutionary path to the market adopted by Hungary and China" (Jeffries 1993, 100–101). However, the major critics of Yegor Gaidar and his team were the hardliner, interventionist ministers and deputy prime ministers coming from the communist "big business"—the petrol, military, heavy-industry complex. Likewise, in Romania it was not the reformist market socialists who defeated Petre Roman's neoliberal stabilization and adjustment attempt, but rather political hard-liners who provoked the violent conflict with aggrieved and manipulated miners that ended the Roman government.

However, neoliberal reformers in the East might have worried about ideological and, at times, bureaucratic and political challenges from their rivals: reform economists and reform communists in early reformer countries, and political hard-liners and representatives of the communist big business elsewhere. How did neoliberals master this triple challenge? This is the topic of Chapter 3.

Chapter 3
The Loneliness of the Economic Reformer

As Chapter 2 discussed, neoliberalism under postcommunism faced a triple challenge. To apply Peter Hall's explanatory framework, it simultaneously had to prove its *economic viability* (theoretical appeal and problem-solving capabilities for economic professionals), its *administrative viability* (capacity to replace existing state institutions with new ones that would support the process of reform), and its *political viability* (usefulness to politicians for coalition building and retaining political support) (Hall 1989, quoted by Kahler 1990, 58).

In many countries neoliberalism underwent a successful process of administrative and political institutionalization under postcommunism. In the following pages I discuss neoliberalism's administrative and political viability. To understand it, I concentrate both on state institutions, which constitute the administrative-bureaucratic environment, and political institutions, which are the political vehicles of neoliberal transformations. Again I adopt a comparative view. Although the particular forms vary across countries, state and political institutions central to Third World neoliberal transformations have frequently exhibited a syndrome that I term the "loneliness of the economic reformer."

A Syndrome in Brief

The syndrome is a metaphor for a certain bureaucratic and political style of economic policy making used to enhance state autonomy and state capacity during neoliberal transformations under economic stress. Briefly, it denotes a politico-bureaucratic situation in which top domestic policymakers, allied with their foreign advisers or supervisors and equally committed to a specific version of the market-oriented policy approach, acquire discretionary influence and power in initiating and implementing sweeping economic adjustments and transformations. "Lonely" reformers have the privilege and the responsibility of acting alone, beyond any political or societal control, in a kind of political (and sometimes cultural and societal) vacuum.

The syndrome has been characterized in the literature by a country-specific mix of common symptoms. One of these is a remarkable concentration of decision-making power in coherent reform teams that are insulated from the influence of other bureaucratic groups and from business associations, labor unions, various civil organizations, and political parties. While their insulation is attributable in part to their educational, ideological, social, and cultural backgrounds, it is also reinforced through bureaucratic and political arrangements.

Bureaucratic insulation is typically secured via the leading policy makers' placement on strategic committees, advisory boards, and cabinets backed by, and subordinate only to, the top political leadership—that is, the president or the prime minister. It also frequently involves secrecy in the decision-making process in that members of the reform team do not have to consult with other actors, including other bureaucratic bodies. All this is more often than not accompanied by the weakening or elimination of opposing bureaucratic strongholds or, in extreme cases, even rival scholarly approaches.

Moreover, the above arrangement has frequently implied omitting negotiation or even consultation with representatives of conflicting societal interests, weakening their capacities for collective action, or at least profiting from their disarray. In many cases the new decision-making apparatus has exhibited authoritarian traits, including attempts at expanding presidential powers, the frequent use of presidential veto rights, governing by decree, and in some cases pressure or violence against the parliament or other political actors. From the viewpoint of democratic politics, the authoritarian elements of this bureaucratic solution are what give it the aspects of a syndrome.

While this pattern was originally observed in the Third World transformation context, there have been attempts to expand it to cases of postcommunism (Nelson 1994; Stark and Bruszt 1996). Below, I analyze the bureaucratic and political innovations associated with postcommunist neoliberal reforms by contrasting them with worldwide evidence on the politics of neoliberal economic adjustment.

Blueprints and Reform Teams: Chicago Boys, the Berkeley Mafia, and the Princes

Based on my survey of selected evidence, first I ask who the members of the reform teams were, where they came from, and what accounted for their internal coherence. As a starting point I use a prototypical case, which is by far the best documented in the international literature. It is the career of the "Chicago Boys," the University of Chicago-schooled architects of Chile's neoliberal transformation between 1975 and 1990 under General Augusto Pinochet's dictatorship. Stenzel notes (1988, 332) that the group "originated in 1955, when Theodore Schultz, Earl Hamilton, Simon Rottenberg, and Arnold Harberger went on an AID-financed mission to Argentina and Chile, in order to recruit bright young economists into postgraduate training at the University of Chicago." By 1961 about 150 students had been brought to Chicago. Upon their return to Chile they gradually attained important positions at the Catholic University, conservative think tanks, influential media organizations, and large business firms (Collins and Lear 1995).

By the time of the military takeover in early September 1973, the Chicago Boys were ready with their economic reform plan, which they presented to the junta. Their intellectual position in Chile "was consolidated after the coup with drastic purges of the economic faculties along the lines of dissent from the neoclassical dogma" (Stenzel 1988, 332). Following the coup, at first they could obtain only advisory jobs in various ministries, but from 1975 until the fall of the junta twenty-five Chicago Boys (and one "Chicago Girl") occupied key policy positions (Silva 1994, 209–10).

A few attributes of the Chilean case may deserve attention for comparative purposes. Some of them, in line with Peter Evans's discovery, denote "non-bureaucratic elements of bureaucracy" (Evans 1992, 153). Others allow for the identification of a number of additional important subtypes of reform teams different from the Chicago Boys.

Analysts repeatedly note that many neoliberal reformers, largely irrespective of their national, societal, or political origins, acquired some education in the United States or Western Europe prior to becoming "the Berkeley Mafia" of the Indonesian reforms (Gács 1993) or "the Princes" or "two-passport Turks" of Turkey (Önis and Webb 1994). In connection with this phenomenon, Barbara Stallings stresses their acquisition of "specific knowledge relevant to their profession provided within the paradigms acceptable in the industrial countries" (Stallings 1992, 52–53).

In this sense, neoliberal reformers and reforms for the rest of the world had their intellectual roots in the United States, the U.K., or France, and at the University of Chicago and Harvard University, the London School of Economics, and the Sorbonne respectively. This geographical concentration reflects factors as varied as the internationalization of social-science education, its domination by English-speaking countries facilitated not least by the expanding activity of U.S.-based foundations, the change of the economics paradigm, which took place in these education centers, and the increasing interest of the upper-middle classes and political elite in the Third World and elsewhere in educating their children and successors abroad.

This is true even for some East European reformers, although under communism very few people were able to study abroad. Still, the Czech reform leader Václav Klaus had the opportunity to study in the United States before 1968. However, Constance Meaney notes that he was "declared a 'counterrevolutionary' in 1970 as a result of his economics writings while in the Economics Ministry during 1968–70" (1995, 292). Similarly, Polish reformer Leszek Balcerowicz studied economics at Saint John's University in New York, and did research at the University of Sussex in England and in Marburg, West Germany (Balcerowicz 1995).

Most of Hungary's top reformers, including Lajos Bokros, the radical reformer finance minister of 1995–96, were not trained in the United States but at the University of Economics in Budapest. In fact, it was not Bokros but the reform-communist apparatchik economist Miklós Németh who, during a career that began at the University of Economics and led through the Central Committee apparatus of the Communist Party to the office of Hungary's premier, spent more than one year at Harvard University.

Important as it is, a shared educational experience and intellectual perspective is not the only nonbureaucratic element of bureaucratic cohesion within reform teams. Another characteristic of at least some of the teams has been their members' common social background, which has produced similar ideological and cultural beliefs. The Chicago Boys were sons of the Chilean right whose origins in the middle and upper classes gave them a "conservative and religious background, a visceral rejection of socialism, and a contempt for Chile's free-wheeling mass democracy" (Constable and Valenzuela 1991, 167, quoted by Collins and Lear 1995, 24). Similarly, Mexico's neoliberal reformers of the mid-1980s "came from a common social background, had attended elite schools in Mexico" (Kaufman, Bazdresch and Heredia 1994, 397).

In 1980 Turgut Özal, who led Turkey's neoliberal reforms in the 1980s, did not select his first reform team from the upper-middle class but from his earlier colleagues with lower-middle-class backgrounds who were loyal to him personally. Members of Özal's team were "not committed to the etatist ideology, but were more inclined toward the development of private enterprise" (Krueger and Turan 1993, 354). Turkey's example highlights new elements of cohesion that appear to be important. First, there are often strong ties of personal loyalty between the members and the leader of the reform team, and, second, neoliberal reformers are more often than not newcomers to bureaucracy.

Members of neoliberal reform teams have typically been excluded from policy making prior to their takeover of its commanding heights, either for political reasons, the incompatibility of their professional and ideological beliefs with those of the ruling bureaucratic elite, or simply their youth and different career orientations. Variations of these factors can be identified in cases as distant as Chile and Poland or Turkey and Czechoslovakia.

In Eastern Europe, for example, the Balcerowicz team exhibits a complex mix of political exclusion, shared beliefs incompatible with the regnant politico-bureaucratic view, and youth. Balcerowicz himself has remarked that "The shared background, commonality of purpose, similar age (around 40), and the common pressures created what quickly became known as the 'Balcerowicz team'" (1995, 303–4). These were the young reform socialists, originally recruited by Balcerowicz in 1978, who, in response to Poland's economic malaise, became committed to neoliberalism and entered the government in September 1989 (Balcerowicz 1995, 341).

It is also true that most reform teams consist of members who are political outsiders or neutral to politics; they function as technocrats rather than politicians. As Collins and Lear noticed, it was part of the appeal of the Chicago Boys for the Chilean generals that they "were not affiliated with a political party, for the men who carried out the coup d'état intensely despised political parties and politicians. The Chicago Boys appeared self-sacrificing. They presented themselves as dedicated to the salvation of the nation and impervious to political pressure, exactly as the men in uniform perceived themselves" (Collins and Lear 1995, 44–45).

A similar technocratic and apolitical orientation characterizes many other cases ranging from President Hurtado's reform team in Ecuador to General Prem Tinsulanond's reformers in Thailand. Not infrequently, the reformers' neutrality and technocratic approach to politics offers various political advantages for both the top political leaders and the reformers. The October 1982–March 1983 stabilization and adjustment period in Ecuador was run by technocrats whom President Hurtado consciously selected because they did not belong to Democracia Popular, the president's small Christian Democratic party (Conaghan 1989). Similarly, advisers, bureaucrats, and nonparty politicians dominated the decision-making bodies in Thailand in the years 1980–1988 and during the simultaneous democratization and marketization in Senegal in 1981. (See Doner and Laothamatas 1994, 436–37, for Thailand, and Ka and Van de Walle 1994, 311–12, for Senegal.)

Freeing himself from his compromised and disintegrating Communist Party might have been the ambition of Miklós Németh when Károly Grósz, János Kádár's successor in Hungary, passed the premiership to him in November 1988. Németh, who continued the reformist economic policy, was politically more acceptable to the emerging opposition, and he remained prime minister during the political transition in 1989–90. He built his own and his government's image on nonpartisan professionalism. József Antall, Hungary's first democratically elected prime minister, continued this tradition to some degree, appointing nonpartisan experts to some key economic positions.

The political neutrality and technocratic credentials of the Balcerowicz team in Poland seem to have been important in their rise to decision-making power. Specifically, it seems very probable that the Balcerowicz team was attractive not least for its relative political "innocence." The radical program, which sharply contradicted the economic ideas of Solidarity, their major political supporter, could only be initiated by people who had not lost their political capital in open political conflict with that movement. Their absence in the crucial Round Table negotiations may have proved to be a competitive advantage for the Balcerowicz team. Later, while serving as vice prime minister, Balcerowicz "tried and largely managed to keep the economic programme outside" the political dispute (Balcerowicz 1995, 305).

Shared educational backgrounds and social origins, personal ties of loyalty, and their status as newcomers to bureaucracy and outsiders in politics were the extrabureaucratic factors that may have contributed to the networks of confidence among members of the liberal reform teams once they advanced to top bureaucratic positions. At the same time, these very features may have insulated the neoliberal groups from their fellow bureaucrats, politicians, and other representatives of society.

Nevertheless, the reform teams' internal coherence and, at times, social insulation, were not the only factors helping to institutionalize neoliberalism in the South and the East. It is the characteristic bureaucratic and political environment in which this took place that I now examine.

Political Support, Secrecy, and Insulated Strategic Institutions

The support of the top political leadership appears throughout my survey of cases as the crucial element in the successful institutionalization of the neoliberal strategy. Chile's leading "Chicago Boy," Sergio de Castro, who was minister of economy between 1975 and 1982, stated, "It was our good fortune that President Pinochet understood and had the character to withstand criticism" (quoted by Collins and Lear 1995, 44).

Bolivia's 1985 stabilization and adjustment program is also especially interesting because it indicates not only the importance but also the nature of presidential support. Gonzalo Sánchez de Lozada, an architect of the program and Bolivia's minister of planning during its implementation, recalls that President Víctor Paz Estenssoro regularly visited the emergency task force as they developed the program and "kept saying, 'If we don't do this now, we'll never do it. Do it! Do it!'" (quoted by Conaghan 1994, 249). Other cases of strong political support to reform teams include Thailand's reforms in the 1980s under General Prem (Doner and Laothamatas 1994), Ghana's reforms under the military rule of Jerry Rawlings (Callaghy 1990), and Nigeria's reforms under General Ibrahim Babangida in the years 1986–88 (Herbst and Olukoshi 1994).

In Eastern Europe, Balcerowicz remembers that he got strong support from Prime Ministers Mazowiecki and Bielecki and also from President Lech Walesa (Balcerowicz 1995, 305–6). Though insufficient for their success, Boris Yeltsin's support was instrumental for Yegor Gaidar's team to initiate Russia's stabilization package. As Yeltsin said, "We have been criticised because this critical operation is led by an inexperienced, young team, but their youth and dynamism is an asset, in our view. To support those young ministers' reform, I am ready to risk my own position" (quoted by Balcerowicz 1995, 367). In Hungary János Kornai, while analyzing the draconian stabilization and adjustment program of 1995, pointed out that "the prime minister of the Hungarian government took political responsibility for the program from the start" (Kornai 1996, n. 2; my translation).

Political support was also apparent in the reformers' central location within bureaucratic structures. Their units—ministries, strategic committees, advisory boards, and cabinets—became centers of discretionary decision-making power, and often the starting points of bureaucracy-wide restructuring aimed at the weakening or elimination of opposing bureaucratic strongholds. In 1975 in Chile, Pinochet decreed the centralization of all economic policy under the Ministry of Finance and appointed a "super minister," Jorge Cauas (Collins and Lear 1995, 28). In Thailand General Prem headed the Council of Economic Ministers, "in effect, a supercabinet authorized to make economic decisions that were binding on the entire cabinet" (Doner and Laothamatas 1994, 436). Similar reorganizations of the bureaucracy under the Özal government in Turkey aimed at taking power from the old, interventionist bureaucrats who opposed the economic program.[1]

In Russia the lack of consolidation of important bureaucratic functions may account in part for the reformers' failure.[2] However, the bureaucratic pattern just described fits the Polish case. As Balcerowicz remembers it, he knew that the state's bureaucratic capacity was rather weak, but he also realized that rapid change for the better was impossible (Balcerowicz 1995, 348). Thus, when he became the top policymaker of the Mazowiecki and, later, the Bielecki government, he assumed full responsibility for the makeup of the economic team, including his deputies in the Ministry of Finance and the main economic ministries. Balcerowicz also chaired the Economic Committee of the Council of Ministers. "The committee acted as a vehicle for co-ordination and the preparations of decisions to be taken by the Council of Ministers" (Balcerowicz 1995, 303–5). In addition, Balcerowicz made structural changes in the Ministry of Finance by abolishing the Department of Prices, creating a department dealing with financial institutions, and strengthening the departments responsible for the budget. In his vice prime minister's office, he set up a group of strategic advisers and several coordination committees, including one responsible for the political aspects of the program.

Another characteristic of the neoliberal reform process is its secrecy and failure to consult with other bureaucratic and political actors. In some cases secrecy is explained by the nature of the policy decisions under consideration. For example, a sharp currency devaluation could not be widely discussed without becoming self-defeating. However, secrecy has more often been prompted by the potential for powerful opposition to the reform measures inside or outside the bureaucracy. This was the case of the Chilean shock therapy in 1975. Collins and Lear point out (1995, 29) that the Chicago Boys "worked on the detailed plan inside and outside the government without the knowledge of the minister of economic coordination, Raul Sáez," an influential opponent of the free-market prescriptions.

Another example was Turkey's experience with the 1980 reform package, where it was not just the opposing bureaucratic strongholds who remained unaware of the program under preparation, but even officials in the Ministry of Finance, where parts of the program were being developed. Önis and Webb note (1994, 160) that "Demirel and Özal briefed the top military leaders, and presumably officials of the World Bank and IMF as well, to assure their support but did not tell all of the ministers what would be in the package. Even the finance minister was not informed, although many of his staff had worked on bits and pieces of the program."

While secrecy has been a favored way of preempting bureaucratic sabotage of reform measures, political tensions have not infrequently led to authoritarian methods aimed at sidestepping, or in extreme cases destroying, the political opposition. The direct consequence has been to weaken political institutions and civil organizations and to limit political rights and freedoms.

Authoritarian Elements in Neoliberalism's Institutionalization in the South

There are abundant examples of would-be reformers' attempts to expand presidential powers, govern by decree, use presidential veto powers, and in many instances to apply pressure and even violence against legislators and other political figures. For example, Conaghan reports (1994, 250) that before enacting Bolivia's economic reform policy, "Paz sequestered his cabinet in a twenty-four hour meeting, explaining the plan and bullying cabinet members into supporting it. On August 29, 1985, Paz decreed the New Economic Policy in a single executive decree: D.S. 21060." When trade unions responded with protest actions that included a general strike and a wave of marches, roadblocks, building takeovers, and hunger strikes, Paz declared a state of siege and sent more then a hundred protest organizers to internment camps.

Likewise, economic-adjustment programs in the Philippines under Aquino after 1986 and in Ecuador under Hurtado in 1982–83 were decreed, not legislated (Haggard 1990, 250), and President León Febres-Cordero used his veto power during his neoliberal experiment in Ecuador in 1984–86 (Grindle and Thoumi 1993).

Authoritarian features abound in Turkey's, Nigeria's, Senegal's, Ghana's, and Thailand's reforms as well. In extreme cases presidents have used outright force against parliaments to push through their economic and political experiments.[3] In this sense, Boris Yeltsin's bloody conflict with the Supreme Soviet was just a variation on a theme well known from the neoliberal experiments in the South—for instance, in

Ecuador and Peru. Clearly, all the above attributes are best illustrated by Pinochet's extremely repressive dictatorship, under which the parliament was closed, all political parties were banned, the activities of labor unions were severely curtailed, and freedoms of speech, press, and assembly were restricted (Stallings and Brock 1993, 81).

In a number of cases of neoliberal reform in the South, dialogue between policy makers and representatives of various societal interests has been sharply curtailed. While trade unions have most often found themselves the targets of exclusion, even business associations have been so restricted. Isolation from the representatives of various socioeconomic interests seems to have been perfect in the Chicago Boys' case. It is less surprising that they omitted communication with representatives of labor, the major losers in their strategy, however, than that from 1975 to 1982, as their policies were being implemented, they had a similarly distant relationship with business.[4] However, in this last respect the Chicago team seems to be an extreme exception rather than prototypical. To mark them as an exceptional case may help in identifying less extreme cases and in defining alternative forms of neoliberal institutionalization. This may result in a better understanding of both the Southern and the Eastern evidence.

Pacts and Neoliberal Reformers

In other instances of adjustment in the Third World, the rejection of social dialogue originated much less in ideological than pragmatic reasons, such as previous failed attempts to negotiate and consult (Grindle and Thoumi 1993, 142). While some reform teams attempted to create consensus or even a social pact in support of their neoliberal adjustment strategies, there were very few success stories. However, Spain's Moncloa Pact of 1978 and Mexico's Economic Solidarity Pact of 1988 constitute alternative models for the adoption of neoliberal economic measures. The serious inflationary crisis that hit Mexico in 1987, for example, precipitated ongoing debates in the state bureaucracy about the merits of a stabilization pact. "Characteristically in the Mexican system, the executive elite provided the most important source of initiative. Especially important for the pact was the network of financial officials allied with Carlos Salinas in the Ministry of Budget and Planning, the Bank of Mexico, and the Ministry of Finance" (Kaufman, Bazdresch, and Heredia 1994, 377). Business played a very important role in the implementation of the pact, which in order to stop hyperinflation included a wage-and-price freeze. Large businesses used their market networks, on which smaller firms had been dependent, to facilitate the price freeze. Without their assistance, the stabilization plan would have been doomed to failure (Kaufman, Bazdresch, and Heredia 1994, 380).

The Mexican experience provokes more general questions about the role of business in neoliberal adjustment. Upon closer examination, it turns out that there were reform teams in the Third World whose members were adherents of neoliberal ideas, just like the Chicago Boys, but at the same time were more receptive to intellectual and financial input from certain business groups. Indeed, there were cases where leaders of diversified and internationally integrated, export-oriented large corporations or their associations took direct personal or ideological control over the neoliberal reforms. Their pattern constitutes a type opposite to the Chicago Boys' approach to reform: the business-controlled reform team.

Reform Teams of Neoliberal Business Leaders

In some Third World countries it was not the academic circles but business groups and their associations that "became a hotbed of neoliberal thinking" and took the most active role in "reinventing" their countries as free-market economies (Conaghan 1994, 243). Ideas for the fundamental reform of Turkey's economy originated partly in the Turkish Industrialist and Businessmen's Association (TÜSIAD), which represented the business elite and large corporations. "TÜSIAD had become interested in the development of a comprehensive reform package during the 1970s" (Krueger and Turan 1993, 347). In 1978 they published an article "in which Özal argued for most of the policies ultimately included in the package" (347). Similarly, in the early 1980s, the Confederación de Empresarios Privados (Confederation of Private Businesses, CEPB), Bolivia's leading business association, became an active supporter of a market-oriented "new economic policy." Led by Fernando Candia, an economist and graduate of Harvard's Kennedy School, a research group in 1984 published the recommendations of the business association for economic recovery, and the proposals were very close to those of the 1985 program (Conaghan 1994, 242–43).

While such cases reveal that big business may occasionally have been active in pressing for fundamental economic restructuring, preparing blueprints, and supporting its executors, Bolivia, Ecuador, and Argentina provide examples of the direct involvement of business leaders in neoliberal reform teams. After his August 1985 inauguration, "President Paz created an economic task force to formulate an econom-

ic plan. He turned to Gonzalo Sánchez de Lozada, the CEPB leader...
to head the group" (Conaghan 1994, 248). The team also included two
independent economists (one of them was a banker as well), another
influential leader from the CEPB, the minister of planning, and the minister of finance.

In Ecuador's presidential campaign of 1983–84, León Febres-
Cordero, a successful businessman and former president of the
Guayaquil Chamber of Industry, won on a campaign platform of "anti-
statism, deregulation, and market liberalization. . . . For his economic
team, Febres-Cordero selected individuals committed to liberalism and
with extensive experience in business and with international financial
agencies. The government had strong and vocal support from a wide
spectrum of the business communities; the right had come into its own
politically with Febres-Cordero" (Grindle and Thoumi 1993, 143–44).

In Argentina, big business obtained direct control over economic pol-
icy making in 1989. "During his first year in office Argentine President
Carlos Menem went so far as to give control over the powerful economic
ministry to executives of the Bunge & Born corporation. . . . Bunge &
Born was the country's largest multinational corporation, and
Peronism's most truculent adversary in the business community"
(Gibson 1995, 20).[5]

In sum, the academic-technocratic Chicago Boys appear to be the
loneliest of all lonely reformers, resistant to all societal and political pressures. In this respect they are an extreme type. Many of their fellow
reformers were less insulated and less suspicious of social dialogue. In
some cases they were able to identify societal partners and initiate and
implement successful stabilization and adjustment agreements. In other
cases they were insulated from some societal actors, such as labor or certain business groups, but they were penetrated by some others, such as
financiers and the export-oriented big business. Most empirical cases in
the Third World seem to represent a combination of the above types:
insulated technocrats, reformers involved in negotiations or pacts, and
business-led reformist teams.

How Is Eastern Europe Different?

To turn finally to the East European transformations, the question is
where they fit within the cases and patterns I have presented. While I
identified some similarities in the ways neoliberalism proved administra-
tively viable in the South and the East, now I mention some differences
between the two regions.

First, in the East we do not see much business involvement in designing and directing the transformation. Business-controlled reform teams and blueprints seem to be essentially missing.[6] Typically, the East European transformations have been initiated and controlled by teams of technocrats with academic backgrounds that make them resemble the Chicago Boys more than the business-dominated reformer groups in Bolivia, Ecuador, and Argentina.

If there is any commonality to be noted at all, the Eastern example that appears most similar to the latter Southern cases is the Hungarian team of reform-communist neoliberals. This is because of its members' constant rotation between leading semiprivate and private jobs and public policy-making positions. From the mid-to-late 1980s until recently, top technocrats like László Békesi, Lajos Bokros, Péter Medgyessy, Ferenc Barta, and György Surányi, or István Tömpe—to mention only some of those who assumed central positions during both the last communist and the initial postcommunist period—appeared to be equally capable public and private bankers (Bokros, Medgyessy, Barta), private entrepreneurs, top managers of Hungarian subsidiaries of multinational corporations (Tömpe), reform-communist and postcommunist neoliberal financial technocrats (Medgyessy, Barta, Surányi, Békesi, Bokros, Tömpe), and officials of international financial organizations (Surányi, Bokros). In this sense they also exhibit the most visible case of the circulation of the elite, which has been so passionately criticized by populist and leftist thinkers in Hungary. One possible implication is that coalition-based interpretations of certain transformation measures, such as the consolidation of the banking sector, may be more relevant for the Hungarian case than elsewhere.

Secondly, however, there is one more important difference between the Southern and the Eastern cases: the typical political environment in which neoliberalism is institutionalized. In this respect, and in the East, Boris Yeltsin's autocratic measures, such as governing by decree, postponing the local election scheduled for 1992 until 1994, and gunning down his Supreme Soviet seem to be the exception and not the rule. However, it is true that other Eastern presidents and prime ministers in the postcommunist era considered expanding their power as well (Jeffries 1993, 383, 436–37). In most cases, however, neoliberal strategies enjoyed strong political support, and while this may have deteriorated later, an opposition sufficiently strong to block the reforms could not develop either. (On some of the reasons for this see Chapter 5.)

Fundamental measures regularly won parliamentary majorities, enabling reforms to continue under democratic conditions.

In sum, as far as the political environment of neoliberal transformations is concerned, the seas of "blood, sweat, and tears" observed in many Southern cases seem fortunately to be missing in the East. Instead, there are the short moments of "extraordinary politics," the honeymoon periods of emerging political actors who, as Balcerowicz stated, manifest "a stronger-than-normal tendency to think and to act in terms of the common good" that seem to characterize the breakthrough year of 1989–90 (Balcerowicz 1995, 311).

However, the unexpected and interesting development is that the political "good times" for market-oriented reforms have lasted much longer than just the brief moments granted by extraordinary politics. Clearly, the democratic implementation of the neoliberal project has advanced without much political disturbance well into times of "normal politics." In this respect, too, there are differences between the political dynamics of the Southern adjustment and the Eastern transformation. As we have seen, it was much more typical in the South than the East that, in the absence of broad political support or acquiescence, conditions of "extraordinary politics" were created or prolonged by force.

What Accounts for the Similarities?

Apart from the identified political differences, however, we are still faced with the challenge of explaining the documented similarities in the implementation of neoliberalism in the South and the East. What accounts for the parallels of the reformer ethos and attitude and of the bureaucratic arrangements? One explanation would point to the similarity of the task, the fact that the appropriate therapy was so similar in both instances. One may argue that in the East, just as in the South, there were no alternatives to neoliberal stabilization and structural-adjustment policies, and that their implementation naturally led to similar bureaucratic and personal arrangements, regardless of the specific country or region. The view that the proper therapy is essentially similar for every country has been expressed frequently by both Western and East European policy makers.[7]

However, the application of uniform solutions to the allegedly unprecedented cases of postcommunist transformation may raise doubts either about the widely touted uniqueness of the transformation or the appropriateness of the chosen reforms. In principle, both may be correct, or not. Perhaps these transformations are far less exceptional than is widely thought. Alternatively, it may be that they are unique but that for some reason there is disinterest in, an absence of, or outright rejection of solutions specifically tailored to them.

This latter assumption is often expressed by the critics of neoliberal reformers, who have charged them with being "utopian social engineers" and with using uniform policies and methods of socioeconomic system construction based on "a blueprint of the end state of society, which usually has little in common with present arrangements" (Murrell 1992, 6–7). The reformers are wrong in assuming that they have a good understanding of how a market economy works, their critics charge, and in thinking that their knowledge is relevant outside developed capitalist economies; their utopian engineering may thus turn out to be unproductive and even dangerous (Murrell 1992, 9). According to this criticism, it is not the similarity of the necessary reform measures but the questionable and sometimes forceful, ideology-driven application of uniform approaches in different historical and economic contexts that may account for the observed similarities in neoliberalism's institutionalized forms. Other approaches are possible, however, including conservative or piecemeal social engineering (Murrell 1992) or "interactive methods . . . eliciting the desired changes by generating a process of social innovation resulting from social interaction" (Hausner 1993, 3).

The problem with this second explanation is that reference to the moral, ideological, and political commitment or the inadequate knowledge of decision makers tells us little about why this type of reform leadership has prevailed both in the South and the East. Clearly, reformers had themselves to be chosen before they could implement their preferred policies. Also, as I have discussed, typically (although not always) reformers did proceed either alone or in a uniform way. Sometimes they acted directly on behalf of particular business groups. In other cases, reformers did not automatically opt for authoritarian methods but instead sought to interact with other social constituents, in some cases successfully. It is clear that a few more variables may have been at work than just the neoliberal reformers' preferences or personal characteristics. To understand them, let us recall how reformers themselves interpreted their situation in the South and the East.

As Chile's Sergio de Castro remembered, "Public opinion was very much against [us], so we needed a strong personality to maintain the policy" (Collins and Lear 1995, 44). If their analysts are correct, the Chicago Boys were impelled by a "crusader-like" missionary drive that aroused "a nation of enemies" whom they had to convert. Stenzel, for instance, asks (1988, 332), "Why did Chicago economists consistently advocate escalation into the position of free market extremism for which they simply had no allies in Chile wherever, certainly not among the military, steeped in their corporatist, organic-statist traditions and beliefs, and certainly not in a business community that for more than two generations had lived in the artificial economic environment created by a subsidiary and protectionist state?"

It was not just the Chicago Boys who found themselves without societal allies. Here is how Osvaldo Hurtado, Ecuador's president, describes the loneliness of the economic reformer: "I decided not to waste time trying to develop a consensus that no one wanted and that carried the risk that information would be abused. . . . The parties didn't want to build consensus; they saw my policies as a termination of their political careers—they wanted nothing to do with them. . . . And I couldn't build consensus with the business associations because . . . they were waiting for me to fall on my face. Every person who spoke to me, who advised me, told me the government would fall. It was like swimming completely against the tide" (Grindle and Thoumi 1993, 138–39).

Surely it would be an exaggeration to generalize this pattern unqualifiedly, but it is equally mistaken to deny its relevance at least for a large number of cases. The scenario of the lonely economic policy maker faced with hostile political and societal actors is from time to time replicated in the world arena of neoliberal reforms. For example, Jeffrey Sachs described Russia's economic reformers as "a small group facing a hostile, corrupt bureaucracy, a hard-line Supreme Soviet and a Cabinet in which conservatives always held a numerical majority" (Sachs 1994, 15). Likewise, Leszek Balcerowicz saw the major difficulty of his deputies in the Ministry of Finance as having to "defend the tough economic measures within the government structures, in Parliament, and against the public" (Balcerowicz 1995, 304).

These examples invite us to examine the crucial issue of the social context of neoliberal transformations. As we have seen, the reformers themselves often felt they had no societal allies. I argue below that their perception was essentially correct and that their loneliness originated much more in the broad nature of the reform project than in the much-criticized specifics of its implementation. To put it differently, the socioeconomic interests supporting neoliberal transformations were not in place at the start of the reforms but were still to be created in the process. They could be created only by political decision and action.[8] If this is true in the Third World context, however, it may be even more so in the postcommunist countries. As is frequently pointed out, the bourgeois revolutions of Eastern Europe occurred in the absence of a bourgeoisie. The collapse of communism preceded both the foreign investors and the rise of a domestic bourgeoisie. The dominance of socioeconomic sectors whose interests were threatened by the neoliberal transformations, and the absence of a supportive social base, may have had a strong bearing on the particular forms that institutionalizing neoliberalism took in the South and the East.

But here we may ask how exceptional the neoliberal reform project is in this respect. There is evidence to show that it probably is not. Other reforms in the history of economic change, ones that are far from being neoliberal, have exhibited many or most of the neoliberal project's documented characteristics. Let us recall, for example, the history of import-substitution industrialization in Latin America. As Hirschman observed, the shift to the later capital-intensive phases of ISI was especially difficult both in societal and political terms because it provoked strong resistance. Even some industrialists in established import-substituting sectors fiercely opposed the advance of the process (Hirschman 1968, 18). Thus, in the experience of ISI in the 1950s and 1960s we meet the archetype of the technocratic reformers of the later decades. The leading figures of this earlier shift in developmental strategy were bureaucrats guided by developmentalist rather than neoliberal beliefs, but they were similarly lonely in their task of pushing for structural change in an unprepared and hostile society.[9]

A similar argument is made by Stephan Haggard in the broader context of explaining shifts between import-substitution and export-oriented development strategies in Latin America and South East Asia. Haggard comments that "Explaining the shift to secondary ISI, and particularly to export-led growth, in terms of business interests is particularly difficult." His conclusion is similar to Hirschman's. State actors, rather than preexisting societal interests, have to be considered in order to understand the strategy shifts (Haggard 1989, 39).

This suggests that whenever social and economic structural change is to be pushed through and enforced by the state, this fact itself will quite naturally provoke the entire complex syndrome discussed above in the specific context of the neoliberal reforms. In this respect, Taiwan's and Korea's development-strategy shifts, Allende's populist-socialist reforms, and Perón's or García's populist reforms appear no less technocratic, authoritarian, statist elite based, and exclusive in societal terms, than the neoliberal transformations. (For the latter three cases see Dornbusch and

Edwards 1991.) To be sure, the former excluded and created different socioeconomic actors than the latter, but it is the composition of the favored and disfavored groups that seems to be the real difference rather than the methods or the political and bureaucratic environment.

Therefore, my final point is that the documented similarity of symptoms in the Southern adjustment and Eastern transformation cases may have to do more with the nature of politically enforced social and economic change in general, whatever its direction or ideology, than with the fact that in our particular cases the chosen ideological objective was the same: neoliberalism.

What is left, then, is to ask about the forces impelling the neoliberal transformations. According to Stallings, in the 1980s and 1990s in the Third World, these factors have been essentially external—both financial and ideological—in nature (Stallings 1992, 82–83). While I believe external influence was important in postcommunist transformations as well, its role still has to be qualified. This is my aim in Chapter 4.

Chapter 4
Local Reformers and Foreign Advisers

In the introduction to his edited volume on foreign advisers, Paul W. Drake provides a thorough analysis of their roles in complex domestic and international arenas. In this chapter I use Drake's framework to examine their roles in the Southern and the Eastern transformation contexts, comparing them with those played by the top domestic policymakers' reform teams. I also look for similarities and differences between the Southern and Eastern cases and consider the interaction between these two influential kinds of politico-economic agents.

Sources of New Economic Knowledge and Institutions?

According to the simplest interpretation, in the South what Drake calls "fiscal physicians" have been called on to "teach the natives how to curb inflation, trim budgets, improve the balance of payments, and service the foreign debt" (Drake 1994, xviii).

The necessity of foreign advising was the standard and least-debated element in the category "western aid and assistance" in every significant foreign economic blueprint of the postcommunist transformation (Jeffries 1993, 346). The result has not infrequently included cases of mere "advisory tourism" to the East. The never resting, lonely nomads of the international scientific and policy community, who traveled from the Budapest Hilton to the Forum in Warsaw and then on to the Daiti in Tirana, offered intellectual fast food in the form of brief economic analysis, some sort of policy advice, perhaps even a forecast, before departing for the Hotel Kreshchatic in Kiev or the Rossiya in Moscow. There the show was repeated, and after short stops in Washington, London, or Paris, the advisers resumed their travels, perhaps to Ghana or Senegal. This type of technical assistance was often legitimately criticized as irrelevant because the so-called experts lacked both country-specific knowledge and time to acquire the needed information from local informants.

In other cases the usefulness of Western experts was questioned not because they were insufficiently informed to have any effect but because their impact was negative. This was in essence Jagdish Bhagwati's criticism of Jeffrey Sachs's involvement in postcommunist economic restructuring—that he was unwilling or unable to distinguish between tasks as different as the transformation of Poland and Russia (Bhagwati 1994).

The most important question here, however, is not whether the Western advisers had country-specific knowledge that would have determined their success or failure.[1] It is more interesting to ask whether it was their internationally recognized, "therapy-specific" knowledge and intimate familiarity with neoliberal policy prescriptions and techniques that made the participation of international money doctors indispensable in formulating correct transformation blueprints for communist economies. A number of economists and policymakers—deeply convinced that a technically flawless program is all that is needed for successful reforms, and that failure is explained by imperfect or partial implementation, improper timing, or sequencing—would argue that it was the crucial factor. However, international evidence provides us with a complex and contradictory picture.

Home-grown Stabilization and Adjustment Programs in the South

Drake, in the context of Third World countries, for instance, has argued that many countries could have designed comparable blueprints without relying on foreign experts, most of whose recommendations were little more than truisms based on monetary and fiscal relationships that were already well understood prior to their arrival. Further, the fact that reforms had not been implemented earlier was not for lack of theoretical or technical knowledge but for other reasons. Last, in many cases reform blueprints not actively opposed, and in some cases even supported, by local socioeconomic or political power groups had been prepared before the money doctors arrived (Drake 1994, xviii).

This was the case in Chile, where the neoliberal experiment advanced without significant direct intellectual input from such international actors as the IMF and the World Bank. Of course, the Chicago Boys got significant intellectual and financial support from the international financial organizations, but this was after their prescriptions had been implemented rather than before. The Chicago Boys were pioneers of their project. In many aspects, their reforms both preceded and anticipated the IMF- and World Bank–sponsored structural-adjustment programs of the second half of the 1980s. Also, some of their reforms were implemented more rapidly, and radically, than had been suggested by the international financial organizations (Collins and Lear 1995, 272, n. 18; Stallings and Brock 1993, 98).

Similar, in this respect, was the Bolivian case, where Jeffrey Sachs's arrival had been immediately preceded by five unsuccessful attempts at stabilization that, in technical terms, were very similar to the successful 1985 program. What was really different in the Bolivian case was the political situation in 1985: trade unions, the main opponents of the stabilization program, had been discredited by the time the new program began (Morales 1988, 391). There were many more home-grown stabilization and adjustment programs in Third World countries that got much less international publicity, probably not least due to the fact that there were no internationally reputed money doctors involved.

However, many reform teams and their supporters in the Third World did rely on direct advice from the IMF and the World Bank. Very often persons with extensive relationships with international financial organizations or even former officials of these agencies were placed in key domestic technocratic positions. Conversely, particularly following a successful stabilization and adjustment program, the leaders of the reform team had a good chance to secure a job at the IMF or the World Bank, and many of them used this opportunity. In extreme cases, the IMF and the World Bank took control of the initiation and implementation of economic programs entirely.

Reform Teams of the IMF and the World Bank

These latter cases constitute another extreme type of neoliberal reform team operating in the Third World—those ideologically or personally dominated by officials of international organizations. While examples of more or less direct and strong international influence abound, two cases—Zambia and Ghana—exemplify extreme levels of intervention.

In Zambia in the mid-1980s, officials of the IMF and the World Bank conducted the necessary studies and analysis, established the basic framework for reform, and designed policies to fit it. Comments Callaghy, "Without these external efforts, a coherent neo-orthodox adjustment program could not have been put together. But many Zambians felt that the Fund and the Bank had become the de facto finance ministry in Zambia. The Zambian economic team was often not unified, its members were rotated frequently, and it received little understanding or support from political elites" (1990, 126; see also Bates and Collier 1993).

Ghana's reforms were very similar to Zambia's, with the difference that they succeeded. Callaghy adds, "To compensate for the administrative weakness [of the Ghanaian state], the economic recovery program has generated a real and quite visible resurgence of expatriate influence in Ghana—the nearly constant presence of IMF and World Bank personnel, visiting missions, hired consultants, and seconded bureaucrats and managers. . . . The World Bank, for example, sent more than forty missions to Ghana in 1987" (1990, 127; see also Leith and Lofchie 1993).

Homegrown Transformation Programs in the East

What has been the role of foreign expertise in the East European economic transformation? Certainly, officials, missions, and blueprints from the international financial organizations have been present throughout the transformation period. For example, almost all the inflation-stabilization programs implemented between 1990 and 1995 in twenty-five postcommunist countries were explicitly IMF stabilization programs, involving both financial and technical support (Fischer, Sahay, and Végh 1996, 63). But unlike in the poorest of the poor countries of the Third World, which undertook neoliberal adjustment under the direct control of the international financial organizations, the transformation plans of postcommunist East Central Europe, though varying across countries, appear to be more homegrown.

In Hungary analysts stress that the reform was very different from both the theory and the practice of the transformation policies adopted by other East European countries. In fact the path of changes resulting from the country's long history of gradual reforms corresponded to the goals of radical programs designed for other countries after the collapse of communism (Kornai 1995).

Although, especially after 1989, all important steps had been discussed with the IMF and the World Bank, each Hungarian program—during the Antall government in 1990 and 1991, and in the Bokros-Surányi stabilization package of early 1995 during the Horn government—was designed by Hungarian economists and bureaucrats. In each case there was little foreign involvement. Sachs, Aslund, and other international experts have not advised the Hungarian government. The transfer of new economic knowledge, techniques, and institutions was not the result of the money doctors' missions but rather the more gradual process of increasing the integration of Hungarian experts into the worldwide academic, financial, and policy networks through scholarships, conferences, study trips, and educational grants. This integration process for Hungarians began earlier than elsewhere and was facilitated by Hungary's rather open political system and its relatively early membership in the Bretton-Woods institutions. All this is not to deny that expatriate experts were present in transforming Hungary, but they had other functions than blueprint formulation or program design.

In his statements on the economic transformation of Czechoslovakia and the Czech Republic, Klaus similarly rejects that there was any grand design and social engineering (Klaus and Jezek 1991, 37–38). Noting that structural adjustments in Czechoslovakia and later in the Czech Republic (but not in Slovakia) resulted in much lower unemployment and fewer bankruptcies than in other countries, Stark and Bruszt depict the Czechoslovakian reforms as a case of genuine gradualism disguised with neoliberal rhetoric. These authors contrast Klaus's "pragmatic" approach to structural change with the "shock implementation" of Hungarian bankruptcy law, and judge the former to be a success story partly explainable by proper choice of strategy but also by the impact of Czechoslovakia's distinctive political institutional system (Stark and Bruszt, 1996).

However, the pragmatic Czechoslovakia did have its "zero hour" of reform with a large devaluation and rapid price and trade liberalization, elements that were absent in Hungary at least until March 12, 1995, the start of the stabilization and adjustment package initiated and implemented by Hungarian radical reformers. Also, while Klaus's mass-privatization program might have been a good idea politically in both the domestic and external context, it reflected anything but economic pragmatism. Ironically, considering Klaus's criticism of blueprints, it was a constructivist grand design with doubtful results, at least with respect to the emergence of strategic interests and actors pushing for disciplined corporate governance and structural change (Brada 1996, 82–83). On the other hand, it appears that wherever reformers of Czechoslovakia, and later the Czech Republic, opted for more cautious approaches to structural adjustment, they did so at the cost of sluggishness and delay in structural change. Thus, I understand recent Czech gradualism in terms of political rather than economic efficiency. In this respect, rather than accepting Stark and Bruszt's characterization, I agree with Peter Murrell, who wrote, "[E]ven an advanced reformer such as the Czech Republic continues to delay broader economic restructuring as a means of social protection" (Murrell 1996, 35–36). Finally, however, and unlike other countries, Czechoslovakia could afford a suboptimal strategy mainly because of the country's relatively favorable initial conditions, relative domestic macroeconomic balance, and low indebtedness. As the economic and political events of 1997 have shown, Klaus had to pay a high price for the strategy of delay.

Even so, judging by the available information, the radical program of the Czechoslovakian stabilization and adjustment and the subsequent caution related to structural change seem no less homegrown than Hungary's gradualism.[2] One might guess that in Czechoslovakia, just as in Hungary, foreign experts were concentrated in areas different from the design of the stabilization and adjustment program.

Poland's "big bang," which—especially after growth had resumed—became the number-one success story and case study in international money doctoring, is even more interesting from my viewpoint because in the literature there is more controversy or at least uncertainty related to its degree of international influence than in the Hungarian and Czechoslovak cases. Regarding the Balcerowicz team's strategy, I found two important references related to the role of foreign advisers and the involvement of international financial institutions. As to the first, Balcerowicz wrote, "This strategy was developed into a detailed pro-gramme in 1989 in co-operation with an IMF team and the assistance of a group of Polish and foreign advisers" (Balcerowicz 1995, 321).[3] On the role of the IMF and the World Bank, we find that "In negotiations with the IMF, multilateral banks and Western governments, there was very little pressure with respect to economic strategy and its crucial details because the Polish programme was basically in line with the goals of these organisations" (310). In a similar vein, Marek Dabrowski, Balcerowicz's deputy in the Ministry of Finance until the summer of 1990, says that "the economic program presented to the International Monetary Fund (IMF) in September 1989 was primarily prepared by the Balcerowicz group itself, although Sachs and Lipton advised them on the draft" (in Johnson and Kowalska 1994, 195).

While Jeffrey Sachs never indicated that he considered himself to be the architect of the Polish reform, but remained loyal to Balcerowicz and supportive of his program, there seems to be an opinion prevailing in international literature that he was not just one of the experts assisting Poland's government but that he had a crucial role (Norton 1994, 233; Graham 1994, 199). Indeed, almost forgetting about other important actors, Jagdish Bhagwati seems to have attributed both the alleged Polish success and the Russian failure to Sachs personally: "Sachs's mis-fortune may be that his theories were so successful in Poland that they were tried again in Russia. What was bold in Poland turned out to be rash in Russia. Poland earned Sachs a place in history. But Russia over-whelmed him, laying waste, not for the first time, to a great ambition" (Bhagwati 1994, 39). In contrast, other analysts seem to worry that insufficient attention might be paid to the role of foreign advisers. "It is perhaps not surprising that some of the principal Polish participants downplay the U.S. advisers' role," Johnson and Kowalska comment (1994, 195). Even faced with these confusing interpretations, however, it appears that the Polish program was no less of an indigenous design than the Hungarian and the Czechoslovak transformation strategies. And in fact, both Bhagwati (41) and Johnson and Kowalska (195) seem to accept this in their final evaluation.

In this respect, the Hungarian, Czechoslovakian, and Polish reforms seem to be much closer to the Chilean or Bolivian than the Ghanaian or the Zambian patterns in that their transformation strategies were essentially homegrown. This may be true of Russia as well. It is hard for me to imagine that the country that once outcompeted the United States in sending humans to space would lack the intellectual and technical expertise to fabricate economic transformation strategies without significant external intellectual input.

Ironically, Serbia, the most communist country of the postcommunist region and presumably the one least exposed to external assistance, is praised by Stanley Fischer et al.: "The Serbian stabilization program, not part of this study, was also highly successful in reducing inflation in early 1994 . . . without an explicit IMF arrangement" (Fischer, Sahay and Végh 1996, 63 n. 16). Similarly, while Romania and Bulgaria have been considered to be notoriously lagging behind the leading reform countries, (unsustainable) neoliberal stabilization and adjustment measures have still been attempted in those countries, and reformist political leaders have cooperated with committed native reform teams led by respected liberal economists. (See Jeffries 1993, 451–57 for Romania, and 371–73 for Bulgaria.) However, it might well be the case that external involvement in the latter cases or in Albania and some post-Soviet republics was stronger. The above observations have several implications.

The More Integrated, the Less Dependent

In order to explain variations in the relative significance, forms, and intellectual content of policy and institutional transfer in postcommunist Eastern Europe, it appears to be important to assess the nature and degree of various countries' integration into worldwide academic, organizational, and policy networks. It may also be useful to combine these explanatory factors with such structural variables as country size, political and economic importance, levels of indebtedness, and general integration into worldwide capital, financial, and goods markets.

Paradoxically, being integrated in the 1980s and 1990s is, I believe, a condition for relative independence and sovereignty in policy making. This assumption, however, runs counter to views expressed in the nationalist (and, to some extent, the left-wing) discourse of transformation in Hungary and elsewhere in the East. Integration of a country's academics, policymakers, financiers, and bureaucrats into international intellectual and organizational networks and markets has frequently given rise to conspiracy theories. The external connectedness of these and other social and political actors—or, in Stallings's formulation (1992, 52), their tendency to identify with, or at least consider, "the interests and outlook of international actors and to support coalitions and policies reflecting them"—is often mentioned as both a symptom of, and a reason for, the loss of national sovereignty and economic policy autonomy.

However, international evidence seems to support the opposite view. While, in general, feasible policy choices appear to be limited to variations of the mainstream approaches epitomized by the Washington consensus, the relative freedom of choice within these limits seems to be positively correlated with high levels of policymakers' external connectedness. To recall the Chilean case, clearly one important source of the reformers' relative autonomy was that they simply "knew better" what was to be done. Similarly, by the second half of the 1980s, Mexico's internationally reputed technocratic team, backed because of their country's political importance for the Reagan administration, managed step by step to improve their bargaining position relative to the "orthodox" economists in the United States and the IMF. By 1988 Mexico's neoliberal technocrats had made the international financial community accept their unconventional, heterodox therapy, concentrating on inertial elements of Mexican hyperinflation even though mainstream policy analysts had little trust in such innovations and advocated more conventional solutions (Kaufman, Bazdresch, and Heredia 1994).

In sharp contrast to these cases, when Zambia and Ghana became dependent upon external financing, their total loss of national policymaking authority was not because of their policymakers' strong external connectedness but for the opposite reason. They were unable to meet the standards set by the international financial community because of their lack of competence and capacity in policy implementation.

Thus, in this view, integrated and/or large countries would appear to be less dependent upon intellectual transfer by external advisers, and less directly exposed to international pressure, than smaller, less developed nations isolated from international intellectual networks and markets. When designing adjustment or transformation strategies, the former may rely much more on their own technocratic and intellectual capacity than the latter.

Let us locate the Eastern cases in this picture of international influence and national autonomy. The fact that, by the time of the collapse of communism, Hungarian and Polish experts knew and, more to the point, had already tried most of what they could have learned from international advisers, and that they also understood the international financial organizations' expectations, may have contributed to their relative autonomy. These factors may have been enhanced, or supplemented, by the country's relative size and importance in the case of Poland and by low indebtedness in the case of Czechoslovakia. However, the less integrated countries of the region, like the Ukraine, Romania, or Bulgaria, probably had much less autonomy when they finally opted for adjustment.

These considerations seem both to confirm and to supplement the view of Roberto Frenkel and Guillermo O'Donnell on the convergence of external and domestic determinants of economic strategies in the postcommunist context:

> It is simplistic to believe that "somebody" imposed these programs from abroad. But it is also simplistic (or diplomatic) to assert that a given government "freely" elected a certain program that was "later" approved by the IMF. What we are really facing is a convergence of determinations, or better still, a case of overdetermination. Even without the need for the IMF's blessings, the stabilisation program of these cabinet ministers would have been similar to the one they agreed on with the IMF. But even if the respective economic teams did not believe that these policies would succeed, the need to formulate a program to satisfy the IMF and the international financial community would also have determined a policy package similar to the one actually approved. (Frenkel and O'Donnell 1979, 19)

My point is that while the "convergence of determinations" hypothesis appears to be true, the degree and specific form of the convergence negatively correlate with policymakers' educational, cultural, and institutional links and the country's structural integration in the world, among other factors. I do not think, however, that the above factors sufficiently account for the variation of the roles played by foreign advisers in East European transformations. After all, an expatriate presence was strong even in Poland, Hungary, and Czechoslovakia.

External Assistance in Various Policy Areas

An alternative view can be built on the observation that international assistance, including the role and function of foreign advisers, varied according to policy area. While focusing on the adjustment experience of a group of Asian, African, and Latin American countries, Stallings found that three policy areas—debt management, stabilization, and structural adjustment—exhibited different levels and mechanisms of external pressure and involvement (Stallings 1992). In Eastern Europe, even in countries essentially capable of designing their own transformation strategies, there were a few areas—primarily debt management and connections to international financial and capital markets, and privatization—in which external assistance and advisers appear to have been important.

Drake has pointed out that international money doctors in the Third World context may have helped to justify and fund governmental growth in the host country. Foreign advisers assisted in obtaining foreign loans or in providing "proof to the international community that the government's program was 'economically correct' and committed" (Drake 1994, xx). Conaghan adds, "Perhaps Sachs's greatest contribution to sustaining the NEP [new economic policy] came in his role as adviser in Bolivia's foreign debt negotiations. Sachs emerged as an influential spokesman not just for Bolivia but for the cause of Third World debt reduction" (1994, 256).

This role of money doctors appears to be no less significant in East Europe than in the Southern cases. Regarding Sachs's role, Balcerowicz mentions that he "was especially helpful in working out this part [of dealing with the Polish foreign debt] and in presenting the Polish case to the Western public" (Balcerowicz 1995, 296 n. 5). Other analysts of the Polish reforms consider Sachs's involvement even more significant: "Nevertheless, Sachs and Lipton were extremely influential not only at the inception of the program but also during negotiations with the IMF and the G-7 governments and until at least the end of 1991" (Johnson and Kowalska 1994, 195).

However, in the East it was the exception rather than the rule that expatriate debt-relief missions succeeded. In the case of Hungary the

absence of significant Western political interest in this relatively unim-
portant, small country, combined with the absence of government commitment to ask for debt relief, resulted in a failure to obtain it. This happened despite the fact that in 1989, in order to ease the country's debt
burden, expatriate and local experts formed several teams under various
ideological banners to discuss its prospects (Meszleny 1995). A mission
that included István Csillag, György Surányi, István Szalkai, Márton
Tardos, and Ferenc Rabár, and backed by influential expatriate
Hungarian experts such as Pál Tar and György O'sváth, gathered in
1989 in London. Under the sponsorship of George Soros, the group
met to discuss various alternatives to servicing the debt regularly—such
as a moratorium, rescheduling of debt payments, and massive debt-equi-
ty swaps—with experts representing prominent Western banks, such as
N. M. Rothschild and S. G. Warburg. The above ideas were in the end
rejected by both the Western and Hungarian participants. The consequences of such a shift in the approach to the debt issue were regarded
as far too risky by most Hungarian economists, and their Western partners were not eager to convince them of the irrationality of such fears.
The issue was taken up a second time with similar results. In the spring
of 1990, shortly before the inauguration of the first democratically elected postcommunist government of József Antall, there was a meeting of
would-be top policymakers—Béla Kádár, Ákos Bod Péter, György
Matolcsy, and Sándor Demján, backed by the Hungarian-Canadian
businessman Andrew Sarlós. Like the earlier team, the participants of
this meeting did not find any alternative to disciplined and regular debt
service.

As for the case of the Soviet Union, in May and June 1991 a joint
Soviet-U.S. team met at the Kennedy School at Harvard University to
design a Western aid package of Marshall Plan proportions in return for
radical economic reforms. The plan of the "Grand Bargain" included a
special status with regard to IMF and World Bank loans, large-scale
technical assistance, and massive financial aid (not loans) from the
United States, Europe, and Japan (Jeffries 1993, esp. 75–78).
Nevertheless, very little of this or subsequent attempts at negotiating a
grand bargain ever materialized.

However limited in its success or criticized for its failures, assistance
in foreign aid and debt negotiation was definitely one of the areas where
foreign intellectual input in postcommunist transformation scenarios was
the most significant. It was at least as important in privatization, the
other policy area where foreign assistance loomed.[5]

In the field of privatization, a mass process triggered by the collapse of state-owned economies, one can observe a duality of actors and forms of foreign assistance. Belying the fact that privatization at the given scale was the very process of marketization under postcommunism about which the least could be known in advance and for which indigenous Western or Third World experience seemed to be insufficient, there has been a proliferation of various privatization blueprints of external origin. Paradoxically, attempts at transferring new economic knowledge and techniques appeared most frequently in the policy area, where, in the absence of any comparable experience, Western intellectuals had the least comparative advantage. "Teach it if you do not yet know how to do it" might have been the slogan for this type of technical assistance. Many foreigners advising the privatization process had no prior experience in selling state assets, such as in consulting and investment banking firms. Neither were they the authors of the various blueprints for privatization, although sometimes, especially in the beginning, it was the students of the latter and other activists who were sent by Western aid missions to help Eastern Europe.

In Poland, first, it was the elaboration of the mass-privatization program that attracted foreign assistance. Meaney notes that "Jeffrey Sachs and other Americans were involved with the plans as well and brought some young MBAs to Poland." Other foreigners connected more or less closely to the newly established Ministry of Privatization and working on the mass-privatization scheme included "Peace Corps and World Bank people, supported with grants. MBAs from Harvard University and from the Kellogg Graduate School of Business at Northwestern University came for the summers" (Meaney 1995, 283).

Another example is the task force of retired executives, American MBAs, and Polish graduate students created under the Council of Ministers and funded by the United Nations, and the German Marshall Fund. Initially their task was enterprise restructuring, but soon they had split and formed two consulting firms: one private and working for companies on a contract basis, and the other working for government agencies as "a strategic management consulting firm" (Meaney 1995, 290–91).

In Czechoslovakia, in September 1991, a group of American investment bankers—former directors and partners from Drexel Burnham, Prudential Bache, Dean Witter, First Boston, and Brown Brothers Harriman, and funded by the U.S. Agency for International Development (AID)—came to "handle the sales of selected enterprises to foreign buyers on behalf of the Czech government." They formed the Crimson Capital Corporation, and their activity was overseen by an American-born Czech on salary from the U.S. AID, who served as a key assistant to the minister of privatization. The Ministry of Privatization was just forming, and Meaney notes that in this period much of its staff consisted of young American students brought in "to help on a voluntary basis, as there was a crisis atmosphere created by the government's deadlines." In this setting, in which the American team heads attended weekly cabinet meetings in 1991–92, Meaney comments, "it is reasonable to assume that for a time the investment banking group represented, to a certain extent, a kind of 'privatised ministry of privatisation.'" Subsequently, Meaney notes, Crimson re-formed itself as "a private investment bank with operations throughout Eastern Europe" (1995, 293–95).

In Hungary, where the entire privatization process was more decentralized and where it was initiated mainly by enterprise managers, the role of foreign actors was considerably reduced. At least foreign graduate students and aid volunteers do not seem to have advised Hungarian government officials on privatization, although foreign investment bankers and consulting firms were an important influence, as in the Polish and Czechoslovakian cases.

Foreign Power Brokers in International and Domestic Politics?

Until this point I have focused on the forms and significance of intellectual transfers by foreign advisers during postcommunist economic transformation. All in all, and with the modifications I have noted, I think Drake's observation on the more developed countries of the Third World might hold for at least the western rim of Eastern Europe as well: "In technical terms, the transfer of technology usually has been quite small, and, despite appearances, it has not been the primary significance of money doctors" (Drake 1994, xviii). Specifically, I have argued that the significance of foreign intellectual input varied according to country characteristics and policy area. In negotiations of aid and debt relief, and in privatization, foreign assistance was more present and significant than in those concerning stabilization or trade reforms.

As far as these policy areas are concerned, foreign advisers might have played an important political role in the East just as in the South. They might have acted as power brokers between the host government and the international financial community and foreign investor groups even

in countries and policy areas where neither the lack of indigenous intel-
lectual-technocratic capacity nor the specificity of the policy area would
predict them as essential or indispensable.

To explain this it may be helpful to recall that in different contexts,
many authors stress that the real difficulties facing economic reforms are
not technical but political. While the crucial ingredients of most policy
reforms are relatively simple, one major difficulty they share is to distribute the burden of the reforms without creating social unrest.
Another is to protect the implementation of reforms against pressures
from opponents (Alesina 1994, 40; Balcerowicz 1995, 368).

This argument leads us finally to trace the significance of external
assistance in the political arena rather than simply in the realm of economic ideas and techniques. To understand why host governments
might regard foreign advisers as crucial to their reform strategy, we have
to consider a last important element of their involvement—their possible role in domestic politics. Drake's own conclusion in this respect was
that, "More than conveying new knowledge, foreign economic advisers
have . . . served the aims of political and economic contenders within the
host countries" (Drake 1994, xviii–xix). In concluding this chapter, I
review two Southern and one East European example in order to
hypothesize the possible forms and significance of the foreign advisers'
role in domestic politics.

Several analysts agree that the 1975 visit and lecture series by prominent Chicago economists, including Milton Friedman and Arnold
Harberger, had an important role in Chile's turn to shock therapy and
later to radical neoliberal structural reforms (Silva 1994, 211). Stenzel
notes that "Friedman was giving lectures on national television [and]
Harberger's press conferences were given the space usually reserved for
visiting heads of state" (1988, 330). The Chicago professors legitimated and popularized the ideas associated with their students' economic
reforms both locally and internationally. There are indications that the
Chicago gurus' visit also influenced the outcome of a bureaucratic rivalry between the Chicago Boys and their powerful "business-type" opponents within the government (Collins and Lear 1995, 28–29). Sachs, in
addition to offering technical advice, may have played a similar role in
1985 in Bolivia. When Sachs was invited by a major business association
to advise the government on economic policy, "In addition to policy
adjustments, he [successfully] argued for a change in the personnel of
the economic team" (Conaghan 1994, 253).

In the Polish case, some analysts write that Sachs and Lipton had a very important domestic political role: "As accomplished U.S. economists Sachs and Lipton could offer the opinion of independent, objective analysts, and in the summer of 1989 many of their arguments were more important politically, particularly within the Solidarity Parliamentary Club, than those of Beksiak, and Balcerowicz" (Johnson and Kowalska 1994, 195). Using every available public-relations tool— speeches before parliament, groups of workers, and economists, TV programs, and interviews to newspapers and magazines—"Sachs galvanised public opinion" and helped turn political attention toward radical solutions (Norton 1994, 233).

However, as I noted in Chapter 3, in Poland and elsewhere in Eastern Europe, and unlike in Chile, the activity and domestic political influence of the foreign money doctors unfolded in a democratic setting, a fact that lends their role in the East more positive moral connotations. Why? In Chapter 5 I explore the diversity of the postcommunist experience by arguing that communism left behind certain structural, institutional, and cultural legacies that put a brake on effective opposition to neoliberal transformation strategies.

Chapter 5
The Social Response to Economic Hardship

Much has been written about how economic crisis may threaten democracy. Similarly, according to some analysts, the exclusionary logic of rapid marketization is in conflict with the participatory logic of democratic politics. One stream of theories, which I call the postcommunist breakdown-of-democracy literature, expected radical collective protest, anomic movements, massive strikes, and political violence to follow the economic crisis and rapid marketization in the region. For precedent for this negative outlook, social scientists sometimes referred to the so-called IMF riots that swept over Latin America and other parts of the Third World from the late 1970s to the mid 1990s. However, nothing of the magnitude or intensity of those riots has happened in Eastern Europe. In Hungary, Poland, the Czech Republic, Slovakia, Slovenia, and the Baltics, no escalation of political protest has been apparent. Why? Why is it that, despite severe economic hardships, political life in Eastern Europe has exhibited less instability and violence during the transformation than the politics of adjustment in many Southern reforming countries?[1]

The East Has Not Become the South

East European political trends have raised a question about the link between crises associated with the systemic collapse but also with the neoliberal strategies and the intensity and typical forms of social response. It is mainly to the conceptualization of this question that I would like to contribute. The general perspective underlying my argument is that history conditions the relationship between economic hardship and the degree and form of citizen response. Different historical settings characterized by distinctive socioeconomic, structural, institutional, and cultural features put different constraints on, and open up different opportunities for, social responses to crises and reforms. It is primarily the structural factor that I examine, for I think this analytic dimension is neglected or misconceptualized in interpretations of postcommunism.

More specifically, I argue that at the start of the transformation it was certain structural, institutional, and cultural legacies of communism, coupled with the demobilizing effect of the crisis and reforms, that paved the way for relative political stability in the East. In order to explain the differences in the political dynamics of transformation, we have to understand better the differences between the socioeconomic structures and political institutional systems and mechanisms, and their implications for collective action in Latin America and Eastern Europe. The lack of detailed and reliable statistical documentation of the Southern and even more the Eastern transformations, combined with the limited comparability of data, make such comparisons difficult and the results questionable. Being aware of these difficulties, I stress that what I am able to present is not much more than tentative and hypothetical statements inviting further in-depth inquiry.

Collective Protest in the South

The economic crises and social grievances in the South and the East share, to some extent, common origins in the collapse of both regions' earlier economic-development strategies (and of course, in the case of the East, the system itself). They also experienced economic reforms that rapidly replaced earlier patterns with radically new strategic and systemic orientations and institutions. Socioeconomic change has been accompanied by extensive social losses both in the South and the East. These were manifested in dramatically decreasing standards of living, rapid polarization of income and wealth, erosion of the social safety net, skyrocketing unemployment, and new impoverishment.

In the case of the South, early fears of the political risks inherent in adjustment were borne out by events from the late 1970s to the 1990s. Specifically, in the 1980s Latin America was shaken by an eruption of severe protests called the IMF riots (Walton 1989, 299). In thirteen countries there occurred at least fifty serious protest events involving mass participation. Recurrent protests across the continent were frequently violent and included looting, clashes with the armed forces, many hundreds of casualties and injuries, and many thousands of arrests. This unrest was not without serious political consequences. Some officials refused to make concessions and instead focused on containing the disorder by declaring a state of emergency and imposing martial law; others responded by withdrawing economic reform measures, offering compensation, replacing key ministers, or returning to civilian government (Walton 1989, 310).[2]

Fears of similarly disruptive social responses to uncertain and deteriorating living conditions have frequently been expressed in the Eastern context by politicians, political analysts, and social scientists alike. In fact, I encountered only a handful of authors—Ekiert and Kubik (1996, 3), Crowley (1994, 589), Balcerowicz (1995, 150), and Urbán (1991)—who have recognized the relatively peaceful and nonviolent character of the East Central European transformation process. Confusing in this respect may have been the fact that some countries have seen bloody ethnic and civil wars during the transition period. However, these wars in the former Yugoslavia and former Soviet Union have not resulted from economic crisis or the neoliberal reforms.

In this respect, then, and paraphrasing Przeworski (1991), the East does not seem to be becoming the South. Belying scholarly expectations, East Europeans have remained remarkably patient. Contentious collective action stabilized at surprisingly low levels, and economic reforms in the East have thus far advanced simultaneously with democratic consolidation. It is useful to consider why East Europeans have not protested more.

The Logic of my Argument and its Analytic Background

My aim is to explain the variation of the political dynamics in Latin America and Eastern Europe as a function of the differences in the characteristic patterns of social response to economic stress.

Expressions of opposition to current policy are chosen from existing patterns or from newly available possibilities. In various conceptual contexts these are discussed in terms of the repertoire of contention (Tilly 1978), repertoire of collective action (Tarrow 1994), "exit and voice" (Hirschman 1970), or threats to reforms (Waterbury 1989).

Social actors' choices concerning whether and how to respond to economic stress are influenced—both constrained and oriented—by their position in society, and by various economic, social, political, and cultural structures and institutions. If social response is structurally and institutionally conditional, then a comparison of the orienting and constraining factors would take us a major step closer to understanding variations in political dynamics. Thus I will explore how variations in socioeconomic conditions structure politics in Southern and Eastern cases. While I stress the importance of structures, and to a lesser extent institutions, I do not think that socioeconomic structures matter more than, for example, culture or ideology, nor do I claim to have a complete explanation of postcommunist political dynamics. Obviously, neither economic conditions nor the geographic, occupational, organizational, property, or age structures on which my comparison focuses can in themselves determine social responses to economic stress. A multitude of factors are at work in each case.

There are competing views about which major types of politically relevant social action have to be included in a historically based, analytically fruitful typology. It is the various research agendas to which most classifications are adapted, and their application in other contexts can be highly problematic. Therefore, while setting up my classification, I could not build on the available theories directly and exclusively. Rather, I found several perspectives and research results relevant to my topic. I could not avoid the task of conceptual criticism and adaptation, nor could I avoid the risk of being eclectic.

For my purpose, the major analytical attraction of the mainstream of social-movement research—as represented, among others, by Charles Tilly, Susan Eckstein (1989), and Sydney Tarrow—is that it allows for the influence of structural, institutional, and cultural factors as actors choose among various forms of collective response. Tarrow's concept of collective action and Tilly's repertoire of contention—"at once a structural and a cultural concept" (Tarrow 1994, 31), and defined as "the whole set of means (a group) has for making claims of different kinds on different individuals or groups" (Tilly 1986, 2)—are useful starting points for developing a framework for East European cases. Corresponding to specific historical conditions, the typology stemming from these theories would include a wide range of protest forms such as riots, street blockades, hunger strikes, rallies, demonstrations, strike threats, and local and general strikes. However, if our ambition is to assess the totality of politically significant societal responses to economic hardship, a repertoire of collective action tailored to the requirements of social-movement research may turn out to be too narrow a concept. Reflecting Tilly's and Tarrow's preoccupation with social movements, their framework has contentious collective action as its focus with an equal stress on both attributes. People or other actors, however, do not always respond either contentiously or collectively in expressing dissatisfaction with their circumstances. This distinction is especially significant in postcommunist societies, which often lack a strong civil society and consequently the organizational vehicles for collective action.

In this respect it is Hirschman's theory of social response that appears to offer a more promising perspective. As an alternative to "voice"—that is, to collectively and politically expressing their dissatisfaction—individuals or firms may "exit" or abandon their unfavorable circumstances for something supposedly better (Hirschman 1970). The magnitude of the exit response, its frequency relative to voice, and its specific forms may be no less significant in explaining variations in political dynamics than the repertoire of contention. The intensity of contentious collective action is affected by the possibility and forms of exit, and vice versa. Exit and voice may tend either to undermine or reinforce each other.

In line with Hirschman's typology, it is possible to expand the repertoire of contention to a more encompassing typology of social responses. A substantial enrichment may follow at the actors' level because in addition to collective political actors we can include collective economic actors and individual political and economic actors in the analysis. Also, noncontentious exit options may be added to the repertoire of social responses.

Specifically, my typology, expanded in accordance with the above considerations, will include capital flight and a few other exit options that I call "going informal." Thus my classification is similar to the typology of threats to reforms elaborated by John Waterbury in order to understand social responses to neoliberal reforms in Third World countries (Waterbury 1989, 46–49).

The social-movement perspective and the repertoire of collective action appear to have one more limitation. Various approaches to using democratic procedures for protest purposes seem to be excluded from the repertoire. If the neglect of the individual exit option stems from a theoretical concentration on groups and social movements, then the exclusion of the most important democratic form of voice—the protest vote—may be partly explained by the same orientation, as well as by the preoccupation of both social-movement theory and democratic theory with consolidated Western democracies. The latter factor makes it easy to understand why all other forms of political participation, including democratic voting, are usually strictly separated from contentious collective action. Sometimes this analytic separation manifests itself in the contrast between conventional and unconventional political involvement (Barnes, Kaase et al. 1979, 137).

I argue, however, that in this respect transforming societies may constitute an exception for the simple reason that they lack democratic political conventions. Indeed, it is no exaggeration to think about their entire political realm as unconventional almost by definition. After all, one of the core assumptions underlying the theory of noninstitutionalized or nonconsolidated democracies is that politics—from strikes to rallies, and from partisan activity to voting—is still uncommon and unusual for emerging actors.

While positing a clear distinction between conventional and unconventional political participation may be analytically legitimate in consolidated democracies, understanding protest in transitional systems might justify a different scholarly approach. Consequently, I include protest voting and other democratic initiatives, such as absenteeism, abstention, or mobilizing for referenda, into my typology of social responses. This conforms both with what we know about social-movement traditions under communism and with the assumption that political participation has been in evolution from the unconventional to the conventional in new postcommunist democracies.

Mobilizing abstention, negative votes during elections or referenda, or support for noncommunist candidates when it became possible were forms of protest widely used by anticommunist social movements such as Solidarity in Poland or the Democratic Opposition in Hungary. Brady and Kaplan note, "From 1987 to the present, referendums have arguably been as important as strikes, protests, and elections as tools for refashioning authority. They have, in Poland, Hungary, and the Soviet Union, shown Communist party elites that they could not bulwark their faltering power with popular support" (1994, 175).

Moreover, plebiscites had an important role in several East European transformation cases. Why should one assume that the advent of free elections will suddenly eliminate the protest traditions originally present in democratic procedures? I think that the opposite is true: the dramatic reshuffling of support around the political spectrum in new Eastern democracies, or the recurrent attempts to oppose unpopular policies through direct democratic means like referenda, indicate that the above traditions prevail. As I hope to demonstrate, paying attention to protest voting may substantially contribute to our understanding of the Eastern social response to the hardships of the 1990s.

Before concretely exploring how social conditions in the East may have oriented and constrained social actors' choices, I have a few more suggestions about conceptualizing the typology of social response. One issue that is relevant for this analysis is the extent to which social response is organized and coordinated rather than spontaneous and individual. Actors in the economy and polity may threaten political and economic stabilization either by means of organized, common, mostly political actions or through a multitude of individual, unorganized, and mostly economic responses. While strikes, rallies, demonstrations, and (to a much lesser extent, and only under specific conditions) riots, more or less denote the first group, remittance withholding, hoarding, unsecured borrowing, capital flight, and certain forms of "going informal" represent the second. The two groups of responses consist of actions that differ both in their preconditions and in their political or economic aims. Organized and coordinated responses need organizers, while the actions of the second type do not. Events of the first type constitute political action that seeks economic or economic and political results combined. Responses of the latter type—without a primary intention to halt reforms, or to overthrow democratic and reformist governments—constitute economic adaptation or passive resistance with only a contingent political impact. There are different implications for short- and medium-term political stability depending on which type of response is dominant.

A second analytic possibility is to differentiate among forms of protest, which, in my classification, constitutes only one of the important subsets of social responses to economic stress. Clearly, there are expressions of discontent that are strictly bound to specific social or economic structures and groups and are unavailable to others. Conversely, there are socioeconomic groups who are limited in the forms of protest that are available to them. For example, a strike is strictly anchored in labor organization, while elderly people, or specifically pensioners, do not have many alternatives to voting against the crisis or the economic transformation strategy if their living standards are threatened. Undoubtedly, the political dynamics of transformation under economic stress are crucially affected by the availability of diverse and effective contentious responses to its major losers and opponents or, in line with my earlier point, by the characteristic pattern of social protest.

Structures, Institutions, and the Pattern of Social Responses

In accordance with the ideas just outlined, my typology of social responses to economic stress under transformation has five categories: *riots* (and violent demonstrations, street blockades, and hunger strikes); *strikes* (including strike threats and lockouts, but also general political strikes); *hoarding, unsecured borrowing, and capital flight* (but also other practices, like lobbying for subsidies, cartels, investment restraint, or disinvestment); *going informal* (tax evasion, illegal employment, illegal street trading, organized crime, and stripping public firms of their assets), and *protest voting* (but also protest by abstention, and by mobilizing for referenda).

I now turn to a more detailed description of the individual types of social response, including a characterization of what we might call their structural and institutional embeddedness under postcommunism and placing the discussion in a comparative perspective.

Riots may not only adversely affect or halt economic reforms by forcing the targeted policies to be withdrawn but, especially when supported by other antireform actions, may shake up or oust reformist governments, whether democratic or not. Riots are often triggered by policy attempts to "slaughter the sacred cows" of the preceding economic or social system, mainly by decreasing subsidies and raising prices for basic consumer items. Riots are protest forms characteristic of urban, unorganized, and low-income groups, such as the unemployed and the poor (Waterbury 1989, 47). Indeed, unorganized and poor groups rarely have an alternative to these most dramatic forms of protest. Therefore, a hypothesis concerning the sociopolitical risk of riots and related manifestations of political instability may be derived from comparing such

Table 5.1: Indicators of Poverty, Inequality, and Urbanization in Latin America and Eastern Europe

Country	Infant mortality rate (per 1,000 live births) (1989)	Daily calorie supply (per capita) (1988)	% share of income of highest 20% per lowest 20% of households	Urbanites as a % of total population (1989)	Population in cities of 1 mil. or more, as a % of total	% of rural population
Bulgaria	13	3,614	–	68	13	32
Czechosl.	12	3,564	3.1	78	8	22
Hungary	17	3,601	3.0 (1983)	63	20	37
Poland	16	3,451	3.6 (1987)	62	18	38
Romania	27	3,357	–	53	9	–
Argentina	30	3,118	11.4[a] (1970)	86	42	14
Brazil	59	2,709	26.1 (1983)	75	35	25
Chile	19	2,584	11.7[a] (1968)	86	36	14
Ecuador	61	2,338	19.9[a] (1977)	56	28	44
Mexico	40	3,135		73	32	27
Peru	79	2,269	11.8 (1985-86)	70	29	30
Venezuela	35	2,547	10.8 (1987)	91	27	9

Source: World Development Report 1991.

[a] The Economist Book of Vital World Statistics. (1992)

indicators as the level and growth of per capita GDP, income distribution, size of social groups below or near the poverty line, the level of urbanization, share of population of large cities, educational standards, and traditions of political instability in the South and in the East (see Table 5.1).

Data on levels and growth of per-capita GDP indicate that Eastern Europe has not yet managed to escape from the poverty and stagnation that is associated with a high risk of political instability in the less developed countries (LDCs) in general (Londregan and Poole 1990). Low per-capita incomes and poor growth performance under postcommunism make the region comparable to Latin America in terms of the risk of riots. However, inherited egalitarian income-distribution patterns and the still-limited extent of poverty in East European societies, relative to the extremes prevalent in Latin America, may have contributed to defending the Eastern transformation from violent forms of political destabilization. Moreover, many of the Southern riots and violent demonstrations were rooted in the grievances of marginalized shantytown dwellers of megalopolises, while Eastern Europe is much less urbanized than Latin America and there are no impoverished masses concentrated in metropolitan shantytowns, factors that may also have contributed to stability. The higher overall level of education in the East may reduce the likelihood of inarticulate outbursts becoming a major protest form as well.

In principle, history may be a factor protecting the East from another type of political extreme, the frequent military coups associated with the above-mentioned violent forms of political destabilization. According to the quoted research by Londregan and Poole, a country's experience of the violent seizure of executive power may increase the chance of future coups. Coups soon breed other coups, a tendency that may also be true of riots and other forms of political instability. In this respect, East Central Europe's recent record has been better than much of Latin America's.

Strikes may adversely affect economic transformation either by paralyzing the economy (specifically by targeting rail and ship transport, or strategic industries) or by provoking destabilizing wage-price spirals. Not infrequently, strikes have led to government or regime collapse. Organized labor—blue- and white-collar unions, and professional associations—may initiate strikes that pose an effective threat, especially if the actors concentrate on key sectors of the economy. A tentative assessment of the socioeconomic risk of strikes may be reached by comparing such indicators as the level of unionization of the workforce, the extent of organized labor's concentration in strategic branches, the country-specific institutional bases and traditions of union activity, and the credibility and organizational capacity of labor unions.

Table 5.2: Level of Unionization and Strike Activity in East-Central Europe and Latin America during Hard Times (Selected Years)

Country	Unionization as a % of labor force	Number of strikes
Czechoslovakia	77 (early 1990s)[a]	24[c] (1990-93)
Hungary	37-76 (early 1990s)[a]	61[c] (1989-90)
Poland	26-40 (early 1990s)[a]	432[c] (1989-93)
Former GDR	–	107[c] (1989-93)
Chile	25 (mid-1970s)[b]	416[d] (1983-89)
Mexico	20 (mid-1970s)[b]	1,538[d] (1983-89)
Brazil	22 (mid-1970s)[b]	286[e] (1980-82) 11,693[d] (1983-89)
Peru	37 (mid-1970s)[b]	3,779[f] (1974-80) 2,832[e] (1981-84)
Venezuela	45 (mid-1970s)[b]	566[e] (1980-84)

[a] My estimates based on Fischer, and Standing 1993.
[b] Haggard, and Kaufman 1992, 276.
[c] Ekiert, and Kubik 1996, Table 2.
[d] Heredia 1994, 276.
[e] Epstein 1989, 175.
[f] Haggard, and Kaufman 1995, 62.

Note: The data are not comparable and are only illustrations.

Eastern Europe has in general been more unionized than Latin America (see Table 5.2). Eastern unions are well represented—even more than their Latin American counterparts—in sectors that are of strategic relevance for the entire economy: iron and steel, mining, transportation, and industries having military significance. However, while there are important country-specific differences, most Eastern labor movements have suffered from impaired credibility, rooted in their close links with the outgoing communist regime. Later, due to rapidly growing unemployment, competition among unions, and government actions, unions and the strike weapon seem to have declined as important risk factors for economic adjustment.

The *hoarding* of imported raw materials while facing devaluation, *unsecured borrowing* from banks and forced credits from suppliers, *monopolistic output cutbacks* and inflationary price rises to cover efficiency gaps, and *lobbying* to sidestep stabilization policies are attributed specifically to public enterprises in the literature (Waterbury 1989, 48). Responses like these may threaten economic and, indirectly, political transformations by disrupting stabilization plans, the financial system, and foreign balances, as well as by causing bottlenecks in producers' markets and shortages in consumers' markets.

Capital flight (or investment restraint or disinvestment), associated mainly with the private sector (private importers, financial-services firms, foreign-exchange brokers), may cause the sudden collapse of the exchange rate and of the entire financial system by exhausting currency reserves. Capital flight has been considered by a number of analysts to be one of the main threats to sustainable economic and political stabilization in many of the reforming LDCs (Commisso, Dubb, and McTigue 1992) (see Table 5.3).

Table 5.3: Estimate of the Volume of Capital Flight in Latin America (Bn US $ without Interest)

Country	1976–87	US$ per capita
Argentina	29.1	924
Brazil	20.4	144
Mexico	60.6	745
Venezuela	40.1	2,195

Source: Dornbusch, 1993.

A tentative assessment of the socioeconomic risks of hoarding, unsecured borrowing, and other practices may be reached by examining such indicators as the public sector share of GDP, employment, and investment, further the reactions of state-owned enterprises (SOEs) to economic reform measures as reflected by the stock of bad debt, forced interfirm credits, and to price liberalization. A comparison of such factors would reveal that state ownership in the East expanded far beyond the scope of any populist or statist government in Latin America. This legacy has been clearly reflected in the long traditions of firm behavior under soft budget constraints, as explored in the paradigmatic analysis by János Kornai. Public firms' behavior in communist shortage economies involved hoarding, unsecured borrowing, applying various forms of pressure for subsidies, and asserting suppliers' power against buyers and consumers via price increases and poor quality (Kornai 1980). These practices represented more serious threats to economic stabilization in the East than did the public firms' preemptive reactions to adjustment measures in Latin America. Unlike "textbook" firms, state-owned firms in the East initially reacted to early radical reform steps—price liberalization and elimination of subsidies—by unexpectedly high price increases coupled with output and real-wage contraction. Moreover, the state firms' ability to escape credit cuts, even in cases of insolvency, and their power to force "credits" from suppliers and from social security funds substantially slowed the progress of economic stabilization attempts. As a consequence, a complex web of forced credit relations and insolvent firms has emerged all over Eastern Europe, posing a formidable burden to national budgets, the entire financial system, and the success of the economic transformation in the medium term (see Table 5.4).

Table 5.4: Bad Loans in Selected East Central European Countries

Country	1991	1992	1993	1994
	As % of bank loans to enterprises and individuals			
Hungary	9.4	20.7	42.6	30.2
Poland	16.5	26.8	27.4	29.0
Czech Rep.	2.7	19.3	22.1	38.8
	As % of total assets			
Hungary	4.1	7.5	15.7	11.0
Poland	6.9	10.2	9.7	9.8
Czech Rep.	1.2	10.4	10.5	20.1
	As % of GDP			
Hungary	3.5	5.4	11.9	7.9
Poland	2.2	3.3	2.7	3.2
Czech Rep.	1.9	14.2	16.9	30.4

Source: Anderson, Berglöf, and Mizsei 1996, 15.

The fact that the rapidly growing private sector has had a subordinate role in the East for the time being does not mean that reformers have not worried about capital flight when initiating and implementing policy reforms. The threat of capital flight in the East may be related not only to private (mostly foreign) firms or institutional owners of (sometimes "hot") currency deposits but also to better-off local individuals and households holding significant currency reserves in foreign-exchange accounts at home or—illegally—abroad. Estimates of these accounts point to significant potential losses that would threaten national financial balances in cases where reform policies were judged unacceptable by the owners.[3] Worries about currency flight have shaped policy makers' views wherever they have attempted to target the "correct" exchange rate or plan risky steps toward convertibility or unified taxation.

However, in order to make a useful comparison of potentially threatening social responses, a distinction between the South and the East is necessary. One certainly has to take into account that the emerging private sector in Eastern Europe has not ended its dependency on the public sector. Rather, for the time being, privatization in the East implies the emergence of a hybrid sector regarding ownership, resources, and regulation, as opposed to a clear separation of the public and private sectors.[4]

While in the East the private sector has often emerged in the shadow of the public sector, close interrelationships have often been maintained between the two during the transformation. As a consequence of privatization, many of the transformed state-owned firms have mixed ownership structures (Voszka 1992). Many new private or hybrid (public and private) entrepreneurs came from the public sector, as is evident in their skills, habits, attitudes, and—what is most important—their networks of acquaintances. Many emerging entrepreneurs initially retained their jobs in the state sector. Using public resources for private aims has deep roots in the East European tradition, and this practice continued at least in the beginning of the transformation (Laki 1993).

Private or hybrid firms often assert monopoly power in economic transactions—again a legacy of the communist economy but also the result of certain privatization practices. The lack of a clear separation of the private and public sectors is further reflected by both the heterogeneity of membership and the strategy of new and old business associations to encompass diverse interests (Tóth 1992). The private sector, just like parts of the public one, has been subsidized and supported in other ways by the state during the initial years of transformation. Eligibility for various subsidies was extended to the hybrid sector, which was correctly considered a dynamic area of ownership transformation.

Through this policy approach, hybridization not only helped the private to penetrate the public (forcing the SOEs to become more efficient) but had the opposite effect as well. Subsidies may have contributed to maintaining typical public-firm practices: dependency on state paternalism, competition for subsidies and exemptions, and economy-wide risk aversion (Laki 1993, Major 1992). Multinational corporations (MNCs), "the heavy artillery of capitalism," joined indigenous public, private, and hybrid firms in benefiting from the Eastern governments' support for privatization. Competing host governments in the region have lured MNCs with a wide variety of privileges, and there is evidence that the corporations' own requirements often exceeded the generosity of the hosts.

The implication is that hybridization of the economy hybridizes the public and private economic agents' attitudes as well as their politico-economic weapons. In the East it is the inventive combination of typically "public" and "private" responses by actors of the hybrid economy that reformers have to fear probably much more than do their fellow reformers in Latin America.

While *protest voting* against economic transformation or reformist parties and governments is not a threat in regimes that restrict democratic rights, anticipated electoral behavior may constrain economic reformers in democratic societies. But even there, voting plays a less decisive role in the interelection period when reformers may act relatively free from electoral concerns. However, market-oriented transformation strategies may obviously be stopped or adversely affected through democratic elections. Voting may therefore pose a crucial threat to economic adjustment in democracies and democratizing systems.

All citizens eligible to vote may threaten reforms aimed at radical economic transformation by voting against them. However, while some groups or individuals may pose other threats as well, pensioners, for instance, basically have no other defense. Elderly people in general, and pensioners in particular, cannot strike or riot when they feel aggrieved. The same is often (but not always) true for people in rural areas, who live dispersed in the countryside and typically lack organization. Notwithstanding this generalization, well-organized and vocal rural groups in Poland and Hungary, for example, have passionately opposed unwanted policies employing a broad repertoire of protest actions.

A comparative assessment of the importance of voting as an expression of discontent requires a comparison of the proportion of pensioners, or elderly in general, and of unorganized, rural sectors in the entire population and in the electorate in the South and the East. In addition one has to assess these groups' chances to vote freely, as supported or constrained by the electoral system and by other institutional, educational, or cultural factors.

Such a comparison suggests that the structural importance of socio-economic groups who lack the means to express opposition to reforms except by voting against them (groups that include the old, retired, and rural population) tends to be substantially larger in Eastern Europe than in much of Latin America (see table 5.5). Also, it should be noted that, due to higher educational standards, old and rural people in the East may be generally less constrained in using their only weapon of protest—voting—than is the case in the South.

Table 5.5: Age Structure of the Population in Latin America and Eastern Europe (1990–91)

Country	(a)15–59 years as % of total	(b)60+ years as % of total	(c)Senior citizens as % of "politically potent" population = (b) per [(a) plus (b)]	Rural population as % of total
Bulgaria	60.5	18.9	23.8	32
Czechosl.	60.8	16.7	21.5	22
Hungary	61.4	19.2	23.8	37
Poland	60.2	14.1	19.0	38
Romania	60.9	14.4	19.1	47
Argentina	56.8	12.9	18.5	14
Brazil	57.7	7.1	10.5	25
Chile	60.4	7.7	11.3	14
Ecuador	55.0	3.7	6.3	44
Mexico	57.8	5.7	9.0	27
Peru	54.0	7.0	11.5	30
Venezuela	56.0	5.7	9.2	9

Source: Tények könyve, 93 (Book of Facts, 93).

Tax evasion, illegal employment, and street trading as well as organized crime, and the drug economy constitute the type of social response that I call *going informal*. On the various kinds of informal economic activity, their political effects, and the difference between the informal economy and the communist "second" economy, see Sík (1994). While certain ways of going informal can be seen as strategies for coping with economic hardship rather than as weapons to oppose reforms, others have different implications. The danger in going informal consists in the fact that effective economic and political reforms depend in part on the willingness of social actors to adhere to certain societal conventions or formalities and to accept the rule of law. Going informal, therefore, may threaten the required level of conformity to these norms.

Economic and, in the medium term, political transformations may be undermined by actors from both the popular sectors and better-off groups, including some elites, as they go informal along different, often group-specific paths. The significance of the groups, and their characteristic paths in the South and the East, may be assessed by comparing factors such as the growth rate of unemployment; declining GDP and the number of consecutive recession years; the resulting drop in earnings and living standards; regional and country-specific respect for formality and legality; the level of tax burdens, social security, and unemployment-benefit contributions; traditions of blurred boundaries between the private and public economy; freedom of travel enabling tourists to trade; regional political and military instability and the resulting waves of refugees; and geographical proximity to international routes for illegal trade (of drugs, cars, fur, arms, and the like).

Needless to say, it is difficult to get beyond anecdotal evidence to collect reliable data on the "informalization" of economic activity, not to mention the difficulties in comparing the Southern and Eastern experiences in this respect. Nevertheless, while it is not easy to interpret the potential threat associated with going informal, even in a qualitative way, most estimates available on recent Eastern trends suggest that the risks are increasing. In the following section I present tentative conclusions about how the typology outlined above might be useful for comparative interpretations of the political dynamics of postcommunist politico-economic transformations.

On the Political Economy of Protest and Patience in the South and East

My aim in this discussion is limited to stressing some probable and important differences in the politics of Eastern transformations as compared to Southern cases, rather than providing a credible political assessment and forecast.[5] Explanations for the nonviolent nature of the Eastern transformation process have tended to focus on the peaceful takeover of power in 1989–90, or have emphasized elite attitudes and behavior. Regarding the latter, I share Ost's view that "by turning state property into their own private property," the old elite "only further undermine the reasons why they might ever want to restore the old communist system" (Ost 1992, 49. For a similar argument see Urbán 1991, 309, and Lipton and Sachs 1990, 2–3).

The comparison with Latin America may in turn help to explain why changes have proceeded in a nonviolent way from 1991 to the present writing. Moreover, it provides us with the chance to enrich the general picture with a couple of society-centered arguments. Some such explanations start with the view, favored mainly by economic reformers, that citizens of the postcommunist countries who had become deeply frustrated with the economic performance of the previous regime genuinely *like* capitalism and market reforms. Thus, in David Ost's formulation, they "approve of the economic values behind the policies making their lives worse" (Ost 1995, 179). However, after their initial strong political support of the reforms, people increasingly became disappointed with them. Still, they voiced their discontent with less intensity and in less politically disruptive forms than was expected and than citizens had done in many Latin American and other Third World countries. Therefore, society-centered explanations, which stress the importance of factors that would have worked even in the absence of strong initial support to the capitalist transformation, and actually restrained disruptive protest even after support gave way to increasing discontent, may both complement and correct the above view.

My own explanation for the relatively peaceful transformation is that communism left behind societies lacking in the structural, institutional, and cultural factors associated with violent collective action. The lack of extreme income inequality, the smaller number of marginalized poor, the relatively lower degree of urbanization of the population, and the absence of recent, violent experiences with coups and riots may all have contributed a stabilizing influence under postcommunism. It is also important to mention in this context that reformers in the East have not been in a hurry to eliminate the "premature welfare states" (Kornai 1995) left behind by communism. Indeed, from 1990 to 1993 social consumption increased as a share of GDP in several East European countries. (The other side of the coin, of course, is that the relative increase paralleled a deterioration in both the quality and quantity of social services.) In sum: in contrast to the South, large sectors of the population in the postcommunist region could avail themselves of relatively substantial reserves to survive hard times. This may have lessened the risk of violent and disruptive social response to economic stress in the East.

Still, poverty exists in the East as well. There are groups living under desperate conditions who lack access to resources that could carry them through hard times. However, they are more dispersed geographically and their numbers are smaller than is the case for their counterparts in Latin America or elsewhere in the South. It is not solely for this reason that organizing political action has generally turned out to be impossible for them; potential organizers and allies seem to be missing as well. We see little solidarity across social groups in the newly democratizing postcommunist states. Instead, there is some evidence that, in close association with the transitional situation, it is mostly rivalry, struggles for legitimacy, exclusivity, and attempts to monopolize constituencies, rather than the solidarity and cooperation essential for successful political action, that characterizes relations among political parties, labor unions, social movements, and other civil actors. While any further deterioration of their livelihood may be fatal for them, so long as they are left alone by the most vocal social organizations, the poor have few alternatives to political "patience."

Given that Eastern Europe's workforce has been far more unionized than those of many LDCs, and that unions are well represented in many strategic sectors of the economy, it is noteworthy that relatively few strikes have occurred. As a consequence, labor protest has not significantly shaped transformation politics either. While much of the region's labor movement has suffered from impaired credibility, it is also true that the few credible unions, like Poland's Solidarity or Hungary's Democratic League of Independent Trade Unions, initially took a pro-reform position. Later, however, the transformation crisis, declining living standards, and the loss of job security associated with rapidly growing unemployment may have hampered labor's ability to take collective action. Three institutional factors, also partly a legacy of the communist past, however, may contribute to the cooperative stance adopted by most unions. One is the tradition of collusion between labor unions and management, and of common lobbying, originating in pervasive state ownership. The second is that the labor movement has frequently felt an affinity for the ruling political force, an example being the close relationship between Solidarity and Poland's first government. Later there was a similar alliance between the incumbent communist successor parties and the communist successor labor unions in both Poland and Hungary. From time to time, although not always, these alliances have implied explicit or at least tacit union support for the incumbents' economic policies. A third factor is government tactics of either *divide et impera* or strategic compensation, sometimes in the framework of social pacts. As a result, not only the poor but also the more numerous, and in principle more vocal, labor groups have had to remain patient in the face of hardships associated with the crisis and the reforms.

In different forms and to varying extents all population groups, including workers and the poor, have had an important alternative to voice during the entire transformation period—that is, massive exit from the formal economy, or from legality in general. Noncriminal exit forms as alternatives to disruptive, collective protest might have had a stabilizing effect at least in the short run (Sík 1994). Also, the delayed adaptation of firms to the harsh conditions of the postcommunist economy might have brought some short-term relief for their employees. By remaining overstaffed initially, firms may have decreased the risks both of strikes from organized labor and of other disruptive types of threat at the crucial beginning stages.

Attracted by the blurred boundaries between formal and informal, legal and illegal, as well as oriented by their traditionally ambivalent attitude toward the rule of law, Easterners have gone informal or exploited their employers' capacities to enforce protective state intervention instead of protesting violently and collectively under the pressure of need. Rather than voice, it has been exit that has dominated the pattern of social responses to economic stress in the East, and it is partly to this that political stability is due.

This does not mean, however, that there was no massive protest but only that its form was specific. All in all, it is not just the poor and labor groups who have been sentenced to political patience. They were joined by those major social groups whose only defense has been voting: elderly people in general, and pensioners in particular, and sometimes, although not always, segments of the rural population. Both groups had basically no way to protest the economic reforms apart from voting out their executors. This is the context in which we have to consider the importance of the fact that, because of the structural, institutional, and cultural legacies of the previous system, the societal significance of those who had no alternative to the protest vote as a weapon against economic hardship has been relatively large under postcommunism.

Consequently, the characteristic postcommunist pattern is that voice has been biased in favor of using democratic procedures for protest rather than the rest of the repertoire of contention. This, in turn, has had important implications regarding the political dynamics of transformation. Unlike all other contentious groups—such as rioters, strikers, hunger strikers, or violent demonstrators—who pose direct threats to politicians, protest voters cannot disregard the institutional, chronological rhythm of democratic procedures. As Przeworski formulated the process of reform under democratic conditions, "all groups must chan-

nel their demands through democratic institutions and abjure other tactics. . . . They must adopt the institutional calendar as the temporal horizon of their actions, thinking in terms of forthcoming elections, contract
negotiations, or at least fiscal years" (Przeworski 1991, 180).

However, this pattern of social protest, biased in favor of democratic
procedures, has provided economic reformers and democratic politicians
in the East both with more chances for political calculation and a longer
grace period to implement and consolidate economic and political
reforms than has been the case in the South. While it is impossible to tell
whether the lengthier grace period will be long enough, this argument
suggests that there has been a greater possibility than is frequently
assumed both for economic reforms to be implemented and for democracy to be consolidated in the East. Thus we come to a few more preliminary conclusions on the political structures that characterize the new
Eastern democracies.

Firstly, if voting is a significant weapon of protest in the East, any
(planned or unplanned) increased occasions for voting may risk shorten-
ing the grace period granted to economic and political reforms in general, and threaten unpopular reforms with being postponed, adversely
reshaped, or even stopped. Any time when the electorate is given the
chance to protest through voting, economic transformation may become
a major and sensitive campaign issue. The chronological rhythm of
democracy can speed up, and the institutional calendar can be rewritten,
by referenda, presidential elections, and no-confidence votes resulting in
governments' dissolution between regular election terms. This is a point
where country-specific variants of the democratic institutional system
have to be considered. In principle, country-specific differences in the
institutional calendar of democracy may have some bearing on country-
specific patterns of economic transformation. So may political institutions (including the characteristics of the party system) and state institutions, specifically the autonomy, coherence, and capacity of state bureaucracy and its strategies in general.

Secondly, in democratic theory there is not yet agreement about the
relative sociopolitical weight and significance of the three public realms
of society under postcommunism—the state, the polity, and civil society.[6] The theoretical assumption underlying the debate is that in different political systems the center of political gravity can be found alternatively in civil society, the polity, or the state. Each of three arguments
finds supporters in the literature on postcommunism: (1) that state institutions, which have remained relatively the most powerful through the

systemic collapse, continue to distort and suppress the civil realm; (2) that it is the emerging political institutions—that is, the parties—that became most powerful after civil society was "demobilized" by them; and (3) that it is civil society and its characteristic attitudes and behaviors, rather than the state or the polity, that dominates the sociopolitical arena during postcommunist transformation.

Here is the first view, as expressed by Dietrich Rueschemeyer: "Though varying across countries, the overall strength of civil society in Eastern Europe, its organizational density is not great. The state apparatuses, by contrast, may lose functions, and become fragmented, but relatively they often remain strong and, as they are being restructured, they do not find a substantial counterweight in the autonomous organization of the civil society. This is aggravated to the extent, that many interests stand in a relation of a clientelistic dependence to the state" (Rueschemeyer 1992, 26).

Proponents of the "demobilization thesis," however, posit that it was instead the emerging, consolidating political society and its central institutions, the parties, against which civil organizations lost ground shortly after their "hour of truth"—the breakthrough years of the new system: "Although the democratic parties which emerged out of the civil society needed the active support of society during the transitional period, afterwards, due to the demobilising aspect of transition, they had to discharge those 'revolutionary' tendencies" (Bozóki and Sükösd 1993, 230). The resulting political formula under postcommunism is generalized as "partyist" or "partocratic" democracy, "in which parties are the only actors and they try to exclude all the other political and social actors from the policy-making process, monopolizing all the decisions in macro politics in the parliamentary level" (Ágh 1994, 3–4; see also Ágh 1991).

Finally, in contrast to both these views, Grzegorz Ekiert and Jan Kubik reject the idea that anything like a demobilization either by the state or the parties took place in the Polish case. In Poland, they argue, "Given the relative weakness of the state and political society, civil society became the strongest and most rapidly developing realm of the polity" (Ekiert and Kubik 1995, 12, 21–24).

My argument in the preceding and forthcoming chapters contradicts Ekiert and Kubik's interpretation, while it is close to both the first and the second view presented above. In Eastern Europe, the bias toward expressing discontent either individually (by exit) or, in the field of politics, through democratic procedures (the protest vote) appears to suggest that it is the political parties that predominate over labor unions, business associations, and other civic organizational forms. As I have argued, because of their structural, institutional, and cultural legacies the latter could not play a central role in organizing collective protest action and—except at the very beginning—never really shaped transformation political dynamics.

It is certainly not accidental that in 1992, one of the worst years of the transformation recession, there were altogether only a handful of strikes in Hungary involving a few thousand participants. The picture was not much different in other countries of Eastern Europe. In their preliminary analysis of political protest in Poland, Hungary, East Germany, and Slovakia, Ekiert and Kubik themselves conclude that protest events had not significantly outnumbered those of the West European countries, and in some cases their number was actually smaller (Ekiert and Kubik 1996, 4).

Nevertheless, year by year millions of Hungarians choose the exit option, as demonstrated by the fact that one-third of the Hungarian GDP is produced in the informal economy. In addition, millions of citizens participate in elections whenever they get the chance to express their political preferences, including their dissatisfaction with economic hardship and the reforms. Moreover, my point is that the apparent, relative lack of direct, synchronous protest actions and the dramatic realignment of support around various points of the political spectrum are just two sides of the same coin. The more Eastern societies seem to be "sentenced to patience" in interelection periods, the greater are the pent-up demands released during elections and furiously seeking to punish those who supposedly caused injury to citizens' interests.

Parties mobilizing protest votes have been in such great demand that, within the first seven years of the postcommunist period, politicians representing much of the political spectrum have had a chance to be elected and to tackle the difficult tasks of transformation, even the initially handicapped socialists. However, this means that leftist governments can be as furiously voted out as their predecessors, if the economic situation fails to improve substantially or if the therapy requires too much sacrifice, as recently happened in Lithuania, Romania, and Bulgaria.

However, while I think that it is political parties, rather than other organizations of the civil society, that dominate the political arena and shape the political future of Eastern Europe, they certainly do not do so alone. In accordance with the view expressed above by Rueschemeyer, in Chapter 9 I present evidence that state institutions also try to dominate

civil society and, at least in the Hungarian case, they have been successful.

Finally, if my statement on the dominant role of parties is valid, it is
important to ask about the parties' economic and political visions and
practices in order to predict future directions of change in the East. I
examine these in Chapter 6 and Chapter 7 in the specific context of an
analysis of populism and populist parties under postcommunism.

However, at first glance a striking uniformity of policy options is
apparent in the East Central European transition. Neither the country-
specific characteristics of the political system nor the ideological preferences of the incumbents seem to be closely reflected in the economic
policy choices of the respective governments. This implies that the most
widely used political weapon against the crisis and the reform in the East,
the democratic protest vote, may have less impact than is assumed.
Citizens vote out economic policies injurious to their immediate interests, only to witness their stubborn recurrence under different party banners.

Chapter 6
Rethinking Populism under Postcommunism

In the initial years of the transformation, populism has become a hot issue academically and politically. However, much of what has been written about it has contributed to confusing rather than clarifying what populism means.[1] One reason for this may be that the subject was first introduced into the transformation discourse in a negatively biased way. Warnings against "the populist threat" to economic and political transformation preceded or totally replaced careful analysis of populism's real attributes under postcommunism. Another reason may be its inconsistent interpretation in social science in general.

Inconsistent Interpretations

Some commentators point to the difficulty of aiming at a moving target: "Populism, anyway, belongs to those ideas that are most difficult to define and that in certain historical situations, regions, and societies have emerged in an ever changing form" (Bozóki and Sükösd 1993, 232). Other analyses, however, put the blame on social science: "like the proverbial blind man trying to describe an elephant by feeling its individual parts, conceptions of populism are shaped by selective attention to its multiple components as well as by national and regional peculiarities" (Roberts 1995, 84).

This observation appears to apply to much of the sporadic theorizing on populism under postcommunism as well. Populism is often linked with a single negative component such as irresponsible promises or the antagonism between the nation and the "alienated elite." Then it is argued or tacitly assumed that the larger social construct exhibiting the negative component will tend toward other predictable attributes, such as a multiclass sociopolitical coalition or a package of protectionist, expansionist, and redistributive economic policies adopted in response to societal pressures.

This brand of populism, however, has never existed under postcommunism. My aim is to describe the subtype that does exist. First I present a critical review of populism as it is depicted in academic and political discourse, in terms of the "populist threat." I also review some reasons for the term's popularity in political language. Then, given the worries expressed in social science, I seek to explain why postcommunist economic history has lacked any notable populist politico-economic episode. This in turn leads me to conceptualize a subtype of populism under postcommunism from its empirically observable attributes in the Hungarian case, which I think will help us to understand similar phenomena in other East European countries. Finally, I show how an underlying logic integrates the subtype's features.

Conflicting Views of the "Populist Threat"

Soon after the transformation began, professional economists and economic policy makers began to express anxiety about the possibility that populist politics might derail economic reforms and, consequently, democracy itself. Sachs was probably the earliest and most influential with his warning published just two weeks after the Polish stabilization program began: "Populist politicians will try to hook up with coalitions of workers, managers and bureaucrats in hard-hit sectors to slow or reverse the adjustment—just as they have, successfully, in Argentina for more than a generation" (Sachs 1990, 21; Lipton and Sachs 1990, 18–19).

Such warnings were accompanied by advice to sidestep the populists by rapid and resolute reform initiatives: "Only decisive actions by a reformist government can keep these populist pressures in check" (Lipton and Sachs 1990, 18). Thus, radical economic reformers seek to undermine their opponents by establishing "the principles of free trade, currency convertibility and free entry to business early in the transformation" (Sachs 1990, 21). Lipton and Sachs were not alone in perceiving the populist danger as an argument for reform radicalism.

The most dramatic formulation of the same view by an economic politician was a speech delivered in December 1992 by Yegor Gaidar, then acting prime minister of Russia. If the reforms are not pursued, he warned, "then we will develop not according to the American or Swedish pattern, but according to African or Latin American patterns . . . [leading to] the chronic poverty and political instability, the populist politicians and dictatorships so common in Third World states" (in Jeffries 1993, 482–83). Corresponding views were expressed by analysts and politicians in varied contexts (Balcerowicz 1995, 307; Aslund 1991, 19).

There were, however, entirely different opinions on the causes and nature of the populist threat, proposed either by economists critical of the radical reforms or social scientists worrying about their social and political consequences. The critics saw the sweeping economic reforms and underlying political project as the surest way not of avoiding but of *provoking* populism, mainly in politics but also in the economy. Populism thus came to be seen as a consequence of radical economic reforms rather than an obstacle to them: "Paradoxically, then, what pushes Eastern Europe away from democracy and towards populist authoritarianism is precisely the neoliberal program" (Ost 1992, 50). The logic of the argument, Ost explains, is that if the majority of people and "particularly workers . . . in the still-dominant state sector" see no role they can play "in building the new society" and no alternative to marginalization, "they become receptive to demagogues" (48–51).

A similar argument—that neoliberalism, or more specifically its collapse, breeds populism—was raised by Jerzy Hausner. Continuing the liberal-monetarist policy, he argued, will condemn the government to failure, "which will open the way for populist solutions" (Hausner 1992, 128). Liberal monetarists will have neither the will nor the means to solve "'the financial crisis of the state' . . . the root cause of the populist threat in the transformation process of socialist societies," Hausner continues. However, "in such a situation, the social masses, disoriented and burdened by the effects of the socioeconomic crisis, lose their faith in the governing elite and their ability to overcome the situation. Thus, they feverishly look for new hope and identity" (124–27). Gérard Roland suggests a similar scenario (Roland 1992, 1), while Attila Ágh wrote that the populist-authoritarian threat would be activated if East Central Europe's integration in the European Union should fail or be only marginal (Ágh 1991, 116).

Other authors have argued less against the radical reforms than against the political perspective "that the process of economic restructuring and the maintenance of competitive politics can only be sustained amidst popular demobilisation and political fragmentation of mass constituencies" (Commisso, Dubb, and McTigue 1992, 27). The latter authors' suggestion for avoiding populism is the same as Ost's—*inclusion:* Any populist threat is likely to originate in a popular sector that is inadequately represented by strong labor unions and left-wing political parties (53).

Who Are the Populists?

While there is an essentially opposing logic underlying the two streams of thought presented here, they also have many things in common.

Both, for instance, perceive populism as a threat, and they relate the likelihood of its activation to the dynamics of economic transformation, either to its exaggerated, or to its insufficient speed. Similarly, they refer to the Latin American experience, albeit with a different interpretation. However, the discourse on the populist threat resulted in confusion regarding the particular ideological, political, and socioeconomic identity of Eastern European populists. While some analysts refer to specific countries, such as Poland, others consider Poland, the Czech Republic, Hungary and Slovakia, while for many writers populism is a threat to all East European reformer nations.

There is also disagreement concerning the socioeconomic source of the populist danger. Sachs points at the multiclass coalition of bureaucrats, managers, and workers in the shrinking sectors, while many other authors refer to lower social groups: "disoriented social masses," the "millions of people marginalized," or the economic "losers." Still other analysts are anxious about the populist tendencies of the upper or propertied classes: "If there is a threat of populism, it is likely to come from these groups" (Commisso, Dubb, and McTigue 1992, 53). Bozóki and Sükösd similarly posit that "In Hungary, Poland and Slovakia, it was not so much a populist protest by the masses that one had to fear as that, in the period of 'political hangover' following the radical change, some power groups, playing the 'populist card,' referring to the 'people's' dissatisfaction, would try to overcome other politically elite groups" (1993, 231).

Finally, the problem of who the populists actually are or, more specifically, which political actors are prepared to play the populist card, seems to be either the least interesting question or the major unsolved puzzle in the discourse over the populist threat. Their concrete program and their historical, ideological, and cultural backgrounds have not been extensively studied.

Their references to the Latin American experience indicate that Lipton, Sachs, Gaidar, and others worried about the emergence of a similar social phenomenon under postcommunism, with all the core features from fiscal indiscipline to authoritarianism. However, one has the impression that for the radical reformers, anyone opposing the radical program might be labeled a populist, including their fellow economists and policy makers with alternative reform proposals. (See Lipton and Sachs 1990, 81. A similar criticism of radical reformers is raised in Hausner 1992, 128.) Balcerowicz, in turn, mentions "influential trade unions that played a large role in toppling communism only to turn increasingly populist (Solidarity in Poland, Podkrepa in Bulgaria)" (Balcerowicz 1995, 163). Thus populists reveal their identity mainly by their attitude to the pace and concrete design of the economic transformation strategy. "Populist" becomes a synonym for "opponent of neoliberalism" and vice versa.

Disinterest in the actual ideological, political, and social positions of real-world populists is most explicit in the framework used by Roland for assessing the political economy of the transition period. Proceeding from the assumption that it is the distinction between "conservatives" and "reformers" that really matters, he argues that "Conservatives are those in favour of status quo and who oppose concrete moves towards the market, whatever their ideological convictions, Stalinist or populist. On the contrary, reformers approve moves towards the introduction of market institutions. One could introduce additional dimensions, but this would unnecessarily complicate the task" (Roland 1991, 48–49).

There is one obvious explanation why the discourse on the populist threat helped little in defining and identifying it. It is the fact that this debate was not about populism but the proper approach to economic and political reform. Political economists and economic politicians expressed conflicting expectations regarding the feasibility and political and social impact of reforms, and used the same catchword, populism, to invoke all sorts of negative consequences that would result from their opponents' suggestions. As Commisso and her collaborators put it, the debate was between a liberal "utopia" and its populist "pathology" rather than between empirically verified concepts (Commisso, Dubb, and McTigue 1992, 27).

This also may explain why proponents of the conflicting views neglected additional dimensions that could better have identified the populist threat. Any specificity concerning its meaning would have limited the term's expressive power as an encompassing "pathologic" danger. The thin historical, ideological, and social "local content" with which, if at all, postcommunist populism has been endowed were labels of anticommunism, anticapitalism, anti-Semitism, xenophobia, and nationalism (Ost 1992, 49).

In addition, there have been sporadic attempts at conceptualizing populism under postcommunism by combining negative elements originating in conflicting interpretations. Bozóki and Şükösd, for instance, assume, "A general trait of East European populist politics is that, more often than not, it uses *national* and *social* rhetoric at the same time. . . . The national-populist rhetoric can be coupled with anti-West feelings, xenophobia and anti-capitalism which, in a period of increasing unemployment and a painful economic transition, can be conveniently completed with social demagogic demands for 'fair' central distribution" (Bozóki and Sükösd 1993, 231–32).

The scholarly perspective on populism under postcommunism was thus dominated by the notion of a complex "pathology" exhibiting an assortment of political and economic ills ranging from anticapitalist to anti-intellectual attitudes, and from illiberal nationalism to statist protectionism. I have argued in Chapter 2 that market socialism and "the third way" underwent a similar transformation into pathologic terms in the policy discourse. Sometimes the two groups of terms became combined, with market socialists and proponents of the third way becoming the populists. Powerful as it was, this characterization proved to be more useful as a resource for political competition than as sound scientific generalization.

Further on in my discussion I will challenge these conceptualizations by noting crucial elements that are missing from the presented conceptual mix. It will suffice here to point out one of the best-known cases to contradict such ideas, that of the populist Stanislaw Tyminski's remarkable victory over Tadeusz Mazowiecki in Poland's 1990 presidential campaign. The victory was not based on anticapitalist and anti-Western prejudices but just the opposite: inexperienced and uncritical pro-Western feelings (Balcerowicz 1995, 298; Johnson and Kowalska 1994, 221).

Populism Becomes a Bad Word

As Commisso and her colleagues argue, "utopias and pathologies supply the raw material for political debates about the paradigms they express" (Commisso, Dubb, and McTigue 1992, 27). Uncorrected by social science, politicians in Eastern Europe made full use of the pathologic interpretation of populism. They capitalized on the opportunity to enrich their vocabulary with "a catch-all term which lumped together aspects belonging in very different contexts" (Boeckh 1993, 1). One need not stress the practical political value of a complex label implying social demagogy, economic irresponsibility, and reactionary authoritarianism that could be used to stigmatize adversaries with quite varied political and ideological backgrounds.

The result was a notable success in constructing populism as a bad word in the language of politics. Clearly, economic hardship, which was said to breed populist fervor, has been present in the region. And some groups have in fact made irresponsible appeals and put forth demands that have threatened both liberal democracy and economic stabilization. However, the fact that almost no government, interest group, political party, or social movement has escaped charges of populism leveled by one or another competitor (and analyst), and that demagogic populism seems always to be on the agenda, reflects the term's alarmingly inflated use.

Thus we are left with some essential unanswered questions. Is it true, for example, that everybody who opposed the radical program of economic transformation was a populist? After all, one cannot ignore the emergence of influential opponents with entirely different social origins and ideological beliefs, such as social democracy or classical conservatism. The implication is that the proper conceptualization of populism under postcommunism should not include opponents of reform radicalism from within the democratic political camp to which the reform radicals themselves belonged.

Conversely, is it true that all chauvinist, nationalist, and racist political actors under postcommunism would automatically favor economic populism and radically oppose the neoliberal mainstream? In Chapter 7 I argue that the answer is no. Finally, if concerns about equity and acceptable living standards on one hand, and national, ethnic, or racial identity on the other were as central to postcommunist politics as some social scientists suggest, then how could it happen that, alone among political parties, it is only the populists (the only political actors allegedly campaigning on the supposedly popular platform combining national and social rhetoric) who have never succeeded in winning control of politics and economic policy making in East Central Europe? This is the puzzle to which now I turn.

The Prototypical Experience: Populist Episodes in Latin America

How has it happened that the East's recent economic history has lacked any notable populist experiment? Why is it that no populist movement has managed to take control of macroeconomic policy? In developing my explanation, I use a concept of economic populism reflecting the experience of Latin American populist economic episodes.[2] In accordance with Kaufman and Stallings, the episodes I refer to include the governments of Salvador Allende (Chile, 1970–73), Juan Perón (Argentina, 1973–76), Alán García (Peru, 1985–90), José Sarney

(Brazil, 1985–90), and Luis Echevarría and José López Portillo (Mexico, 1970–76 and 1976–82) (Kaufman and Stallings 1991, 16).

There is both a contextual and a methodological argument supporting the use of the Latin American experience as a point of comparison. The former is that there were numerous references made to it in the discourse on "the populist threat" under postcommunism both by the radical reformers and their opponents. Methodologically, however, I find it helpful to assume, with Roberts, that an "integral, prototypical populist experience such as that of Argentina under Perón would . . . aggregate the core features [of populism]. . . . By disaggregating, it is then possible to identify populist subtypes that share a 'family resemblance' and manifest some but not all of the core attributes" (Roberts 1995, 88). What I am specifically interested in below, then, is why it is that, contrary to expectations, nothing like a Latin American–style populist episode occurred in Eastern Europe. It may have to do with the fact that, first, the structural antagonisms that have been conducive to populist economic experiments in Latin America, such as dramatic income inequalities and a sharp division between the traditional export sectors (mining and agriculture) and producers of nontraded goods, have never been characteristic of East European societies. Second, since the transformation began, neither the political nor the economic conditions favored a populist economic experiment. At times, economic populism was feasible from a strictly macroeconomic point of view, but the necessary political conditions were missing. Conversely, there were moments when political factors seemed to favor a populist turn in economic policy making, but macroeconomic factors prevented it. While there has as yet been no convergence of political and economic factors favorable to populism, this may occur in the future.

In Latin America, populism has meant an economic policy mix designed to mobilize political support from organized labor, the lower-middle class, and domestically oriented business. This entailed the political isolation of the rural oligarchy, foreign enterprises, and the large-scale domestic industrial elite (Kaufman and Stallings 1991). Typically, this policy package, aimed at steering economic activity into domestic sectors producing goods for basic consumption, includes budget deficits to stimulate domestic demand, nominal wage increases with price controls to effect income redistribution, and exchange-rate control or appreciation to cut inflation and raise wages and profits in the nontraded goods sectors.

Analysts agree that populist economic policy makers, while concentrating on income redistribution by macro-policy means, have tended to disregard macroeconomic constraints. More specifically, the populist approach to economics "emphasises growth and income redistribution and de-emphasises the risks of inflation and deficit finance, external constraints and the reaction of economic agents to aggressive non-market policies" (Dornbusch and Edwards 1989, 1). The literature stresses that the rejection both of efficiency criteria and of concern for macroeconomic balance was based on principle and was not the accidental by-product of populist episodes. However, populist programs cannot be treated as mere aberrations; as Drake stresses, they responded "to the problems of underdevelopment by expanding state activism to incorporate the workers in a process of accelerated industrialisation through ameliorative redistributive measures" (Drake 1982, 218). Experiments with economic populism have been much more coherent than just the incorporation of a few politically based priorities into the process of economic policy making. The latter is a general characteristic of political regimes. A populist episode occurs, however, when populist measures dominate the macroeconomic policy mix (Bazdresch and Levy 1991).

The failures of populist economic experiments are associated with both inaccurate assumptions and the neglect of structural constraints. Neglect of the inflationary impact of budget deficits leads to rapid inflation or hyperinflation. Neglect of international constraints leads to a swift drying up of international reserves and to a rapid deterioration in the trade and current-account balance. Neglect of the macroeconomic constraints on large-scale income redistribution leads to dramatically adverse distributive consequences. Organized labor and lower-middle income groups, targeted as the main beneficiaries of populist redistribution, have actually been much worse off after populist episodes than before. All this did not happen without grave political consequences.

These are some of the realities that may have made the reformers and their foreign advisers anxious about the turn to economic populism in Eastern Europe. It is not the focus of my discussion, however, to analyze in any depth why populist economic policies failed. (See Dornbusch and Edwards 1989, Bazdresch and Levy 1991, Sturzenegger 1991, and Lago 1991 on the most important reasons.) Despite these evident failures, however, new populist episodes recurred in Latin America at least until the 1980s. And why are populist economic policies tried at all? One answer is that they can produce short-term economic and political benefits. Economic populism is tempting precisely because it does not back-fire immediately. That occurs only later, when budget and current-account balances deteriorate and international reserves dry up. Under specific conditions, important macroeconomic indicators like growth, inflation, and real wages may actually improve dramatically in the short run. In other words, populist policies pay politically.[3]

Structural explanations for the recurrence of populist episodes in Latin America point to two particular features. One is the extreme income and asset inequality characteristic of many Latin American countries. Income polarization may intensify redistributive pressures. The second structural problem is the distributional struggle pitting employers and workers in industry and services against the primary-products export sector dominated by the traditional oligarchy. Populist policies that penalize the rural export sector have been politically popular because export earnings benefit only a small fraction of the population while those targeted for populist redistribution constitute a large and vocal group of voters (Sachs 1989, Kaufman and Stallings 1991). The class and structural divisions in Latin American societies do not constitute a satisfactory explanation, however, because populist episodes have also occurred in countries characterized by more balanced income patterns as well as by closer ties between the export sectors and the rest of the economy.

Also important are features of the political institutions and of the regime that translate socioeconomic structural tensions and pressures into political behavior and policy choice. Two types of party structures have been found to facilitate populist experiments: the exclusionary and the unstable multiparty patterns. Perónistas in Argentina and Apristas in Peru represented popular sectors that were periodically excluded from the political process (Kaufman and Stallings 1991, 24). Multiparty systems without exclusionary elements and fragmentation, however, limit the chances for populist turnabouts.

With regard to regime type, both established authoritarian systems and consolidated democracies are unlikely to experiment with economic populism. However, transitional democracies that have only recently moved from authoritarian to democratic rule are extremely susceptible. All democracies in postcommunist Eastern Europe are in transition. None, however, has experimented with populist macroeconomic policy episodes so far. One reason may be the profound structural differences between Latin America and Eastern Europe. Another might have been the catastrophic macroeconomic situation in the early transformation period.

Structural Differences of the East and the Macroeconomic Constraints

None of the structural characteristics conducive to economic populism in Latin America can be found in postcommunist Eastern Europe. Take income and asset distribution. Despite rapidly increasing income polarization since 1989, postcommunist income distribution has remained far more balanced than in Latin America (which is extreme even by Third World standards). There is also a sense that populism is not necessary in Eastern Europe since communism left these countries with a legacy of relatively egalitarian social welfare benefits. Much of the former social, educational, and health-care systems remains in place, putting extreme pressures on the state household even in the absence of additional populist economic initiatives.

Another important difference is that the export sector in Eastern Europe is less sharply divided from other economic sectors than is often the case in Latin America. Rather, it functions as a complex of developmental, productive, and marketing activities focused on competitive markets and unevenly spread in the active structure of firms (Greskovits 1987). Populist pressures for redistribution at the expense of the export sector are thus weaker. Sectors oriented to domestic markets have had less opportunity to enforce the kind of economic policy turnabouts typical of Latin America. Of course, just as sharp structural divisions alone cannot explain the intensity of redistributional pressures placed on governments, their absence is no guarantee that there will be no such pressures.

My argument is that even if such pressures existed and East European policymakers felt tempted by them, the latter would still be firmly constrained from pursuing populist policies during the early transition period. This is because one cannot simply "go populist" at will. The Latin American experience demonstrates that even populist adventures, which ostensibly disregard macroeconomic constraints, are still dependent on specific macroeconomic conditions. The most important point is that populist episodes rarely begin during extreme macroeconomic instability and deep recession. This is, however, not to say that populism has nothing to do with economic crisis. (See Boeckh 1993 on the roots of Latin American economic populism in the Great Depression.) Rather, under certain external and domestic political conditions, populist episodes may begin immediately afterwards, when there is a little "breathing space." None of the Latin American populist episodes started in a deep recession. Out of six such periods in Argentina, Brazil, Chile, Mexico, and Peru, only the 1985–90 Peruvian experiment was initiated during a slight recession. The others were preceded by economic growth, even if policymakers thought actual growth was below its potential. Other macroeconomic indicators were also more or less acceptable prior to populist experiments in Chile (1970), Argentina (1973), Mexico (1970 and 1977), Peru (1985), and Brazil (1985). No short-term macroeconomic catastrophe was forecast on the basis of macroeconomic indicators alone. These facts are of utmost importance in that populist economic policies need adequate financing. In the pre-populist era, inflation was high although not excessive by Latin American standards. In most cases there was no hyperinflation. Budget deficits, ranging from 2.7 percent of GDP in Chile (1970) to 6–7 percent in Mexico and Peru (in 1977 and 1985 respectively), were high, although dramatically lower than those resulting from the populist episode. In most cases the trade balance was positive, and/or the current-account deficit was low, and substantial international reserves were available. In addition, populist regimes could often acquire additional financial resources by nationalizing differential rents from the country's main export products—copper in Chile and oil in Venezuela and Mexico (Boeckh 1993, Bazdresch and Levy 1991).

The "acceptable" economic situation, though far from satisfactory, was certainly not independent of the standard stabilization and adjustment programs introduced prior to the populist episodes. In fact, orthodox stabilization and adjustment programs can be said to have "bred" economic populism in two ways: first, by improving "the budget and the external balance sufficiently to provide the room for, though perhaps not the wisdom of, a highly expansionary program," and, second, by feeding the dissatisfaction of politicians and the population with poor growth results and the serious distributive consequences of the mainstream adjustment approach (Dornbusch and Edwards 1989, 5).

However, the above lesson contrasts with an argument raised in the discourse on the populist threat in the East European context, to the effect that economic populism would be "an undesirable though unavoidable consequence of [the neoliberal stabilization programs'] collapse" (Hausner 1992, 127). My point is that economic populism can emerge from the temporary success, not the collapse, of neoliberal stabilization programs. Macroeconomic collapse, in turn, would bring about economic and political disorder instead of the fairly systematic enforcement of specific socioeconomic interests to the detriment of others, and the exploitation of political benefits of this process, by which economic populism as government policy is meant.

If moments of relative and temporary balance have provided the macroeconomic conditions for populism in Latin America, the absence of such conditions is what is most striking in the early years of East European postcommunism. From 1990 on, macroeconomic indicators have pointed to a substantially *more* devastated landscape in Eastern Europe than in Latin America prior to populist episodes, rendering any populist approach virtually impossible. The unprecedented recession in postcommunist Eastern Europe has in fact been deeper than the recession that followed the collapse of populist experiments in Latin America. The breakdown of populism implied a 2.9 percent drop of the GNP in 1976 in Argentina. Corresponding declines are 5.6 percent for Chile (1973), 10.4 percent for Peru (1989), and 0.6 percent for Mexico (1982), while Mexico and Brazil actually continued to grow after 1976 and 1987.

The breakdown of communism, however, has been accompanied by a contraction of 11.6 percent in Poland, 11.9 percent in Hungary, 14.2 percent in the Czech Republic, 14.5 percent in Slovakia, 11.7 percent in Bulgaria, and 15.4 percent in Romania.[4] Not only the depth but also the length of the crisis was unprecedented; 1992 was the fourth consecutive year of recession for most of Eastern Europe, and only Poland experienced a modest recovery. One can hardly find anything comparable even in Latin America in the 1980s, a decade characterized as "lost" in terms of growth (Nelson 1990, Appendix, Table 1).

Besides the recession, other macroeconomic conditions have blocked populist adventures in Eastern Europe. Budget deficits have reached or exceeded levels of the peak growth years of populist episodes in Latin America. This is all the more striking since Latin American budget deficits were fueled by fiscal expansion and an overheated economy, while in Eastern Europe they occurred without any new investment programs. The overall rate of inflation was as high or higher in Eastern Europe than in prepopulist Latin America. With regard to international reserves as well as trade and payments balances, most of Eastern Europe has fared the same or even worse than Latin America prior to populism. From 1990 through 1993–94, macroeconomic conditions were never ripe for populist experiments in any East European country. On the contrary, from a macroeconomic viewpoint, Eastern Europe has looked as if it were in a postpopulist era. In fact, one can argue that this resemblance is more than accidental.

Similarities between Communism and Populism

While communist central planning went far beyond any populist experiment in Latin America, communist economic strategy had strong populist-like features. These included:

1. An appeal to organized labor and urban white-collar groups by sanctioning full employment, comfortable wages, and such social benefits as minimum wages, free nurseries and kindergartens, and free health, education, and child-care benefits

2. Import-substitution policies aimed at regional autarky and forced industrialization, prompted by the ambition to "take off" (in Rostow's sense) and "catch up" with the rest of the world

3. A pro-urban and antirural policy aimed at a redistribution of income from rural to urban populations and from agriculture to industry

4. Strong preference for the public over the private sector

5. Considerable restrictions on foreign firms, especially multinational corporations active in the Third World

6. Policies such as budget deficits to stimulate aggregate demand, nominal wage increases with price controls to effect income redistribution, and exchange-rate control or appreciation to cut inflation and to raise wages and profits in non-traded goods sectors

7. An emphasis on growth and income redistribution, and de-emphasis on the risks of deficit finance and of external constraints.

In retrospect, the similarity of the two economic strategies seems to be confirmed by the "medicine" regularly prescribed to cure the resulting economic ills. The internationally sponsored transformation strategy recommended for postcommunist Eastern Europe is remarkably similar to the stabilization and adjustment programs implemented in postpopulist Latin America. As key macroeconomic data show, in the period from 1990 through 1993–94, Eastern European economies were far from cured. They were even far from any "breathing space." In general,

Eastern Europe could not afford economic populism after 1990. Macroeconomic conditions did not provide room for it.

International Constraints

Are macroeconomic constraints the only things preventing a populist turn? The question is more relevant with respect to the Balkans. Evidence from that region shows that under specific conditions the actual state of the economy does not matter. What is important is the maintenance of certain "rules of the game." In the East European context these rules have been mainly of an international nature. They include a collaborative relationship with the IMF, the World Bank, and the international banking community and a desire in the East Central European countries to become as close as possible to the European Community. In the early transformation period a number of countries in the region have tried to maintain the image of committed reformers, reliable debtors, and potential members of an united Europe.[5]

In Eastern Europe, macroeconomic constraints along with a specific international context have limited policy options in general, including any tendency toward economic populism. However, the Latin American experience seems to show that the rules of international financial and economic cooperation can be broken temporarily for the sake of politically motivated policies, provided that macroeconomic performance permits at least short-term internal financing. Thus, Sarney in Brazil, García in Peru, and Betancur in Colombia all broke with the IMF, and both Brazil and Peru announced a moratorium on debt payments when initiating populist policies. For their part, the IMF and the banking community broke with several countries attempting to move toward economic populism. Populism, however, has very poor prospects if it requires challenging international financial sources during times of catastrophic macroeconomic conditions. Under the conditions of early postcommunism, economic populism was simply a nonstarter, regardless of the political circumstances. However, other factors become significant in subsequent transformation phases.

Dominant Economy, Subordinate Politics

In the early years of postcommunism there have been three distinct periods of interaction between political institutions and macroeconomic conditions: the "breakthrough" years of 1989 and 1990; the period of "subordinated politics" from 1990 to 1993–94; and a period of nascent recovery beginning soon after and continuing in 1996–97.

During the first period there was still an economic window of opportunity for a populist turn, in that the macroeconomic situation did not prevent it. The second period—with a deep recession, rapid inflation, large budget deficits, low international reserves, and a domestic politics subordinated to international financial constraints—offered no populist possibilities. The third, most recent period might still see a populist turn should the political opportunity arise.

From a purely macroeconomic viewpoint, the breakthrough years of 1989 and 1990 may have provided the last occasion to introduce populist economic programs in Eastern Europe. This was the "honeymoon" period of the new democratic governments, and macroeconomic conditions did not yet rule out populist experiments, although not all countries enjoyed "permissive" conditions.

Thus in Poland, with a 1989 inflation rate of 639.6 percent, a large budget deficit, a huge external debt burden, and exhausted international reserves, populist policies were never economically feasible. Nor was there any political support for them. Virtually all the important political forces at the time, from Solidarity to the former communists, supported stabilization and some form of "mainstream" neoliberal transformation scenario. Even public opinion at the time showed a willingness to accept hardships as the condition for a better future. Nor was economic populism feasible in Yugoslavia because of the catastrophic economic conditions: a near 10 percent decline in GNP in both 1989 and 1990, with hyperinflation in 1989 and over 100 percent inflation in 1990, and a severe budget and current-account deficit. The subsequent ethnic hostility and civil war only pushed the country into deeper economic chaos, with further devastating economic consequences in the following years. In any case, it was not macroeconomic income redistribution but nationalist and ethnic appeals that were used for political mobilization in the former Yugoslavia.

In Hungary and Czechoslovakia, however, economic populism was viable in principle. In 1989 GDP dropped by only about 1 percent in Hungary and actually grew by 1.3 percent in Czechoslovakia. Inflation was increasing but remained relatively low and far from dramatic in both countries; budget and current-account deficits were also at tolerable levels. Yet economic populism was shunned. In Hungary there was still the memory of the failed quasi-populist attempt at revitalizing the economy in 1985–87 (Ungvárszki 1989). Key macroeconomic indicators at the time resembled those of failed Latin American populist efforts. The failed effort discredited the communists' reputation as competent

reformers and aroused considerable suspicion of hasty attempts to revi-
talize the economy through fiscal expansion and income redistribution.
Caution came to characterize the Hungarian approach to economic policy. Thus in Hungary, as in Poland, both the outgoing and the incoming political forces legitimated themselves through "mainstream" economic approaches, even if the macroeconomic situation could have permitted something different. Like their successors, the outgoing
Hungarian reform communists did not initiate any populist measures in
1989–90.

Wherever macroeconomic conditions in Eastern Europe permitted
politicians to have a say in the desired path of economic transition, they
unanimously chose mainstream and antipopulist policies. During 1989
and 1990, the last time politics could influence economic policy, anticommunist and procapitalist public sentiments were overwhelming.
Large anticommunist electorates—Solidarity and its political affiliates in
Poland; Civic Forum in coordination with Public against Violence in
Czechoslovakia; a more developed, but segmented anticommunist party
system in Hungary; and the Union of Democratic Forces in Bulgaria—
voted for antipopulist economic changes, even though only a minority
of the voters had any idea of their bitter, short-term economic consequences.

The subordination of politics to emergency economic conditions,
external constraints, and earlier political choices became effective later,
when the stable political support for the mainstream strategy ended.
Instead, from 1990 to 1993–94, the implemented transformation strategy seemed to be at risk from the increasing fragmentation of the new
political system and major populist challenges.

Fragmentation in Hungary occurred mainly within the established
political parties in parliament. Within the governing coalition, both the
main coalition force (the Hungarian Democratic Forum) and one junior
coalition party (the Smallholders Party) became polarized over differing
approaches to systemic change. Until late 1992, populists advocating
nationalist appeals had an impact within the coalition, while some major
labor unions and other organizations began to articulate labor and popular-sector demands.[6] The populist leader István Csurka charged that
the "international financial Mafia" and its internal agents were enforcing
restrictive macroeconomic policies, resulting in a substantial decline in
living standards (Csurka 1992). Csurka was soon forced out of the
Hungarian Democratic Forum and in 1993 founded his own "Party of

Hungarian Truth and Life," a name that reeks of prewar extremism. (See Chapter 7 for a detailed account of Hungarian populism.)

While fragmentation in Hungary was mainly an intraparty matter, in Poland it occurred during the process of party formation; and because of substantial initial differences in electoral and legislative rules, the resulting fragmentation was far more extensive than in Hungary. During and after the 1991 and 1992 elections, both the political arena and parliament were invaded by a multitude of small parties, the largest only slightly stronger than the smallest Hungarian parties in parliament. In this context, populists were able to make a much more direct and effective challenge than in Hungary.

Political fragmentation in Czechoslovakia followed the Polish pattern. A multitude of competing parties emerged as spin-offs from the major anticommunist blocs originally mobilized by Civic Forum and Public against Violence (Juberías 1992, 167–68). After their initial political goals were met, fragmentation was quick and brutal. In Czechoslovakia, however, the major fragmentation has occurred along ethnic and national lines. By 1992 populism there reflected national and ethnic frustrations amplified by the hardship of economic transformation. Slovak Prime Minister Meciar's populism addressed the fear and anger of many Slovaks, hit much harder than Czechs by recession and price hikes and principally by unemployment. Notes Juberías, "The tremendous impulse of Meciar's party and the growing success of his populist and utterly nationalist message forced the rest of the political groups to relocate themselves ideologically and to redefine their strategies. Most of them did so by clearly favouring nationalist positions" (1992, 162).

Yet despite political fragmentation and polarization and the populist predilections of many politicians, there was no populist economic turn anywhere in Eastern Europe. Ironically, because of the poor economic situation in Slovakia, Meciar "the populist" had even less opportunity to introduce populist economic policies than his counterpart, Klaus "the liberal," in the Czech Republic. The antireform and propopulist rhetoric during the presidential campaign in Poland did not prevent Walesa from keeping Balcerowicz as his number-one economic policy maker. Even after Balcerowicz's resignation, following the 1991 parliamentary elections, the general economic policy approach hardly changed. In Hungary the first coalition government continued spouting the populist rhetoric, but its spring 1993 financial-adjustment plan was almost pure neoliberalism. Like their Polish colleagues, the officials of József Antall's government had to subordinate political ambitions to macroeconomic crisis management. The limitations of economic policy choice were dramatically illustrated by the striking uniformity of the economic programs of the various parties in the 1994 parliamentary election campaign. A related phenomenon, the relatively low salience of economic issues, was already apparent in the parliamentary elections of 1990 (Commisso 1991, 127).

Even so, another round of gloomy prophecies of economic populism occurred when postcommunist successor parties came to power in Lithuania, Poland, Hungary, and other countries of the region. Nowhere, however, have populist challenges been powerful enough to alter the overall neoliberal policy approach; nowhere did postcommunists turn to populism. To the contrary, they timidly continued what their Christian Democratic, neoliberal, or technocratic predecessors started, or at least none of them was in a position to undo the earlier programs' main principles. After the breakthrough years, prohibitive macroeconomic conditions along with external financial and political constraints, rather than vague procapitalist feelings, led to consistent antipopulist policy choices throughout the region.

This does not mean there was no change. Populist pressures, combined with increasing political fragmentation, retarded the implementation of some reform measures and postponed the development of others. Examples of this are the slowing of privatization in Hungary, Slovakia, and Poland in 1993, and the postponing of comprehensive reforms of the health, education, and pension systems in practically every country in the region. The distribution of "pork" and of "sweeteners" during election times was probably also prompted by populist appeals. The first examples are issues of pace and sequencing of reforms, while the latter concern political business cycles rather than economic populism. As to the relationship between political business cycles and populism, Alesina suggested that "populist cycles in Latin America magnify partisan cycles in OECD democracies" (1994, 47). However, the specific interpretation of economic populism on which my argument is based significantly differs from the political-cycle analogy.

As I argued above, economic populism constitutes a different and much broader policy mix, one that has not yet occurred in the East European transformation. Instead, fiscal restraint, trade and price liberalization, budget cuts, subsidy removals, and privatization have remained government policy everywhere, regardless of the depth of political fragmentation or the intensity of populist challenges. Political action has clearly been constrained by poor macroeconomic and strict international conditions. The implication is a subordination of politics to economic conditions.

Does this mean that politics did not play a role at all? Of course, it did. On one hand, the "bourgeois revolutions" of 1989 and 1990 in Eastern Europe "have sought not only to achieve substantial policy gains within the existing rules of the game, but to change the rules of the game itself." (This was formulated in the context of the developed West's recent bourgeois revolutions by Pierson and Smith [1993, 489].) Certainly, this happened through conscious political actions and choices. However, the crucial, politically governed decisions of the early transformation period limited the freedom of later policy choices.

On the other hand, politics has certainly influenced policy choices even after the breakthrough years. My point, however, is that governments and politicians have been "free to choose" only within the rather narrow limits of the generally accepted mainstream transformation strategy, essentially the neoliberal scenario or the Washington consensus. That is, political actors could choose between fixed or flexible exchange rate regimes, but they could not opt for state-controlled multiple exchange rates, which were the major policy tools of the protectionist late industrialization or the communist economy. They could determine the sequence in which the budget would come into balance, but could not pursue Keynesian fiscal expansion to stimulate economic growth. There was choice in the timing and sequencing of trade liberalization, but maintaining or building up high tariffs or a complex system of non-tariff barriers were not among the feasible options. Politicians could choose among various strategies of privatization, but could not choose not to privatise at all or to (re)nationalize productive capacities. By the 1990s, policy options that just a few decades earlier denoted characteristically divergent development strategies no longer belonged to the repertoire of reasonable tools.

This also implies that only sustained economic recovery and/or the easing of international constraints can broaden the universe of feasible policy options. For the next crucial political choices politicians in Eastern Europe had to wait for better times. Until 1993–94 macroeconomic policies largely failed to reflect the ideological preferences of the governing coalitions, whether leftist, rightist, or populist.[7]

Economic Recovery: A Resurgence of Populism?

The recession did not last forever. But the recovery that began in 1994 does not mean that the structural problems of the postcommunist economies have been solved. It is likely to represent little more, in fact, than a breathing space on the road toward a Western-type market economy. Nevertheless, it is a crucial time since politicians are likely to regain some of their influence over economic policies.

The Third World experience suggests that, "The hardest political challenges often come after the initial package has been launched" (Nelson 1994, 13). Improved macroeconomic performance may release pent-up demands. Moreover, the structural reforms badly needed in all postcommunist economies involve a political and bureaucratic pattern of governance in which political actors and other representatives of social interests may acquire much more influence than in the period of macroeconomic instability. In fact, a second phase of transformation has begun in East Central Europe in the mid-1990s, which has implied much more complex measures than just the first stabilization steps "decided and put into effect by a small circle of senior economic officials." This new phase seems to require more interaction between state and society because "sectoral and institutional reforms usually impose permanent losses focused on specific interests. They therefore prompt tenacious resistance" (Nelson 1994, 14).

Governments can be elastic enough to change their political tactics only if they preside over a framework that can support both stability and structural reform. Reviving distributional pressures, triggered by the first results of recovery and combined with requirements for new, cooperative political and bureaucratic tactics, may significantly restructure the political and policy-making arena, and lead once again to politics controlling economic decisions. Thus politics is likely to be less subordinated to macroeconomic necessities than it has been since 1990. In principle, this provides new opportunities for alternatives to the mainstream, neoliberal transformation strategy, including economic populism. Also, when domestic macroeconomic and external conditions no longer rule out alternative choices, the political system will regain its relevance. In that new situation, the paths of Eastern Europe may change.

By the late 1990s, the specific features of the political institutions of each country may determine, more than before, the path each will follow. The exclusivity or fragmentation of specific national party systems, as compared to stable electoral blocs elsewhere; the behavior of employers' and employees' associations, including their connection to the political parties; the political leaders' personalities, both inside and outside the formal political systems; and the relations between state and society will all shape the character and intensity of political influence over economic policy in each country.

The renewed influence of politics over economic policy will not necessarily lead to economic populism in any postcommunist country. There are, in principle, other alternatives to radical neoliberalism than demagogic populism, such as corporative-type arrangements of negotiated structural reforms or export-oriented, selective growth policies. Politicians seeking sustainable growth and structural change and shunning risky populist swings are likely to be challenged more in the coming period than in the early years of transformation. The age of demagogic populism in Eastern Europe may still be ahead.

It is becoming all the more important to know who the populists are in Eastern Europe. What is their historical, social, and ideological background? What are their short-term economic demands and long-term development strategies? These questions will be explored in the next chapter using the example of Hungarian populist movements and political parties.

Chapter 7

Populist Transformation Strategies: The Hungarian Case in Comparative Perspective

This chapter surveys and interprets the rhetoric, ideology, and economic strategy of Hungarian populists under postcommunism. I do not focus on the occasional demagogic gestures, promises, or demands of governments, parties, or labor unions that are labeled "populist" in everyday political discourse. No political actor has avoided charges of populism leveled by one or another competitor, and the resulting inflation of the term does not enhance conceptual clarity. Nor is it my intention to point out populist features of the petitions and programs of some Hungarian economists. While such ideas abound, they have not yet become policy and thus have not mobilized political support.

Populist Parties in Hungary

István Csurka's movement of the Hungarian Way Circles and József Torgyán's Smallholders Party are different in that they make systematic and comprehensive populist appeals. Although the parties are opposed to one another, their ideas have attracted much public attention and won political support. I expected that their economic agendas would combine the core features of the populist strategy—as Roberts describes it, "widespread redistributive or clientelistic methods to create a material foundation for popular sector support" (1995, 88). What I found, however, did not fit my expectations.

In comparing Hungarian populist manifestos with the ideas of major Latin American populist movements, I found only rhetorical and ideological resemblances. Despite partly similar arguments and expressions, Hungarian populists do not share the economic ideas of New World populist mass movements. I found the opposite when I compared Csurka's and Torgyán's populism with other Hungarian parties' programs. While populist attacks against their socialist and liberal opponents typically reek of prewar extremist, chauvinist, and racist terminology, and their ideological stances could not be more different, paradoxically, there are striking similarities between the populist and the liberal (or the postcommunist socialist) economic transformation projects.

How can we account for the strikingly divergent economic strategies of Latin American and East European populists, if they have in common a hostility toward the capitalist world order and the international financial community, and anxiety about having a dependent and peripheral status in the global economic order? If Torgyán's and Csurka's movements are populist, how is it that their economic strategy is not? How does one evaluate the frequent claims that a populist turn will bring economic catastrophe in Hungary? These are the questions addressed in this chapter.

Is Hungarian Populism Obsolete?

In the critics' view, contemporary Hungarian populism more often than not appears to be an outdated phenomenon. Discussions of its xenophobia and anticapitalism stress its close kinship with the populist-nationalist movements of the 1930s and, in Csurka's case, prewar right-wing extremism (Bozóki and Sükösd 1993, Bozóki 1994). Thus, according to some writers, it is tradition, rather than ideological transfer or innovation, that is most relevant in interpreting the populist political-ideological formula under postcommunism. While this portrait is not entirely false, it is far from being precise or complete.

Csurka's Hungarian pathography—spiritual exhaustion, neuropathy, alcoholism, self-destruction, biological sickness, national indifference, strife, and self-hatred (Csurka 1993, 16)—undoubtedly resounds with prewar anxieties about the "distorted Hungarian build, and deadlocked Hungarian history," as it was put by the great social scientist István Bibó (1986). Similarly, when blaming the alien element for the Hungarian pathology, Csurka revives an idea that was popular among some populist-nationalist and extreme right groups before World War II. (See on the latter Bibó 1986 [572].) From time to time József Torgyán uses similar rhetoric.

Clearly, Csurka also adopted many characteristic elements of the extreme right idiom of the 1930s, and more specifically of the early, plebeian wing of Hungarian national socialism. His political anti-Semitism, belief in conspiracy theory, and concern about the genetic decline of the nation and the Hungarian Lebensraum are clear proofs of rhetorical kinship. This, however, is not true for Torgyán's rhetoric.

If we compare the arguments made by the head of the Hungarian Way Circles—and later of Csurka's Party of Hungarian Truth and Life—

with the views of Zoltán Böszörmény, leader of the National Socialist Hungarian Workers Party in the early 1930s, we find close similarities even to their use of rhetoric. For instance, there is much in common in the way the prewar, plebeian national socialists and the postcommunist populists thought about issues of Hungary's dependence and the cosmopolitan superstructure, the reasons behind the nation's misery, the methods of subordination and its beneficiaries, the alien elements and their janissaries. So close are the similarities that the reader will have to read the following quotes carefully to be sure who said what: Csurka, or the prewar plebeian Hungarian fascists.[1]

On national dependence and the cosmopolitan superstructure:

> Financiers, banking, the Hungarian National Bank's participation in and dependence on the international financial system are all legacies of the last reform-communist period. They also became the least flexible determinants of the changes under postcommunism. (Csurka 1992a)

When Csurka wrote this he was still vice chairman of the Hungarian Democratic Forum (MDF), the largest party of the governing coalition. In 1993, following the political scandal provoked by his pamphlet, he left the party. However, just seven decades earlier Hungarian plebeian fascists had stated:

> What we have been facing for a long time is an internationally organized burglary, a warfare with devastating consequences. The many big banks and cartels are nothing but an organic part and the representatives of interests of cosmopolitan democratic capitalism. They destroy smallholders, artisans, small traders and workers alike. (Gergely, Glatz, and Pölöskei 1991, 280)

Given the nation's dependence upon the cosmopolitan superstructure,

> Hungarians should be warned that the country's alien occupation, the dominating alien element in top positions and, finally, the servitude of the indigenous population all result from the same source: the monetarism of the nomenclature. (Csurka 1993, 19)
>
> We know who is responsible for the people's misery. It is the result of many decades of economic and spiritual predation by profiteers whose spirit and morality are alien. This democratic capitalism devastates every firm or factory unless it cheats its workers. They consciously increase

unemployment and mass poverty just to make their rule complete. (Gergely, Glatz, and Pölöskei 1991, 179)

Furthermore, the cosmopolitan authorities utilize economic methods of subordination, just as they did seventy years ago.

> Devaluation, the consequence of the restrictive policy, is necessary to help their clientele acquire whatever they want from the state's assets at a minimal cost. (Csurka 1993, 20)
>
> Goldfish caper in the muddy waters of privatization: consulting companies specializing in privatization visit bankrupt firms and ask the top management about the bargain price they would charge a private owner. Then they look for a buyer for the bankrupt firm. It is good for the buyer, who will express his gratitude. Similarly, it is the best outcome for top managers of the bankrupt firm because they too will be bribed by the buyer and can keep their jobs. The exorbitant amount of bribes circulating in the Hungarian privatization process is beyond imagination. (Csurka 1992b, 9)
>
> Many cases of so-called bankruptcy are nothing but Talmudic tricks: rather than punishing those allegedly bankrupt, it devastates and cripples their Hungarian creditors and employees. (Gergely, Glatz, and Pölöskei 1991, 179)

The only ones benefiting from all this are the aliens and their janissaries:

> Clearly, the real aim then [in 1945–46] and today has been the same: power and dominance, censorship and profiteering from acquired property. The less solidarity and cooperation Hungarians exhibit, the easier it is to trick national and Christian forces into hostility among each other, and the easier it will be to reach this aim. It is a fertile ground for petty Realpolitik. While its proponents tacitly assist in the execution of their fellow Hungarians, they hope they will get the chance to act in terms of the common good. (Csurka 1993, 16)
>
> It is no wonder that indigenous Hungarians are devastated in such conditions, that even those Hungarians who are weaker spiritually and morally are infected by the alien spirit and adapt to it. However, while the alien parasites merely harm the host race—alien to them—those degenerated Hungarians destroy their own fellows-in-blood. (Gergely, Glatz, and Pölöskei 1991, 179)

While the similarities are striking, I think it would be improper to limit the analysis of Csurka's populism to a comparison with the populist-nationalist or plebeian national socialist tradition. On one hand, a closer look reveals that the sociopolitical and economic strategies of the two programs, while dressed in similar rhetoric, are divergent. On the other hand, the beliefs underlying the rhetoric are not specific to Hungarian populism; rather, they are offshoots of a far-reaching ideological family tree. My point is that the kind of populism represented by Csurka and Torgyán never before existed in Hungary. To understand their program and Torgyán's remarkable political attraction, we have to reach far beyond the "traditionalist" explanation and elaborate a much more complex and modern postcommunist populist formula.

It is well known that the prewar populist-nationalist ideology and rhetoric combined with an economic strategy of a "third way." There was no contradiction between the rhetoric and the economic program (Lackó 1975, Juhász 1983, Szárszó 1983, and Borbándi 1989). The latter observation holds for the statist and populist economic views of the Hungarian plebeian national socialists as well: the economic program conformed with the ideology and rhetoric. In the 1930s, Böszörmény's national socialists, Meskó Zoltán's National Socialist Hungarian Workers and Agrarian Party, and a spin-off of Böszörmény's party, the Party of Hungarian National Socialist Workers itemized their demands as follows: "[A] proportional distribution of material wealth"; "state provision of jobs to every worker, and free distribution of land to agrarian laborers"; "immediate nationalization of large department stores, which have to be parceled out for rent to small artisans; the latter should get priority in government procurements as well"; "nationalization of all socialized firms"; "profit-sharing arrangements in large firms" (Gergely, Glatz, and Pölöskei 1991, 283, 284); "economic planning aimed at production control, and a rational distribution of goods produced"; "nationalization of all large firms and mines"; "a moratorium on the interest on usurious loans of international capital"; "nationalization of creditors' activity" (316, 317); "leaving the League of Nations, which is nothing but an organization representing the interests of Jewish freemasonry and cosmopolitan capital" (349); and "just, socially sensitive and progressive taxation, elimination of turnover and consumption taxes on wage goods (355)."

However, as I show later, contemporary Hungarian populist economic programs are not even reminiscent of these kinds of demands; rather, they represent an entirely different economic ideology. The question becomes why contemporary Hungarian populists use rhetoric reminiscent of the prewar era if they have relatively little use for the underlying economic views and solutions. Does a regard for tradition explain their choice of rhetoric? I do not think so. After all, similar thoughts have been expressed by movements and political thinkers rooted in entirely different traditions.

Contemporary leftist writers in Hungary and elsewhere attack the power of the international financial superstructure, the subordination of less developed nations, and their resulting backwardness with no less vehemence than Csurka and his rhetorical predecessors in the prewar period. Indeed, one charge expressed by both postcommunist populists and prewar national socialists, that dependence through debt is the result of conscious warfare rather than just an accidental and regrettable development, has recently been raised by Susan George (1993, 18). For similar views see George (1992) and Walton and Seddon (1994).

However, with respect to the rapidly expanding influence of the international financial community and the resulting new perspectives on international relations, we need not go too far to the left to meet thought-provoking analyses. They can be found in the studies of less passionate experts as well (Kahler 1992, 92).

Moreover, one of Csurka's most controversial claims, that the multinational financial superstructure presides over Eastern Europe through local intermediaries—its domestic allies and beneficiaries—is not exclusive to postcommunist populism or to prewar fascism either. Essentially the same argument has been raised in the modern historical-structural versions of dependency theory. Its representatives argue that social science should focus "not on direct links between centre and periphery but on intermediaries, specifically groups in Latin America who shared interests with international actors and thus joined forces with them to promote mutual gain often at the expense of other national groups" (Stallings 1992, 45 mentioning Cardoso and Faletto [1979] and Evans [1979] as the best works on this approach). The domestic intermediaries identifying with the interests and outlook of international actors are financiers, externally oriented business people, the military, policy technocrats, and consumption-oriented upper-middle classes: an assemblage almost identical to the groups and their "internationalist coalitions" targeted by Csurka's criticism in the postcommunist Hungarian context.

The implication is that prewar rhetorical and ideological traditions cannot be the only key to populist ideology under postcommunism. The ideological affinity might be better explained by the similarity of the historical situation than by pure tradition. Recently, just as it did seven decades ago, Hungary faced a deep economic crisis and, probably, a crisis of national identity. International factors in the 1990s, just as in the 1930s, have crucially influenced the country's choice of a recovery path. Except for the fact that Csurka continually stresses such issues as the supposed Jewish and communist origins of the "intermediaries" and "billeting officers" of Hungary's "dependent capitalism," one might just as well classify him as a contemporary leftist thinker or follower of modern dependency ideas as an outmoded plebeian national socialist—at least as far as his rhetoric is concerned.

This latter paradox, however, returns us to the comparison with Latin American populism. Old and new theories of dependency and of economically or politically induced subordination and backwardness were, in a more or less direct form, characteristic of the ideological background of Latin American populist episodes.

The Populist Program in Latin America and Hungary

As Chapter 6 discussed, the populist economic program conformed to the ideology and rhetoric of the earlier populist episodes in Latin America. I have argued that these populist economic experiments tended to ignore the fact that "a more complex economy is a delicate mechanism with exigencies of its own that must not be tampered with" (Hirschman 1981, 101). To quote Albert Hirschman further on the subject of populist imprudence:

> The best expression of this attitude is the well-known 1953 advice Perón gave to Carlos Ibáñez, then president of Chile: 'My dear friend: Give to the people, especially to the workers, all that is possible. When it seems to you that already you are giving them too much, give them more. You will see the results. Everyone will try to scare you with the specter of an economic collapse. But all of this is a lie. There is nothing more elastic than the economy which everyone fears so much because no one understands it.' (Hirschman 1981, 102)

A comparison of the economic transformation strategies of Hungarian populism with the kinds of nostrums Perón espoused and their policy implications in Latin America reveals how much less radical and, indeed, essentially different the former are. Neither Csurka nor Torgyán espouse macroeconomic policies of the Latin American populist kind. While both leaders have passionately attacked fiscal and monetary restriction and blamed it for the rapid impoverishment of Hungarians, neither has said that the opposite would be the solution. According to some analysts, "populist politicians can easily argue that the economic misery of postcommunist countries is caused by the restrictive economic and financial politics dictated by the IMF and the World Bank, against which a 'fair' redistribution of the riches and burdens and a central rejuvenation of the economy are necessary" (Bozóki and Sükösd 1993, 232). Hungarian populists, however, were sufficiently cautious not to follow this suggestion. Neither the Hungarian Way Circles nor the Smallholders Party opted for aggregate-demand measures such as fiscal and monetary expansion. Instead, Hungarian populists have urged the reduction of taxes and interest rates, and other initiatives to improve the entrepreneurial climate and taxpayer morale. In contrast to its Latin American counterpart, the Hungarian populist economic project has supply-side measures as its focus.

Populists and Neoliberals in Postcommunist Hungary

In order to understand postcommunist populism in Hungary, it may be helpful to consider its relationship with its major political rival, Hungarian liberalism. I begin by comparing two extremes, the populist and liberal party programs on economic transformation. Another approach might have been to compare the populist scenario with that of the postcommunist socialists, specifically Gyula Horn's Hungarian Socialist Party's transformation project. Horn's socialists formed a coalition government with the liberal Alliance of Free Democrats following the socialist's landslide victory in the parliamentary elections in 1994. But in fact Hungarian postcommunist socialists have been implementing a neoliberal transformation strategy. My reason for contrasting the populist program with the liberal one is that the latter comparison has much richer political empirical content. While at a first glance populist rhetoric appears to be equally anticommunist and antiliberal, in reality Hungarian populists defined themselves much more as the opposite political pole to liberals than to socialists, and vice versa.

Comparison of the populist and liberal economic transformation projects reveals a remarkable convergence of ideas in such crucial areas as the role of the state; the problem of external debt service and the relationship to the IMF and the World Bank; joining Europe and NATO; privatization and the role of foreign capital; and such tools of economic policy as taxes, levies, interest rates, and supply-side measures.[2]

A view commonly expressed in this regard was that East European and specifically Hungarian populists were statist and that they favored increased state intervention (Bozóki and Sükösd 1993, 232). A comparison of party programs, however, reveals little if any difference between the populist and liberal perspectives on the transformative role of the state. Csurka, for instance, wrote, "The nation-building state is leaner than what we have now, but more powerful and secure at the same time. It has the public knowledge of its actions as the source of its citizens' trust. It will not tolerate bias or corruption" (Csurka 1993, 20). The same emphasis appears in the program of the Hungarian Way Circles ("A Magyar Út Körök Mozgalom Programja," 1993). Creating a leaner, less costly state apparatus appears to be a popular theme for other Hungarian populists. Such a demand appeared in the Smallholders' program in 1995: "Economic policy implementation in this scenario presupposes a cheaper, more effective, and modern state and a different role from that which it has recently played: one much more similar to the state's role in developed countries" (Torgyán 1995b, 18). All this is not much different from the way liberals describe the role of the state: "The actor implementing our policies is not the omnipotent 'large state' machinery, but a substantially smaller, cheaper, though more efficient state apparatus" (*A liberális megoldás* 1991, 8).

In sharp contrast to the general belief that populists wanted a moratorium on debt service is the remarkably moderate view expressed in both Csurka's and Torgyán's programs. "What should be the guiding principle of the new economic policy of the Hungarian Way? Should we announce a moratorium on debt payments? Should we ask for debt rescheduling? It's out of the question! To trick national forces into it might be the very aim of the communist nomenclature which is pulling the strings" (Csurka 1993, 19). The Hungarian Way Circles' program reinforces the point: "While it has to be taken as fact that any moratorium on debt payments would place the country on the verge of ruin, it is also clear that the maintenance of the recent situation without any change implies the same" ("A Magyar Út Körök Mozgalom Programja" 1993, 2). Similar is the phrasing of the Smallholders Party program: "Equally harmful to the unilateral moratorium or rescheduling of debt payments is the continuous lamentation that it would result in immediate economic breakdown" (Torgyán 1995a, 63–64).

While European authorities may be concerned that the East European nations may at some point turn to populist authoritarianism, Hungarian populists want to join Europe. Judging by their parties' programs,

Csurka and Torgyán do not oppose Hungary's joining the European Union and NATO. To the contrary, together with Hungarian liberals, they consider membership a pressing priority: "We may like it or not, joining NATO and the EU is not just unavoidable but an urgent task, even if we are not yet fully prepared. . . . However, joining from a dis-advantaged position would be a threat to Hungarian identity" (Torgyán 1995a, 85). "In addition, of course, we have to participate in the polit-ical and economic process of European unification; however, it is not somebody else's but our own task to create the conditions for Hungary's suitable and smooth adaptation" ("A Magyar Út Körök Mozgalom Programja" 1993).

Unlike the late Latin American populists but similar to the liberals (or postcommunist socialists), Hungarian populists have been proponents of privatization rather than of (re)nationalization. Their criticism of foreign capital has been directed mainly against policies and practices favoring certain foreign investor groups over others or over the national bour-geoisie. Just as other Hungarian parties have done, the populists have declared war on the corruption that has accompanied privatization: "We grant tax holidays to foreign firms without knowing much about their real origin, while we strip the Hungarian debtors naked and go through their pockets. In some cases, however, the reputed 'Western' buyer turns out to be either insolvent or someone who does not like to pay. Some people are allowed to acquire a business empire on credit while others cannot buy even a tractor without cash" (Csurka 1993, 20). Or, in Torgyán's version, "The Hungarian people opted for a legal welfare state based on private rather than public property. Consequently, we have to create favorable conditions for private-sector development by supporting medium and small entrepreneurship" (Torgyán 1995a, 128). "In general, we cannot give up capital import; rather we want to increase it. This is a general rule, which of course is not equal to an uncritical application" (Torgyán 1995b, 33).

While populists are not hostile to foreign capital in general, they favor the emergence of a national bourgeoisie, a position they share with Hungary's liberals: "Despite the slogans on the creation of a new Hungarian propertied middle class, the privatization policies of the Antall government did not sufficiently help domestic entrepreneurs and managers to actively join major foreign investors in Hungarian privati-zation. Free Democrats lend support to privatization procedures and policies favorable to Hungarian investors: mainly entrepreneurs and workers or managers of competitive public firms" (*Fordulat, biztonság, felemelkedés* 1994, 65).

In accordance with the above orientation, Hungarian populists share with liberals (and the postcommunist socialists) a preference for supply-side measures oriented to the middle class: "Taxes should be kept within reasonable limits so that we encourage business ventures to expand rather than push them toward tax evasion. Similarly, tax levies and social security contributions should not become obstacles to entrepreneurship. . . . Recently, overtaxation has continued to be coupled with paralyzing interest rates and other constraints on the availability of credit. . . . Rational taxation and a pro-business credit system are thus essential. Parallel to that, however, it is necessary to improve controls on tax collection. Fair taxes are to be paid by everyone. Tax evasion or cheating with the social security contribution should carry serious consequences" ("A Magyar Út Körök Mozgalom Programja" 1993, 2). Similarly, the Smallholders Party urges the fundamental reform of the entire system of taxes, customs duties, and public finances. Change in these areas is essential. So long as duties and taxes remain at the current levels, only the underground economy can expand even as the legal economy is dying. . . . A substantial, general reduction in tax rates must be accompanied by improvements in tax collection and the replacement of gangster morality with Christian morality" (Torgyán 1995a, 129). Accordingly, liberals argue that "Entrepreneurs could not count on a predictable legal framework for the assessment of taxes and customs duties. Only a few could get access to subsidized credit while state guarantees on credit have been entirely absent. Business has had to cope with high taxes and, especially, very high social security contributions. . . . Free Democrats demand fundamental changes in the business environment" (*Fordulat, biztonság, felemelkedés* 1994, 65).

Such evidence suggests that, belying their reputations as irresponsible, anticapitalist, third-way believers or unreliable debtors, neither Csurka nor Torgyán have espoused economic programs that are radically different from mainstream social-liberal prescriptions for economic transformation. To the contrary, on the most crucial questions, populists under postcommunism stand much closer to contemporary liberals (and postcommunist socialists) than to Latin American populists or prewar Hungarian populist or fascist movements. If, in fact, Csurka's and Perón's movements had ever had the chance to operate in the same political arena, their conflicting economic ideas would have made them adversaries, not allies. By the same token, if Hungarian liberals or postcommunist socialists and

Torgyán's Smallholders had not had to compete in the same political arena, they might have been coalition partners rather than political enemies. At least their economic views would not have precluded such an alliance. Clearly, the possibility of such strange combinations is more theoretical than real. There are plenty of important issues other than economic ones that would prevent the alliance of Hungarian liberals or socialists with Csurka and Torgyán, and vice versa. These are paradoxes that I explain below, but first a number of caveats are in order. One could argue that the populist programs are too vague and include various elements that contradict the mainstream economic principles that populists share with liberals. In fact, I have found examples of such contradictions. However, the same is true of other party programs. Parties always have to strike a balance between realistic and politically popular campaign promises, a balance achieved more often than not at the expense of their programs' coherence. Populists are not exceptional in this respect. In general, however, most of the economic propositions advocated by the Hungarian populists do not seem to exceed the bounds of reasonable economic ideas. Two proposals widely discussed and criticized in the press as excessive and irresponsible were Csurka's idea to build a hypermodern higher education center financed by the foreign reserves of the central bank and Torgyán's vision of a housing project aimed at solving the housing problem of young adults (Csurka 1992b; Torgyán 1995a). But, apart from the above, the only fair observation we can make is that their positions in a number of politically sensitive policy debates differ from their opponents'. Torgyán, for example, passionately argued against foreign acquisitions in the Hungarian energy infrastructure and large banks. This may not be a wise criticism and there might be strong arguments against it; however, to dismiss it as irresponsible populist blustering would certainly be an exaggeration.

One can also argue that the political messages expressed in populist rallies and demonstrations and in the mass media are more extreme than, and even sharply contradict, the tenets of the formal, published party programs. In fact I have observed many such disparities. Therefore, my conclusions are valid insofar as the more general viewpoint of populist politics coincides with the formal statements of the party programs.

Finally, one might argue that, whatever the content of movement and party manifestos, the moderate policy stance is nothing but a façade concealing a populist agenda. This façade serves to protect populists from devastating criticism and loss of reputation and permits them to attain positions of power, where their true (irresponsible and anticapitalist)

identity will become apparent. While some analysts may fear such a scenario, it seems to me that the presumption of innocence is owed either
to all political parties or to none. Social science in particular must not be
guided by fear and prejudice. Moreover, the use of deceptive tactics
defies political logic. After all, appeals to voters have to be made before
and not after the elections. Thus, populist parties would presumably not
try to win over voters by promising levels of economic hardship similar
to those occasioned by the emergency measures of their opponents, only
to embark, once in office, on an unbridled spending spree. In fact, both
political logic and recent evidence suggest the reverse, what Drake terms
"bait and switch" populism—i.e., personalist leaders who campaign on a
populist platform only to switch abruptly to neoliberal policies following
election (Drake 1991, 36, n. 11, quoted by Roberts 1995, 92).

Constraints on the Populist Program

How can one explain the remarkable convergence of populist and liberal
party programs—and of all other economic ideas between these extremes?
What accounts for the concord over economic strategy between political
opposites? In the preceding chapter I suggested a general explanation in
the broader East European context. I pointed to constraints on the freedom of policy choice. My argument was that the grave macroeconomic
situation, crucial early political choices, and varying degrees of external
influence had worked to subordinate politics to economic conditions in
the Eastern transformations. It seems much more the case that radical stabilization and transformation policies "preselect" reliable executors in the
political arena than that the various political parties select economic policies that reflect their ideological preferences. For populists the implication
is that, once in office, any attempts to introduce expansionary protectionism and redistributive policies will be strongly constrained. However, in
their recent party programs Hungarian populists have not even planned a
prototypical populist turnabout nor campaigned on the classic populist
economic platform.

One irreverent but not entirely irrelevant explanation would be to
point out that the populists' strategy advisers are recruited from broadly the same professional and bureaucratic circles as those of their opponents. Among these professionals, moreover, there is a basic consensus
about what is acceptable and unacceptable economic policy; classic economic populism appears to be uniformly unacceptable. And because
Hungary is a small country, there are no alternative professional circles.

Thus, the authors of various party programs would simply copy each other's lists of policy measures while their main task would be purely ideological: the populist, liberal, socialist, or Christian-Democratic "orchestration" of basically similar major principles. This, however, does not explain why it is the neoliberal economic project—reduction of the role of the state, deregulation, unification with Europe, foreign capital import, trade liberalization, and privatization—around which all politically significant strategies revolve. Simply saying that the neoliberal project is the outcome of worldwide intellectual trends manifested in the "Washington consensus" is not sufficient. We also have to understand why and how even populist demagogues would come to accept this worldwide consensus.

In part, this has come about through their international political contacts. Clearly, to the extent that domestic political parties seek international recognition it is not just government policies but also party platforms and even campaign promises that may become subject to external influence. External actors do in fact play a crucial role in contemporary politics. European and worldwide ideological alliances, and formal or informal political networks and organizations, reach to the roots of domestic politics. Their contributions may range from personal and material support to consultation, advising, and participation in media campaigns.

Undoubtedly, Hungarian populists have actively sought international contacts and recognition. For example, István Csurka held highly publicized meetings with right-wing movement leaders including the French extremist Le Pen, who spoke on October 23, 1996, a national holiday. Csurka has mainly been oriented toward the West European New Right: Austria's FPÖ (Freedom Party), the Lega Lombarda, Le Pen's Front National, or the German Republikaner. Torgyán, while also flirting with New Right forces, has mainly been seeking entrance into the EDU, the influential European organization of Christian Democrats.

Transnational political alliances generally form between ideological kin, and neither the European New Right nor the Christian Democrats would see equity-oriented classic populism, with its statist, protectionist, and redistributive program, as closely related to their own political agendas. To the contrary, as recent analyses of the West European populist New Right have found,

> Radical right-wing populist parties are radical in their rejection of the established sociocultural and sociopolitical system and their advocacy of individual achievement, a free marketplace, and a drastic reduction of the

role of the state. . . . What distinguishes most radical right-wing populist parties from the established parties is not only their militant attacks on immigrants but also their pronounced neoliberal program. Although varying in emphasis and importance, radical right-wing populist parties have tended to hold strong antistatist positions. They find articulation in a sharp criticism of high levels of taxation, of the bureaucratic state in general, and of welfare outlays. (Betz 1993, 417–18)

European Christian Democrats have also joined the Washington consensus on the neoliberal transformation project. The international political community does not seem to sympathize with extreme alternatives to this consensus, and classic economic populism appears to be internationally unacceptable.

So far I have pointed to several types of domestic and external constraints that have led populists to adopt the mainstream economic-transformation ideas supported by their political opponents. However, one might also examine the political conflict between postcommunist populists and their major rivals, the liberals, and the specific social interests represented by Hungarian populists.

Elite-based Populism?

While populists and liberals appear tacitly to share views regarding many important aspects of economic transformation, there has been much less agreement on this strategy's intra-elite redistributive implications. Let me review some major areas of conflict. While Hungarian liberals have supported spontaneous privatization, management buyouts, and foreign acquisitions in order to speed up the transformation process, even at a certain cost of fairness and moral justification, it was the elite groups favored by them that provoked passionate populist attacks. Csurka's and Torgyán's repeated proposals for continuous retroactive control on privatization, and of confiscation of property acquired in unjust and corrupt ways, targeted "red" and "green barons"—company managers, bankers, and the agricultural elite—and certain foreign businesses (Csurka 1993, 22). Liberals supported, and populists criticized, the wide variety of privileges—subsidies for job creation, tax exemptions, trade-protection schemes, formal or informal discretionary treatment in the privatization process—that favored foreign business, including the multinational corporations, in the early transformation years.

Also, while Hungarian liberals opted against a general cleansing in the central and local state bureaucracy, it has been a recurrent populist

demand to complete the unfinished revolution by replacing the nomenclature bureaucrats with persons having a "real" Hungarian identity.

Finally, there has been continuous disagreement on who should be in
control of economic policy making. Liberals supported the dominance
of macroeconomic policy makers and financial experts over the opposing
sector-specific bureaucratic strongholds in the Ministry of Industry and
Trade, the Ministry of Agriculture, and the Ministry of Education and
Culture. Liberals continued to support the discretionary policy authority of the minister of finance and of the president of the central bank,
whoever they were. Populists, especially Csurka, however, argued that
the Hungarian situation would improve only when economists and "nar-
row-minded financial experts" were replaced by "national strategy
thinkers" in top policy-making positions (Csurka 1992b).

It is thus the redistribution of wealth, income, and jobs within the
elite—specifically from foreigners and domestic "alien elements" to the
new national bourgeoisie, the new national bureaucratic corps, or just
different foreign investor groups—that appears to concern Hungarian
populists far more than any societywide income redistribution from the
wealthy to the poorer classes. For instance, Torgyán, who often passionately criticized foreign expansion and domination in the Hungarian
economy, has repeatedly said that he would warmly welcome the influx
of Taiwanese and other Southeast Asian capital. In addition to the
domestic and external constraints mentioned above, it is their orientation toward certain elites rather than the popular sectors that may help
to explain why there is so little "populism" in the Hungarian populists'
policy repertoire. This orientation accounts for the conspicuous absence
of redistributive fiscal and monetary macroeconomic policies, for
instance.

Hence my understanding of the political conflict between Hungarian
populists and liberals (and postcommunist socialists who are implementing the neoliberal economic transformation scenario) is mainly in terms
of an intra-elite rivalry. This interpretation may help explain the tacit
populist-liberal agreement on many crucial issues of the economic transformation strategy. Clearly, even the fiercest redistributive conflict within the elite would still allow for a consensus in matters vital to elite interests, including a rejection of policies that would work to redistribute
wealth from the elite to the popular sectors. Hungarian populists appear
careful not to demand policies that directly challenge the international
financial community, global policy brokers in Washington and Europe,
and their kin in the international political arena. Both Csurka and

Torgyán appear to recognize very well that a moratorium on debt payments, trade protectionism, distributive egalitarianism, and fiscal expansion would severely harm Hungarian elite positions in general, including the interests of those groups whom they represent.

If my view of Hungarian populists as challenging the emerging pattern of distribution of power and wealth within the elite is correct, it also changes our perspective on postcommunist populism. Instead of stressing populism's obsolete and outdated character, my view may highlight what is modern in both the movement and its major political conflict.

A Populism That Never Before Existed in Hungary

The implication of the above interpretation is that the liberal-populist wrestling in Hungarian politics represents something other than a stereotypical antagonism between good and evil, past and future, obsolescence and modernity, the open society and its enemies, or serfdom and freedom. Instead, what we actually confront is essentially a conflict between two politically distinct and rival approaches within the neoliberal/neoconservative mainstream of postcommunist transformation.

A brief comparison of the Hungarian populist economic program with the ideas of the West European New Right may help us in locating the former in the contemporary European politico-economic sphere. As Hans-George Betz wrote about current New Right ideas,

> The resulting political program marks a revival of radical liberalism. It calls for a reduction of some taxes and the abolition of others, a drastic curtailing of the role of the state in the economy and large-scale privatization of the public sector including the state controlled media, a general deregulation of the private sector, and a restructuring and streamlining of the public sector. The main beneficiaries of these measures should be small and medium-sized enterprises which are expected to play a central role in the further development of advanced western societies, particularly since new technologies allow them to compete effectively with larger enterprises. (Betz 1993, 418)

But there are recent Latin American analogies as well; Latin American populism is no longer the same as it was. The politics of Peruvian president Alberto Fujimori represent a strange new combination of economic neoliberalism with populism including, in his case, antielite and antisystem ideology and rhetoric, elements that also occur in István Csurka's and József Torgyán's populism in Hungary. Based on the Peruvian experience, Roberts commented on "the emergence of new forms of populism that are compatible with and complementary to neo-liberal reforms in certain contexts. . . . Its emergence demonstrates that populism can adapt to the neo-liberal era and that it is not defined by fiscal profligacy; indeed, even when constrained by fiscal austerity and market reforms, personalist leaders have discovered diverse political and economic instruments to mobilise popular sector support when intermediary institutions are in crisis" (Roberts 1995, 83). Moreover, Fujimori is not alone in Latin America with his new version of populism.

Recently, the major populist political force in Mexico, the Partido Revolucionario Institucional (PRI), and Argentinean Perónism have undergone thorough "structural adjustment" as well (Gibson 1995, Heredia 1995). As to their ideologies, "social liberalism" and "popular market economy" have replaced earlier statist and corporatist "revolutionary" paradigms of state-led economic development. Both parties have implemented radical neoliberal adjustment strategies. The turn to new ideologies both reflected and precipitated political attempts at "restructuring the social coalitions that had historically supported Perónism, and the PRI, dismantling entrenched corporatist institutions, and fundamentally altering the representational structures that linked key social actors to the state" (Gibson 1995, 1). Both parties have changed the composition of their electoral base and their party machinery to win political support. Instead of workers, labor unions, domestically oriented business, and some rural groups, now it is internationally integrated and diversified business and their employees whose significance as members of the new coalition has dramatically increased.

Seen in the context of such examples, Hungary's postcommunist populism no longer seems unique or particularly enigmatic. However, it clearly is wrong to conceptualize it as a combination of obsolete nationalist and racist rhetoric with statist, redistributive economic appeals aimed at the popular sectors who have been disadvantaged by the postcommunist transformation. Instead, Csurka's and Torgyán's populist formula combined a modern dependency ideology in a local Hungarian (anticommunist, anti-Semitic, and nationalist) guise with an economic program respecting the radical liberal revival. As suggested earlier, this mixed populist appeal may turn out to be attractive mainly to certain elite groups who fear losing influence relative to other elites, although they feel capable of implementing a similar transformation scenario with dramatically different intra-elite distributional consequences. Thus they assume their losses could be overcome if only their rivals—certain groups of communists, bureaucrats, domestic capitalists, and foreign investors or "some scapegoated 'minority'. . . . Jews, foreigners or some other imagined enemy—[are] persecuted, allowing the True (i.e., prosperous) Nation to assert itself" (Ost 1992, 49–50). My point is that Hungarian populism differs much less in its transformation strategy than in its favored elite executors and beneficiaries. While the above description seems to fit Csurka's supporters well, populism appears to reach a much broader social stratum in the version represented by Torgyán. This takes us back to the analysis of Hungarian populist rhetoric.

The Appeal of Populist Rhetoric

Why do Hungarian populists stubbornly cultivate the rhetoric of the third way if they do not see such an economic alternative? In this respect East European populism under postcommunism differs from the ideas of the contemporary West European New Right. The latter have transformed the ideological perspective underlying their economic project into an anti-system and antiestablishment political weapon. In the Hungarian populists' case, I think something else must be highlighted. If in the transition period there is hardly any space (or intention) to articulate significant differences of economic strategy, then politicians will need to depend increasingly on noneconomic issues, and on rhetorical differences, in their efforts to be recognized by the electorate.[3] Specifically, the less Hungarian populists have been able to define an economic policy position that separates them from their rivals, the more aggressively they have to draw such a distinction rhetorically. Under postcommunist conditions the same seems to be true for many other parties as well.

A different question is to what extent the distinctive extremist rhetoric pays politically. Why is it that Csurka has never really managed to capitalize on populism? Why has Torgyán's populist rhetoric so regularly proved more attractive to the Hungarian electorate? Probably, the answer is that the latter is less bitter and, paradoxically, less extremist and relatively more centrist than the former. Torgyán seems adept at, while Csurka has never been able to master, the fine balancing act involved in choosing among acceptable and unacceptable ideas and slogans.

Torgyán's respectable political career indicates that well-articulated populist rhetoric presented by talented political entrepreneurs can have considerable chances for success. But where do these chances originate? What is credible, convincing, and attractive in the contemporary Hungarian populist argument? Populists of whatever stripe address problems that not long ago were considered real dilemmas by all political forces, including their major rivals. Hence, in many respects, the actual transformation scenario and its populist criticisms stem from closer roots than is suggested by their recent antagonism.

To give only one example, even the debt issue, the litmus test separating allegedly "irresponsible" populists from other Hungarian political actors, was much less polarized in 1989–90 than it appears to be at this writing. At that time it was neither Csurka nor Torgyán but teams of actual and would-be top policy makers, including experts from the Hungarian Democratic Forum and the Alliance of Free Democrats, who attempted to assess the chances for debt relief for Hungary. Only after their missions had failed was any attempt to raise the debt issue labeled as irresponsible populism.

Other criticisms, such as the lack of elite change, unjust privatization, and pervasive corruption, had also become largely identified with the populist parties by the mid-1990s. While other parties have also raised these issues, only in the populist agenda do they appear as central themes. In this respect, Hungarian populist rhetoric has become a kind of "ideological nature preserve" or "living museum" for a number of sensitive and crucial problems that both leftists and liberals seem to have forgotten or have failed to articulate convincingly and coherently. In addition to elite change, corruption, and the shortcomings of privatization, populists raised questions about the future of agriculture and the danger of foreign dependency. Other parties' neglect of these issues may be explained by their assumption that after the early, crucial political choices were made, the revolution was essentially finished.[4]

The appeal of populist rhetoric may, in fact, come from the fact that debate on such crucial issues ended far too quickly—that is, before solutions were reached that were widely acceptable to the Hungarian electorate. This is not to say that other political groups, such as Hungarian liberals, made no attempts at social dialogue or to address the crucial moral problems involved in the transformation and to offer solutions compatible with their political and moral beliefs. My point is, rather, that their suggested solutions failed to generate a societywide consensus. In that context, the populist explanation—that discourse had been closed prematurely and the revolution remained unfinished because the ruling elite perceived their monopoly to be threatened—could become an anti-elite and antiestablishment argument with credibility far beyond certain ambitious elite groups who felt disadvantaged by the new political and economic power structure.

Until now the populist political argument has been only partly effective, mainly because the institutionalized forms of political representation have not broken down. Rather, however incomplete and exclusionary they may appear, they have taken root and stabilized in Hungary and elsewhere in Eastern Europe. But the populists' political appeal may increase if the institutionalized forms of political mediation weaken, and with many facts of everyday life as their central issues. After all, it is commonly accepted by many Hungarians that the country is corrupt, taxes are crippling, the debt burden is exorbitant, public services are eroding, the privatization process is full of injustice and immorality, and some of the old elite is still in power.

What about the political and economic implications? First, however peculiar and politically discomforting it may sound, postcommunist neoliberals and true neoliberals while in power could count on tacit support for their economic policies even from the populist political camp. The neoliberal economic transformation strategy appears to be universal enough to attract tacit supporters from even the "enemies of the open society."

Second, if the arguments I have developed to this point are correct, one should not worry too much about a populist economic turnabout, even if Hungarian populists should come to power. In such a scenario, I hypothesize that the populists will experience external and internal constraints on their freedom to choose policies even more directly than they do now, in their role in the political opposition. One plausible outcome would be no more than a slightly more statist and protectionist version of the mainstream strategy. However, it would combine with aggressive attempts at intra-elite redistribution, carried out most likely in an extreme xenophobic, anti-Semitic, illiberal, and anticommunist political climate. Aggrieved popular sectors supporting such a takeover, I hypothesize, would not gain much more than before. One cannot, however, exclude the possibility that, similar to their Latin American counterparts, new populists in Hungary and other East European countries would discover not only political but also economic means of mobilizing political support. My argument in Chapter 6, however, suggests that this would be possible only in an improved economic climate. Also, politically designed populist economic instruments would be selective and target certain popular-sector constituencies rather than aim at a societywide redistribution through macroeconomic policies. At least this has been the experience in Latin America with the economic methods of new populism (Roberts 1995).

There is already evidence to support such a prediction for Eastern Europe. There is, for example, the story of the short-lived Olszewski government in Poland, formed by parties that had campaigned on a forthright populist platform in 1991. Someone who surely kept a critical eye on them, Leszek Balcerowicz, recounts the story, including the "hour of truth" when populists were faced with limits on their policy options. The Polish parliamentary elections in October 1991 were preceded by two months of campaigning. Most of the participating sixty-five political parties urged "relaxation of monetary and fiscal policy, increased protectionism and more active involvement of the state bureaucracy in the affairs of specific industries and enterprises" (Balcerowicz 1995, 300). Also, and especially throughout 1991, the mass media "bombarded the Polish public with messages that the Polish economy had been struck by economic catastrophe and that there should be a radically new program to improve the situation quickly" involving "relaxation of monetary and fiscal policies, protectionism and state intervention at the industry level" (Balcerowicz 1995, 309). But the new government of Jan Olszewski, formed in December 1991, "gradually toned down its revisionist declarations and basically continued the disciplined fiscal policy" (300). Intra-elite redistributive issues, however, loomed around both privatization and a shakeup in the state bureaucracy. "But privatisation of large state enterprises was practically brought to a halt, and political debate on privatisation got more and more demagogic. . . . In June 1992 the government collapsed after a clumsy attempt at disclosing the former regime's 'secret agents' in the state institutions" (300). My point is that this story reveals much about what can and cannot be expected from a hypothetical populist takeover in Eastern Europe.

Finally, let me assess the prospects for a populist electoral success. This seems much more likely than the possibility that economic transformation in any East European country will follow the classic populist scenario in the foreseeable future. But while I see no chance of economic populism coming to dominate economic strategy, its political prospects look better, as demonstrated by cases ranging from Tyminski to Meciar or Zhirinovsky to Miloshevich. Also, worldwide experience suggests that combining anti-establishment and anti-elitist rhetoric with intra-elite redistributive appeals and a special version of the mainstream neoliberal economic scenario can produce political success. Examples for it abound (Stallings 1992, 81). From this viewpoint, neither the postcommunist populist formula nor its political venture is unique in our contemporary world.

Chapter 8
Compensation as a Government Tactic

In Chapter 5, I presented society-centered explanations for the differing political environments for economic reform in Latin America and Eastern Europe. While I attributed the unexpectedly peaceful political dynamics under postcommunism to the communist inheritance, I have made it clear that I do not think that the postcommunist legacies and structures are all that matters. Institutional variables, such as the quality and level of state autonomy and capacity, and the forms and strategies in which they are enhanced, may also be important in understanding the dynamics of simultaneous transformation under economic stress.

Political Management of Economic Transformation

In Chapter 5 I mentioned the significance of government strategies for maintaining relative political stability during the transformation. I referred to the fact that even the most radical reformers in the East have hesitated to eliminate the inherited public welfare system. Indeed, in many countries, principally in the post-Soviet region, remnants have been maintained of the other major element of the communist welfare system—welfare services provided by enterprises.

This observation takes us to the broader issue of the political management of economic transformation. The political engineering of stabilization and adjustment usually focuses on solving the political difficulties involved with economic reform. Some of these may arise from the distributional effects associated with the reform programs. Stabilization policies, for example, often involve sharp drops in real wages and an increase in bankruptcies. Trade liberalization programs also change the pattern of income distribution, simultaneously causing losses for import license holders and import-competing producers, and yielding benefits for exporters and the rest of the economy. How to distribute the burdens of stabilization and adjustment, and how to implement programs without provoking social unrest, are crucial questions often faced by reformist governments and political systems.

Compensation is one specific set of measures with which governments attempt to address the political tensions that arise from crisis, stabilization, and adjustment. This chapter examines some of the issues and controversies associated with compensation and develops a conceptual framework to explain the diverse forms of compensation that have been employed in specific cases of economic reform. This framework will be applied in Chapter 9 to a compensation pattern used in 1992 in a stabilization and fiscal adjustment program in Hungary.

The critical fact about compensation concerns the uncertainty of its targets and the difficulty of calculating its effects and financial implications. Incentives meant to reward champions of adjustment, compensatory payments to those who will be disadvantaged by reform, and resources absorbed in rents and spoils to supporters may inextricably mix (Waterbury 1989, 41). This may be one reason why the authors of adjustment and transformation blueprints appear to be overly cautious in their suggestions about it. Certainly, capable reformers try to maximize positive signals; they attempt to design and disburse compensatory payments with the maximum political payoff; and they try to minimize rents and spoils. But they do not always succeed.

While some specific forms of compensation may only be observed in connection with concrete programs, it is not my intention here to explain how one or another compensation measure complements specific reform policies. This may be the task of empirical studies aimed at the political-economic analysis of various adjustment episodes in different countries.

Instead I address broader and more general questions: (1) what is compensation? (2) who is (or will be) compensated? and (3) how are they compensated while politically engineered adjustment occurs? In discussing who will be compensated (and how), and once the goals of compensation are clear, I review the justifications for compensating specific economic, political, and social groups affected by reform, including the poor, the working classes, and specific business groups. I also address the role and significance of various organizations with political or economic interests in issues of compensation.

I remain general when defining the stabilization and adjustment programs themselves. In addressing economic reforms, mainstream reform policies, or stabilization and adjustment programs, I refer to Chapters 2 and 3. The following attempt to analyze compensation in terms of the questions I have listed is based on the assumption that neoliberal reforms may encounter political difficulties associated with their effects on income distribution, and that addressing these difficulties may require the use of methods of political engineering. One of these is compensation.

What Is Compensation?

In developing a definition of compensation, I use the logical pattern detailed by Kaufman and Stallings in order to define economic populism (Kaufman and Stallings 1991). Although both the necessity and the appropriate forms of compensation are widely discussed in the relevant literature, some uncertainty remains concerning its precise meaning. Further, there are contradictory interpretations of its goals and targets.

For the purpose of this chapter, compensation refers to ways of managing coalitions of interests with the objective of enhancing the viability of economic stabilization and adjustment programs. It comprises a set of economic policies and political measures designed to achieve a specific political goal. This goal is to overcome political opposition to reform by reducing the motivation and prospects for antireform coalition building and antireform threats in the short and medium term. Compensatory policies and political measures may include:

1. popular-sector policies targeting lower- and lower-middle-income groups, either by making income-producing assets more available (such as land, emergency employment programs, and access to higher education) or through current income transfers (e.g., food aid and price subsidies);[1]
2. policies and programs enhancing the mobility of factors of production (such as migration policies, retraining, housing policies, and deregulation);
3. measures focused on creating trade-offs among different reform policies implemented both in the same reform phase and at various times throughout the sequence of reforms. (see Waterbury 1989, Roland 1991);
4. measures granting grace periods to economic actors in the form of phased implementation of individual adjustment policies (such as gradual price- and trade-liberalization steps);
5. initiatives to extend political benefits by providing improved access either to political power (through the distribution of influential executive or administrative jobs, or participation rights for trade unions) or to political freedom (e.g., via measures aimed at democratization or increased organizational rights for labor).

The policies and political measures I have listed are not compensatory policies per se. They may be implemented for purposes other than compensation. For example, nonreforming governments may initiate popular-sector policies because of their need for political support or—as in the case of pro-poor policies—for general humanitarian or moral considerations. Measures aimed at improving the mobility of production factors or granting grace periods for adjustment may also be important elements of reform, independent of any compensatory intent. However, such policies and measures may certainly be used in order to create trade-offs between the losses and gains of specific actors who are politically important for the success of adjustment. In this discussion, measures will be interpreted as compensatory if their capacity to create tradeoffs is politically relevant for the policymakers.

Of course, compensation is not the only, or even the most significant, set of policies designed to make economic adjustment feasible and sustainable. Indeed, it is of secondary significance relative to mainstream reform policies like price and trade liberalization, exchange-rate adjustments, fiscal and monetary stabilization, and institutional reforms. At least in the medium and long term, these mainstream policies are expected to be the primary vehicles for mobilizing sufficient political support for reforms by creating economic benefits and pro-reform coalitions of beneficiaries. While well-designed reforms may succeed without extensive compensation, they may not be sufficient to sustain political support for adjustment if mainstream policies fail. However, compensation may prove to be important for the prospects of reform in the short and medium term, especially if the supply response of the economic actors is belated.

Compensation differs from the macroeconomic policies that constitute the core of reform not only by its secondary significance but also in the direction of its actions and the economic and political actors who are targeted. Compensation is also meant to counterbalance the primary effects of adjustment to a limited extent and for a limited period. However, its impact often appears to be more complex. While certain kinds of compensation may partly counteract the effects of specific reforms, they may simultaneously enhance the effects of others. While mainstream policies normally target the perceived beneficiaries of adjustment, compensation targets those who lose, or feel as if they have lost.[2]

Moreover, compensation does not constitute the entire repertoire of political measures available for overcoming opposition to reforms and targeting those who perceive a loss. In fact, reforming governments frequently aim at least in part at destroying the economic and political base of opponents to adjustment. Certain privatization or nationalization policies, anticorruption purges of the bureaucracy, and restrictions on unions or political parties are examples of this. Compensation can be distinguished from this third set of measures on the basis that it implies the distribution—as opposed to the deprivation—of economic and political benefits.

Is There a Need for Compensation?

For any further analysis of compensation, it may be helpful to elaborate three more questions regarding its characteristics: (1) Is there really a need for compensation? (2) Who is (or should be) compensated? and (3) In which way are they (or will they be) compensated? The literature has identified various theoretical, political, and humanitarian arguments that justify compensation.

Haggard and Webb, for example, point to the justification provided by classical welfare theory. If a reform involving a typical mix of losers and winners is to result in a situation where the satisfaction of an individual cannot be raised without lowering the satisfaction of another individual (Pareto optimum), losers must be compensated (Haggard and Webb 1991, 29). Several authors note the use of compensation to secure support for, or at least acquiescence to, adjustment policies. (See also Cornea, Jolly, and Stewart 1987.) There is also a humanitarian justification for cushioning the effects of adjustment on the poorest members of society (Haggard and Webb 1990, 21). However, there are several arguments against providing compensation as well.

First, with regard to the poorest sectors, Haggard and Webb refer to arguments holding that the adjustment process may be welfare-enhancing for those groups because they lacked the political power to benefit from the policy regime prior to the reform. There is no need, therefore, to "purchase" their loyalty through compensation (Haggard and Webb 1990, 21).

While leaving unanswered the question of whether reforms afford the poor access to benefits unavailable under previous regimes, this argument assumes at least political indifference on the part of the poor, who cannot lose what they never had. This situation is akin to that of consumers in a shortage economy, whose consumption is constrained by a lack of goods before, and lack of money after, price liberalization. De facto continuity or even modest improvement in the economic situation of the poor, however, does not necessarily translate into political neutrality with regard to overall changes. As Robert Bates and David Collier point out in the context of the Zambian exchange auction in the mid-

1980s, the Zambian poor opposed and helped to stop reform. The reason? They wrongly assumed that their living standard had dropped relative to that of the rich (Bates and Collier 1993). Moreover, even if the poor themselves feel indifferent, this has often been insufficient to keep them from joining coalitions of the reform's opponents. Nelson cites the frequent alliances of the poor with more politically influential middle-income groups (Nelson 1992). These alliances empower the poor with some support for their interests. Therefore, if middle-income groups are politically mobilized against reform, it is easy for them to enlist the "neutral" poor on behalf of antireform actions.

A second argument with a somewhat similar content may be backed by Pfeffermann's notion that while pro-poor distributional policies may be justified on humanitarian or theoretical bases, they may be mistargeted and, in the absence of economic growth, may help the poor only a little (Pfeffermann 1991). This argument focuses on the welfare-enhancing nature of growth-oriented economic adjustment, which rewards even the poor in the medium and long term.

It is easy to accept that economic growth is the leading means to alleviate poverty, but sustained growth is, at best, a medium- and long-term outcome of most reforms. Most adjustment policies have few short-term beneficiaries, however. Consequently, while there is less doubt about future gains, the question about immediate losses and their impact on the sustainability of reform remains open. Obviously, no one can benefit in the long run from reforms halted prematurely because they have brought unbearable short-term hardships.

There is a third argument, based on the needs of the treasury, that compensation is fiscally infeasible (Haggard and Webb 1990, 21). Here again, nobody doubts that fiscal austerity may pose severe constraints on compensatory payments. However, the capacity of the public purse may be measured in relative terms. Governments have to figure out the optimal trade-off between making payments that burden the budget and enhancing the political feasibility of reforms. With regard to the cost of compensation, reformist governments face the usual optimization problem, similar to that associated with the opportunity cost of any other policy decisions.

According to a fourth argument, some compensatory measures may actually undermine reform. For example, if workers are cushioned from the effects of a nominal devaluation by wage increases, this directly undermines the objective of increasing competitiveness (Haggard and Webb 1990, 21). This again may be true, but only if the measures are extreme. Earlier I noted the possibility that reform initiatives may collapse as a consequence of the excessive and careless use of compensation. However, disregarding such extremes, if a form of compensation turns out to be an inevitable political cost of initiating or sustaining reforms, one may still ask what makes more sense: to implement an economically "suboptimal" reform, or to initiate an "optimal" but politically infeasible one? This question challenges the approaches based on an illusory "quick-fix scenario" (Nelson 1989a) in contrast to "muddling towards reform" (Grindle and Thoumi 1993) or the more effective "two-steps forward, one-step back" tactics followed by Özal's government in Turkey (Önis and Webb 1994). I concur with Waterbury that "It should not be forgotten, however, that a regime that alienates most or all of its coalition partners will not be able to pursue the adjustment process" (Waterbury 1989, 55).

Compensation, according to a fifth argument, is not always necessary and thus may be wasteful. For example, there is no need to compensate those harmed by reform if they are possessed of their own resources and can overcome their losses on their own. I fully support this argument.

Nelson has developed a sixth argument that concerns the likely recipients of politically motivated compensation. In contrast with some analysts, she observes that it is typically not the poor who are politically significant in resisting adjustment; rather, the greatest political threat may come from other popular-sector groups, including organized labor, and from the private sector itself (Nelson 1992). Based on this observation, Haggard and Webb argue that it may be difficult to justify compensation for these groups. Clearly, both the theoretical and humanitarian justifications for compensation may be undermined by the fact that the largest beneficiaries of compensation intended for the poor will often be their politically more potent allies.

However, even this assumption leaves the political argument for compensation unchallenged. Indeed, the political efficacy of compensation is enhanced if it helps to overcome opposition from those whose threats to reform may be more serious than those of the poor. Clearly, this statement is not intended to advocate a disregard for the needs of the poor but merely points to the consequences that may stem from the political-efficacy criterion for compensation. It is sad and cruel enough that purchasing the loyalty of the politically influential urban semipoor and working classes may be more effective for the political feasibility of stabilization and adjustment programs (although both morally and theoretically less justified) than helping the politically marginalized poor to adjust and to survive.

In sum, I believe that most of the arguments against compensation listed above are not sufficiently persuasive. While they may effectively question both the theoretical and humanitarian justifications for compensation, they fail to challenge the political argument regarding its necessity. However, from my point of view it is the political justification that seems to be the key argument for compensation. Also, in accordance with my definition, the efficacy of compensation is to be measured in political terms—that is, its success in overcoming opposition to reform measures and increasing their political feasibility. The costs of compensation should be evaluated on the same basis, and measured by the opportunity costs of not using economic and political resources for compensation.

Who Should and Should Not Be Compensated?

Waterbury argues that "a range of discretionary practices in resource allocation—especially those that are designed to compensate partially those interests that suffer the most in the adjustment process—should be accepted" (Waterbury 1989, 55).

Nelson highlights the case of the poor, whose losses in the economic adjustment process make them candidates for compensation. However, she stresses,

> But with the exception of short-term externally financed relief, most pro-poor measures entail shifting resources from better-off groups, including lower-middle and near-poor classes. Such measures inevitably generate strong political resistance. Moreover, these same middle-class and near-poor groups, particularly in the cities, often had been hard hit by depression and adjustment. They are not the most vulnerable, but they may be the most aggrieved victims of the decade's lost growth. Compensatory programs often do help these groups. (Nelson 1989a, 17)

Haggard and Webb are less specific in hypothesizing that successful reform programs involve compensation for "groups negatively affected by reform" in order to reduce political resistance (Haggard and Webb 1991, 20). Elsewhere, these authors explicitly (but generally) refer to "losers" (Haggard and Webb 1990, 21). Who do they believe is (or should be) compensated in such cases? Those "who suffer the most," those who are "the most vulnerable," "the most aggrieved victims," or simply "losers" in general?

All of the quoted authors generally agree that those whose economic interests are damaged by reforms should be compensated. (None of them identifies the beneficiaries of reform as possible candidates for compensation). However, some uncertainty remains about which disadvantaged groups should be targeted. Compensation to those who "suffer the most" (or who lose the most) reflects perhaps theoretical considerations. Compensating "the most vulnerable" clearly points to humanitarian concerns; compensating "the most aggrieved victims" suggests considerations of political efficiency. Finally, any attempt at compensating "losers," however designated, suggests that "losers" can be clearly differentiated from "winners."

These differing criteria specify different groups to be compensated. The most vulnerable, mostly the rural poor, are not identical with those who lose the most, the mostly urban lower-middle class, wage-earning semipoor. These "primary losers" are sometimes joined by other losers, some semirich or even rich, mostly urban private-sector groups, acting in the political arena as the most aggrieved victims.

These differences point to the divergence between morally justified and politically efficacious criteria for compensation. Compensation intended to help the poor may be largely justified by humanitarian considerations, but it is not necessarily effective in political terms. Compensation that is politically effective, however, does not necessarily help those who have lost the most.

Following my own definition, which stresses the political function of compensation, I will use political efficacy as the major criterion for identifying the actors who are (or should be) compensated by reformers seeking to overcome political opposition to adjustment. Compensation is reconsidered in two ways: (1) not all losers are (or should be) compensated; and (2) those whom reformers might wish to compensate are not exclusively losers.

The first statement is in accord with opinions expressed elsewhere; nobody advocates total compensation of all losers. Reforming governments often use political—and not, for example, theoretical or humanitarian—considerations in selecting candidates for compensation. In such instances the kind and amount of compensatory benefits will not exactly match the economic losses associated with reform. Also, the structure of the group of beneficiaries of compensation will probably significantly differ from that of those disadvantaged by reform. This leads me to some broad generalizations.

No matter how large their losses or how vulnerable they are, there is no political justification and therefore no need for compensating actors in the following cases:

1.   Losers who are able and willing to use their own economic resources to overcome their losses without additional assistance. Compensation provided in such cases would fail to shape political attitudes to reform, but would promote processes that would have developed anyway at less public cost.

2.   Losers who lack or do not use their political resources (capacities for collective action) to overcome their losses by shaping the pattern and/or the political prospects of reform.

3.   Losers who are capable of derailing reforms but whose capacity to act can be neutralized by measures that are more effective or less costly than compensation, such as persuasion, obfuscation, and containment (methods noted by Nelson 1989b).

4.   There may be no need to directly compensate losers who are able only indirectly—through their allies or through intermediary organizations—to affect the reform in an adverse way. In such cases it may be more logical to compensate the allies or intermediary organizations instead.

While the categories 1 through 3 limit the scope for compensation to the politically potent losers, category 4 enlarges a reformist government's field of action even within the narrowly defined group of potent opponents. I discuss the implication of this fact later. However, the group of powerful opponents to reform, or the emerging antireform coalition, may not be solely composed of losers. In fact, it may at times be joined by perceived winners. Should they, too, be diverted from antireform actions by compensation?

The Winners/Losers Identification Problem

The idea of limiting compensation exclusively to those whose interests are damaged by reform may reflect a perceived need for theoretical or humanitarian justification. However, as noted previously, such justification may be unnecessary, and compensation may be considered legitimate on purely political grounds, in terms of neutralizing antireform coalitions. Also, as has been stressed, a primary precondition for directing compensation to the losers is the ability to separate them clearly from the winners. However, I argue that while meeting this condition may be easy theoretically, it is not so in reality.

Reformist governments have sometimes encountered remarkably severe difficulties in identifying, politically targeting, and separating groups affected in different ways by their stabilization and adjustment programs. These difficulties remind us of the problems governments also face while initiating industrial policies with arbitrary targeting. In fact, advance prediction of the beneficiaries of policy reforms, or the identification of such groups even in the short and medium term, may prove to be as complex a task for reform politicians as predicting the leaders of future economic development by technocrats responsible for industrial targeting.

Thus, one explanation for the problem in separating winners from losers may have to do with government difficulties with political targeting. A second group of explanations may be related to the behavior of societal actors. On one hand, as Rychard puts it, "The discomfort felt by many social groups results in part from the fact that their representatives do not know whether to count themselves among the winners or losers. Such uncertainty is not any the less frustrating than the consciousness of being a loser" (Rychard 1996, 427). Nelson would counter this by saying that it is only (some) winners who may not know their real situation, while losers are certain who they are (Nelson 1994, 9). It may be true that there is an asymmetry in how accurately losers and winners recognize their situation, and that it is the winners who fail to identify themselves as such, or recognize the corresponding political implications. However, it is enough to confuse political targeting if winners behave passively or react as if they were losers.

Evidence provided, for example, by Nigerian and Chilean country studies shows that some reformist governments simply do not deem it important to know which economic or social groups are affected by their reforms, and in what ways (Herbst and Olukoshi 1994, Stallings and Brock 1993). Dictatorships guided by rigid, ideological prejudices frequently give an extraordinary degree of autonomy to decision makers, who often ignore the distributional effects of their economic policies.

There are also cases where the policymakers' inability to assess the effects of their own policies limits their chances for correctly separating the winners from the losers. As Bates and Collier demonstrate (1993), the Zambian government, due to a lack of technocratic expertise, simply mistook the winners for the losers and thus mistargeted both its exchange-rate policies and its "corrective" social policies. Leith and Lofchie have also shown (1993), in the context of Ghana's trade policies, that a confusing legacy of chaotic trade protection with associated distributional effects made it unclear to the policymakers themselves precisely who did and did not benefit from government actions. Additionally, the reformist governments' difficulties in separating winners from losers may be magnified by factors associated with the winners' inability or unwillingness to identify themselves as such.

Economic actors occupy several different positions at once in the economic structure. They are simultaneously producers, consumers, and recipients of transfers. This may make it difficult for them, as well as for the government, to calculate the costs and benefits of reform or the trade-offs between short-term losses and longer-term gains. One more obstacle to correct calculation is the imperfect information typically surrounding reforms (Haggard and Webb 1990, 2–3). As a consequence, the benficiaries of reforms may sometimes oppose policies that favor them because of uncertainty about their effects.

Provided that a reform package is comprehensive (i.e., contains fiscal, monetary, trade, and other structural reform measures), firms, individuals, and households may simultaneously experience diverse and contradictory effects in each position they occupy in the economy. Calculating costs and benefits may be more difficult the more complex the policy package is.

Individuals, firms, and households also simultaneously hold diverse positions in the political structure as voters and members of trade unions, business associations, or political parties. In each position they have different abilities to influence policy outcomes. Just like their positions in the economy, those in the political structure may be in flux during comprehensive economic reforms. Such changes may also confuse the actors' perceptions of their status as winners or losers, adding to identification difficulties. And given the possible divergence of political and economic distributional effects, the actors' overall evaluation of their true standing requires the calculation of trade-offs between economy and polity as well.

Examples of this problem have occurred in countries where the financial sector, typically one of the winners under reform in LDCs, is reluctant to be identified as such. This is due to justified fears that the government will exploit its status as a winner by making it a political scapegoat for the hardships of the majority. This has actually happened in Nigeria, where merchant bankers who profited from financial deregulation have not actively supported the Babangida government's reform policies because the government has frequently sought to deflect political blame for the increasing "undervaluation" of the Nigerian currency onto "irresponsible" bankers (Herbst and Olukoshi 1994). Other examples are mentioned by Stallings and Brock (1993) and Lal and Maxfield (1993) in Chile and Brazil, respectively.

Nelson also explains how competition among the various groups disadvantaged by economic adjustment may constrain the government's ability to target the most needy groups for relief measures (Nelson 1989b, 97). Further, competition for state resources is rarely limited solely to the losers. In fact, often there is nothing to prevent certain groups of perceived winners from competing with each other and with the losers for public resources. Indeed, the winners' chances in this contest may be substantial if they wield sufficient political power. It would be easy to expose these "double winners" simply and generally as rent seekers and, consequently, to question their eligibility for relief measures if it were not for two additional factors that justify some of their claims on compensation. Nelson and other analysts have noted that during the quick-fix era of the early to mid 1980s, there was often a substantial time lag before the initial losses produced by stabilization were converted into long-term gains (Nelson 1989a, Geddes 1991, Leith and Lofchie 1993).

The phenomenon of short-term losses preceding long-term benefits exposes the difficulties economic actors encounter in assessing their overall well-being. Coupled with other obstacles to a correct assessment, this factor also enhances the possibility that winners will misinterpret their actual positions during the course of reforms. Clearly, if potential winners are severely hurt by some elements of the reform package in some of their economic roles (even if they are later rewarded by other policy effects, perhaps in another role), they can easily perceive themselves as losers. In response, they may fail to support the reform program or even join its opponents in the political arena. Moreover, the hardships long-term winners experience as short-term losers, and the negative attitude toward reforms that may result, may be reinforced by their lack of resources or of the time necessary to advance beyond their disadvantaged status.[3]

Exploiting the potential benefits from structural adjustment requires decisive action from the potential winners. Benefits are often realized only after time-consuming and painful adjustment, restructuring, and reorganization efforts by firms and households. Transcending the losers' position requires ambition, time, and resources for factor mobility. A change from import-substitution business strategies toward export orientation might exemplify this process. Even if the reform program offers clear incentives, the process of implementation may be delayed or fail altogether. This can occur if missing or dysfunctional institutional arrangements constrain or delay the mobility of the production factors, including labor, land, or capital. Consequently, potential winners will not support the adjustment policies or will even oppose reforms.

For example, manufacturers in Nigeria, although perceived as the beneficiaries of trade reforms, were actually active in the coalition opposing the reform program. This happened because many of the manufacturers represented by the MAN (the main Nigerian business organization) seriously doubted that they could reorganize their production and trade activities in order to benefit from trade reforms (Herbst and Olukoshi 1994). Equally paradoxical was the position of Senegalian industrialists, who felt seriously threatened by that country's attempts at trade liberalization. Although the government designed a set of "accompanying measures" to help firms adjust to fierce foreign competition (including measures lowering excessive labor and energy costs, financial assistance to firms seeking to restructure, a new investment code, and increased export subsidies), only a few of those measures were in fact implemented. Senegalian industrialists, who after restructuring stood to benefit from the reforms, never supported them. This was because they lacked the means and institutional support to move beyond their initial position of disadvantage (Ka and Van de Walle 1994). A similar situation may have contributed to the fact that Polish farmers and the organizations representing them became the toughest and best-organized opponents of the Balcerowicz reforms early on. Although in the short run they were disadvantaged by increased input prices and intensified foreign competition, in the medium and long run, as major exporters in an agro-exporting country, they could have been the beneficiaries of the Polish trade reforms. However, reformers failed to provide them either with the necessary grace period to adjust to the reforms or with other supports that would have enabled them to complete the transition successfully. Moreover, even the incentives to export eroded as inflation persisted. These factors help to explain why perceived beneficiaries opposed the Polish reforms.

Similarly, during the tough stabilization periods associated with wage cuts and declining living standards, it is indeed relevant for the political prospects of reform whether the losers remain cemented in their disadvantaged positions "forever" or whether they are enabled by time and resources to improve their position. In the analyses of economic reform, an abundance of positive and negative examples point to the significance of this issue in the context of strategic coalition management, and to the active use of compensatory policies for turning short-term losers into medium- and long-term winners.[4]

As I have explained, many factors may hamper the reformist government's success with political targeting as well as the beneficiaries' perception of themselves as winners. These factors include: incomplete information; uncertainty about the consequences of reform; the complexity of economic and political impacts, which confound the actors' perceptions of their current and future status; political fears; the possibility that losses will precede gains; and the lack of time, means, and institutional support for adjustment. These circumstances may often cause prospective winners, aggrieved by their immediate losses, to become involved in active or passive resistance to economic adjustment. To avoid the emergence of antireform coalitions, supported even by the expected beneficiaries of reform, it may be politically justified to extend the scope of compensation beyond the losers. Sensitive reformers often keep this in mind.

Indeed, compensation of specific groups of beneficiaries of reform for their short-term losses may sometimes be even more effective politically—and therefore more justified—than the compensation of specific groups who are disadvantaged by reform. Of course, both the direct humanitarian and the theoretical justification are clearly lacking in the former case.

Who Is (or Should Be) Compensated: Losers or Opponents?

The foregoing arguments make it clear that the answer to the question of who is (or should be) compensated is neither losers in general nor, more specifically, certain groups of losers. Politically influential opponents of reform, no matter whether winners or losers, are often compensated in order for the political goal of compensation—that is, neutralization of opposition to reforms—to be met. Based on that principle, the opponents best suited to receive compensation may be specified as follows.

1. Losers who are disposed of and are both able and willing to use their political resources to overcome their losses, even at the cost of adversely shaping the pattern or political prospects

for reform, and who cannot be influenced in a more effective (or less costly) way than compensation.

2.   Politically vocal and influential groups who are allied with less influential losers and who are able to adversely shape the pattern or political prospects for reform.

3.   Short-term losers (but medium- and long-term winners) who lack the time, means, or institutional mechanisms to escape from their disadvantaged position, and who use antireform political action only because they feel locked into the losers' camp. The typical forms of compensation for these latter opponents are—and should be—grace periods and policies improving the mobility of factors of production.

Undoubtedly, any particular pattern of compensation resulting from the guidelines listed above is likely to reflect—and probably even encourage—political pressures to a greater extent than theoretical economists, technocratic policymakers, or international organizations would prefer. But this author, in company with many reformist governments, argues that the chances for reform are improved if compensation is permitted at least partly to filter and absorb those pressures, a response that is preferable to delaying, negatively reshaping, or undoing adjustment policies. Compensation, by this interpretation, may to some extent cushion core reform policies themselves from disruptive political pressures.

However, one additional point may be important in explaining the actual patterns of compensation that have been implemented during various reform episodes. When specifying who should and who need not be compensated, I pointed to the possibility of partially avoiding direct transfers to some or all of those whose opposition to reform is to be overcome through compensation. This takes me to the argument below.

Actors Represented and Their Representatives

In this chapter I have explored the political justification for compensation in terms of the specific political goal of overcoming opposition to reform. Meeting this goal presumes a corresponding political behavior on the part of the actors compensated. This can take the form of passivity or sometimes even of active support for reform measures. If either occurs, compensation has been effective.

The crucial question with regard to efficacy is to identify the types or groups of actors who are able to guarantee a predominantly passive (and perhaps even supportive) response to compensation in the political arena. Clearly, politically effective compensation has to target exactly those actors who have a decisive say in what will happen and who possess the power to influence the process and direction of policy making.

It is both helpful and relevant from the point of view of our argument to refer to two basic types or groups of political and economic actors with the power to influence the outcome of economic reforms. Actors disposed of such powers can be individuals—including consumers, producers, households, firms, voters, the members of a political party or labor union, or the members and sponsors of a business organization or lobby. Alternatively, they can be representatives of the political or economic interests of the same individuals, organized into political parties, trade unions, issue lobbies, or consumer or business-interest organizations.

Individuals certainly have some direct influence over the course of economic reforms through the collective effect of multiple personal actions. However, much of their political impact is accomplished indirectly, through organizations representing their economic and political interests. Fragmented individual interests, both supporting and opposing reform, must be aggregated and organized in order for joint political action to be effective. An individual firm may escape the burdens of new taxation by tax evasion, but it cannot by itself change the tax law. Business organizations, however, sometimes can. Similarly, the organization of a strike needs not only workers willing to strike but also a labor union to finance the strikers, formulate their goals, and negotiate their demands.

The significant impact of the organization form and level of political and economic interests on both the pro-reform and antireform coalition management is widely accepted and discussed in the literature of political economy. However, much less attention has been paid to the interest groups' political importance for targeting compensation. Let me continue the argument based on the example above. If, for example, the political goal of compensation is to prevent strikes targeting one or another reform measure, there may in principle be two ways to do this. Compensation may focus on preventing workers from striking or their unions from organizing a strike. In other words, the government may intervene at the level of the individual actors or at the level of their representative, or both.

Choosing a specific form of compensation requires a comparison of the economic and political costs and benefits associated with any of them. Compensating the representative organization, instead of the rank and file membership, may sometimes turn out to be less costly or more politically efficacious. Clearly, one might argue that compensation of the boards of labor unions and political party elites cannot substitute for compensation of their constituencies, except perhaps for a brief period of time. One reason this may be so is that the boards and elites, who are presumably controlled by the individual actors, may be punished by the latter for not representing their economic and political interests effectively.

However, Geddes stresses the "retrospective" nature of the voters' control, noting that, because of incomplete information and the difficulties of acquiring information, the control or punishment may lag considerably behind the injuries caused to the voters' economic or political interests (Geddes 1991). This is a problem for labor unions, business and religious groups, and other organizations of elected and unelected representatives.

Other factors may contribute to the relative independence of a representative from his or her constituency. These include the absence of other choices for representation; the time lags inherent in the electoral system; and the one-sided dependency of those represented, based on inequalities of an economic, political, cultural, or religious nature (Geddes 1991).

Their relative independence, in principle, allows for union boards, political party elites, or other types of interest organizations to receive political or economic compensatory benefits instead of their constituents without fear of immediate retaliation. In compensating such groups, a government entirely or partially avoids immediate, direct transfers to some or all of those whose opposition to the reform is to be overcome through compensation. This situation may have an impact both on the volume and the type of compensatory benefits dispensed to meet the political goal of compensation.

Each government must evaluate precisely the trade-offs among the economic and political costs and gains associated with specific compensation techniques. However, the very existence of forms of compensation involving distribution of political benefits magnifies the government's field of action for compensatory practices, and improves its chances to establish a political environment favoring reforms. The next chapter shows how techniques of compensation were used in 1992 in Hungary.

Chapter 9

Conflict, Social Pact, and Democratic Development in Transforming Hungary

Complementing Chapter 8, this chapter examines a case in which compensation was provided, the Hungarian Social Pact of 1992, as well as the political conflicts preceding and following it. The case study improves our understanding of the type of democracy currently emerging in Hungary and contributes to its conceptualization through some reflections.[1]

Transition to What?

Analysts attempting an adequate conceptualization of the political and economic system emerging in Eastern Europe are faced with the uncertainties surrounding the dynamics and outcome of the process strongly expressed by some students of postcommunism, most clearly Bunce and Csanádi (1992, 221).

One approach to learning more about unfinished and unconsolidated democratization processes is to observe and study democratic agents acting, struggling, and competing in the global context of the political institutional system. There are special moments—such as elections or dramatic sociopolitical conflicts—where events and actions thicken, the political arena becomes heated, and actors face heightened challenges. At such times their responses may reveal much more than is ordinarily apparent about their aims, resources, and strategies, and the adaptability, elasticity, and durability of the system itself. Undoubtedly, social pacts present meaningful moments in the above sense.

To illustrate Hungarian democracy in operation, I have chosen to examine the Social Pact of 1992. My study was partly inspired by this comment from Sidney Tarrow: "The recent wave of movements in Eastern Europe is not yet over—but there is already a danger that its precious findings will be lost as leaders reify their experiences, and the ephemera of popular politics disappear into people's attics and selective memories. For scholars of collective action, the recent movements in Eastern Europe offer an important challenge" (Tarrow 1991, 17).

I begin by reviewing the economic situation and policy context in which the government opted for an austerity program by the autumn of 1992. Following that, I analyze the sociopolitical conflict arising from the hardships associated with the austerity measures. Based on the framework developed in Chapter 5, I identify various threats to the planned reforms—that is, the economic and political means that different socioeconomic groups tried to use to stop or reshape adjustment policies. I also introduce the organizations behind the protests and assess their strength and political clout.

Next I give an account of the tripartite pact reached by government, labor, and business on November 21, 1992. The analysis focuses on identifying the different interests that were brought to the negotiations, and on the way the resulting accord reshaped the original policy and the compensation package. In explaining who was compensated and what form the compensation took, I build on the analytic framework elaborated in Chapter 8. Then I evaluate the aftermath of the pact, focusing on the subsequent reactions and strategies of its winners and losers.

Finally, I consider some materials from the international literature on social pacts. Based on the case presented, and with special attention to some characteristic features of the Hungarian democratic system, I also review the typology of democracies elaborated in the Latin American context by Carlos H. Acuña and William C. Smith (1994) and consider whether it contributes to understanding the Hungarian democratization. Conversely, I also assess how the Hungarian case may test this typology and so perhaps enrich its empirical content.

The Economic Situation and the Policy Context

The year 1992 was among the worst in Hungary's postcommunist economic history. It was the third consecutive year in which macroeconomic indicators revealed a devastated economic landscape. The ongoing deep recession had produced a record budget deficit. High inflation, falling investments, sharply rising unemployment, and rapid impoverishment marked the social losses associated with the transformational recession. Even worse, no improvements in economic performance were in sight. The Hungarian economy was far from "taking a breath"; instead it was struggling with the immediate, grave macroeconomic implications of its structural crisis.

There was much political tension in the air as well. Beginning in August 1992, with the publication of a political pamphlet by István Csurka—then a vice chairman of the main coalition party, the Hungarian

Democratic Forum (MDF)—a widening split was apparent within the MDF. In September and October right-wing and social-liberal mass demonstrations, repeated extremist and government attacks against the allegedly pro-opposition mass media, and a fascist provocation against the president of Hungary all indicated a highly charged political atmosphere. In addition, Csurka and his followers, with increasing rhetorical consistency, called for fundamental change in government policies. Specifically, they urged the disempowerment of the "conspiratorial internal agents" of "the international financial Mafia" led by the World Bank and the IMF, who had allegedly enforced the macroeconomic austerity of recent years that had brought such a precipitous deterioration in living standards (Csurka 1992a). Increasingly, reformist technocrats around Finance Minister Mihály Kupa were openly threatened by MDF extremists.

Moreover, by the early autumn of 1992, Hungarian policy makers were facing a politically risky undertaking. The high budget deficit had to be reduced in accordance with guidelines approved by international financial organizations in order to preserve the country's credibility and the Hungarian government's image as a committed reformer. After his return from Washington in the summer of 1992, the finance minister announced that he would "say no" to any request or pressure that might produce serious budget imbalances in 1993. This was the situation when the Hungarian Treasury, also urged by the IMF, elaborated an austerity program concentrating on the revenue side of the budget, with a Value Added Tax reform as its focus.

In accordance with the need to bring the Hungarian system into conformity with the practices of the European Community, reform concentrated on the introduction of a two-tier VAT system, rationalizing VAT rates at 8 percent and 25 percent and replacing earlier rates.[2] The planned tax reform would also eliminate a number of tax exemptions, such as those for home construction and renovation, while increasing some consumption taxes. Adjustments to increase tax receipts were combined with relatively minor but sensitive cuts in expenditures: a total freeze on both the operational and wage costs of public institutions at their 1992 levels; substantial decreases in financing employment programs; emergency adjustments to the labor costs of the Hungarian railways, implying the dismissal of twenty thousand employees and a streamlining of the railway's social services to its employees; and freezing family allowances per child at the 1992 level.

There was no doubt that policymakers would have to answer the crucial political question of who was to bear the burden of these policies. Therefore, from the start, the reform package outlined a set of compensatory measures designed to sidestep potential political protest against the social implications of the adjustment program. The plan offered a choice between increasing personal income-tax allowances for families with children; a direct increase of family allowances according to the number of children, based on various budget sources; maintaining tax allowances supporting residential building and renovation; or any feasible combination of these and other compensatory measures.

Forms of Protest

In spite of the promised compensation, an extensive wave of protest actions followed the announcement of the austerity plan. Following a collapse in negotiations with the Treasury, on October 22, 1992, a group hunger strike began in the provincial town of Bicske, coordinated by a civil organization called the Association of People Living below the Poverty Line (LAÉT). The six initial hunger strikers demanded that the VAT reform plan be withdrawn and that basic foods, medicines, and household energy should remain untaxed.

From the start, the protest received support from several civil associations, like the Independent Alliance for Popular Representation, the League for Protecting the Interests of the Unemployed, the League for Legal Protection, the Social Chamber, and the Roma Parliament. Many other civil and political organizations subsequently joined the group of supporters and sympathizers, including the Pensioners' Branch of the National Federation of Hungarian Trade Unions (MSZOSZ); the Borsod-Abaúj-Zemplén-County organization of the Democratic League of Independent Trade Unions; the Steel Workers' Branch of the MSZOSZ; the Hungarian Social Democratic Party; the Liberal Citizens' Association–Entrepreneurs' Party; the Association of Hungarian Taxpayers; and the Hungarian Socialist Party.

The hunger strike quickly spread throughout the country. The number of simultaneous hunger strikers, and of those ready to join or replace them if necessary, rapidly became tens and then hundreds. The movement affected a growing number of localities, including the capital and small and large towns and villages in the countryside. As the movement expanded, its demands became more specific. The hunger strikers identified twenty basic food items for which they demanded zero VAT rates in 1993. In addition, they repeatedly demanded more publicity and accurate, undistorted coverage of their movement. Initially, the hunger strike was treated warily by the media, and it even encountered hostility in some parts of the print media.[3]

The protest became more vocal too. Referring to sympathetic statements by some sectoral and local labor unions, hunger strikers threatened the government with the possibility of food riots, linked with simultaneous demonstrations and strikes in strategic industrial sectors. The hunger strikers gained more sympathy in the independent and leftist print media.

A brief introduction to recent Hungarian civil society may help in portraying the organizers and supporters of the hunger strike. Just prior to and following the breakdown of the communist regime, there was an impressive boom in the number and type of civil associations and organizations. However, the dubious legitimacy and representativeness of most of these was well known, and they were dealt with suspiciously by the government, political parties, and labor unions (the latter themselves struggling with similar problems associated with their own transition.) Many organizations backing the civil protest action in 1992 shared the deficiencies of legitimacy and support characteristic of the civil sector as a whole. LAÉT itself was not entirely different in this respect, except that planning and initiating the hunger strike, coordinating it for almost two months, and winning publicity for it in media that were partly hostile indicated considerable organizational capacities.

LAÉT was founded in late August 1991, and was characterized by its best-known leader, Ferenc Valencsik, as the organization that was "gathering disappointed MDF members," (*Magyar Hírlap,* March 3, 1993) including a former MDF member of Parliament, who thought that the national leaders lacked social sensitivity. Thus it had been the task of LAÉT to address the deepening impoverishment in Hungary. The organization was provided with an office by the Hungarian Red Cross. While asking no membership fees, nor providing membership cards, it claimed to have a registered membership; but prior to the hunger strike LAÉT based its sporadic activities on a very small core of activists. Engaged mainly in preparing and distributing leaflets and brochures on poverty in Hungary, this group sought to raise funds from businesses, presumably with little success. Unpaid phone bills amounting to a hundred thousand forints (about one thousand U.S. dollars) after the hunger strike indicated a shocking amount of debt for LAÉT (*Magyar Hírlap,* March 3, 1993). Nothing in LAÉT's history ever suggested a capability to organize countrywide protest actions.

Parallel to the spread of the hunger-strike movement, numerous strike warnings demonstrated labor's discontent with the planned austerity measures. Unions in the education and health-care sectors threatened coordinated protest actions, including the collection of signatures, demonstrations, and strikes. Unions representing steel and railway workers and miners joined them in threatening strikes if the austerity measures were implemented without modification (*Magyar Hírlap,* October 31, 1992).

Again, a brief review of the position of trade unions in postcommunist Hungary may help in assessing the background and significance of the strike threat. The current structure of the Hungarian trade union sector had emerged by the summer of 1990. The level of unionization has sharply declined from about 90 percent of the labor force in the 1980s to around 30 percent by the early 1990s. Estimated union membership may now be around 1.5 million. Following the breakthrough years of 1989–90, the union movement has also been transformed into a pluralistic one. Three groups of unions can be identified.

While the National Federation of Hungarian Trade Unions inherited only a fraction of the rank and file of the Communist Labor Federation (SZOT), it acquired much of its infrastructure and property and the entire leadership and bureaucracy, with the former Party Central Committee member, Sándor Nagy, at the top. The MSZOSZ has been closely allied with the Hungarian Socialist Party (MSZP), the successor of Hungary's communists.

A second set is composed of splinter groups from the SZOT: the Rally of Trade Unions for Intellectual Workers (ÉSZT), the Confederation of Autonomous Trade Unions, and the Reconciliation Forum of Trade Unions (SZEF). The MSZOSZ together with its splinter organizations had the overwhelming majority of organized labor among its rank and file (Sziráczki, Szalai, and Ladó 1993).

A third group is constituted by three new unions that emerged in the transformation process: the Democratic League of Independent Trade Unions (LIGA), the Solidarity Workers' Alliance (SWA), and the Workers' Councils. Lacking the infrastructural and organizational resources of the MSZOSZ and its associates for much of the early transition period, and facing coolness, if not hostility, from the government and most political parties to unionism per se, the new unions have remained heavily constrained. Labor has continued to be dominated by postcommunist federations. While pluralism was characteristic at the national level, for instance in nationwide tripartite structures, in most cases only one of the unions was present at the industrial sector level and in the workplace.

The general picture is of a trade union movement in decline but characterized at the same time by asymmetric strengths and weaknesses. The movement dominated by the MSZOSZ appears to have been rather weak in terms of membership, mobilization capacity, presence, activity, and influence in everyday labor relations in the workplace. The strength of the unions, however, became more accentuated at the macro level, in various organizations and commissions where the comparative advantage of an experienced leadership and bureaucracy could be best exploited. Unions had a strong experience in politics too through their internal rivalries, competition with political parties and civil organizations for the right to represent nonlabor groups (the popular sector in general, and pensioners in particular), and by sometimes politically colored strike warnings when tough economic measures were introduced or discriminatory steps were taken against them.

Even so, union threats remained mostly symbolic throughout the early transition period in Hungary. Stoppages were sporadic and generally local, there were very few regional or countrywide strike calls, and even fewer actual strikes. The few general strike calls, initiated exclusively by the MSZOSZ, regularly failed. The frequency of strike alerts was relatively low and—unlike in Poland and the former GDR, but similar to Slovakia—far exceeded the frequency of actual strikes.

Table 9.1: Strike Alerts and Strikes in Four East Central European Countries between 1989 and 1993

Form of Protest	Poland (1989–93)	Slovakia (1990–93)	Hungary (1989–93)	GDR (1989–93)
Strike alerts	408	29	107	56
Strikes	432	24	61	107
Strike alerts/strikes	0.9	1.2	1.7	0.5

Source: Ekiert, and Kubik 1996, Table 2.

In 1992, the year under discussion, labor in Hungary was very patient (*Heti Világgazdaság*, January 29, 1994). While a basic assumption of the relevant literature is that, in general, strike activity does not indicate union strength (Nelson 1991), in the Hungarian context, the extremely low level of union militancy cannot be interpreted as an indication of union strength. I think the fact that strikes did not happen in Hungary was largely independent of the unions' will.

Political parties did not seem to be committed to the draft austerity package. Parties of the parliamentary opposition signaled their dissatisfaction with the details of the adjustment package early on. Further, the parties within the governing coalition were even more negative than those in the opposition. Not only the fragmented and populist Smallholders' Party, and the allegedly socially sensitive Christian Democrats, but also the pro-Csurka faction of the MDF said that they would reject the austerity program and the proposed budget for 1993 if the plan remained unchanged.

Social Conflict and Attempts at a Solution

In these circumstances it was clear that any government attempt to force through an austerity program might fail. In order to ease the political tension, the government first pursued a strategy of case-by-case negotiations. Members of Parliament tried to calm the aggrieved hunger strikers with visits, requests, and letters. Indeed, by mid-November the government even signaled its willingness to meet the movement's demand, offering to keep four or five basic food items tax free if the hunger strike would end. The government's attempts to curb the expanding protest were complemented by competition between the parties and trade unions over who could do the most for the interests of poor people. Finance Minister Kupa, in turn, paid time-consuming visits to coalition party headquarters to bargain with the parties and factions on possible modifications to the package in exchange for their support in the budget vote. Ongoing negotiations with the most vocal unions also demonstrated the government's intention to implement the austerity program peacefully.

The government's strategy seemed to produce results. Following its announcement that the hunger strikers' demands would most likely be incorporated into the austerity compensation package, LAÉT signaled its willingness to end the hunger strike and to negotiate a solution to the conflict. By November 18 it also became clear that there would be no miners' strike. An initial agreement between the government and the miners' unions was reached on some of the most contentious policy items, and the parties agreed to continue negotiations into early December (*Magyar Hírlap,* November 18, 1992). A similar agreement to postpone protest was reached with the iron and steel unions, while workers in health care and education seemed to await further agreements related to their demands. Negotiations with unions representing railway employees failed, however. Also, it remained doubtful that Finance

Minister Kupa would succeed in convincing coalition factions that the austerity program was unavoidable. In spite of the partial success of the case-by-case approach, sufficient discord remained to make the formation of an anti-austerity coalition a real possibility.

In this atmosphere of continuing sociopolitical tension, the unions called in early November for the resolution of all disputes through tripartite negotiations of the government, labor and business, and the conclusion of a social pact. This offer came just at the right moment for the government. After short exploratory talks, an agreement was soon reached to conduct negotiations within the existing framework of the Council for the Reconciliation of Interests (the CRI, discussed in more detail below), and these were scheduled for November 20–21.

It is not surprising that the trade unions preferred to negotiate rather than push the situation toward open conflict. It must have been clear to the entire movement, and especially the MSZOSZ, that they could gain much more through negotiation and compromise than by forcing strikes. Union restraint may have paid off politically at that time because unions were still struggling with serious deficiencies in legitimacy and organization due to their status during transformation, the grave economic situation, and the government's political style.

For the labor unions there was also the prospect of significant institutional gains. With the CRI as the locus for negotiations, the tripartite forum could be publicly recognized as a body where important policy adjustments could be achieved while, CRI members could enhance their image as having substantial control over economic policy decisions. Another factor was the simultaneous decision about which interests would and would not be represented in negotiations. The tripartite pattern of preselecting the negotiating partners and excluding others (LAÉT, and other civil organizations in this case) had great significance especially because the CRI played an important role in deciding which social groups would be compensated for their losses under economic austerity and what form this would take. To demonstrate the CRI's significance as the forum for the social accommodation of austerity, it may be useful to give a brief account of its institutional history.[4]

The CRI's predecessor, the National Council for the Reconciliation of Interests (NCRI), "was established in October 1988. Its purpose was to provide a forum for agreements on wage increases and exceptions to wage regulation. However, the NCRI was soon expected to deal with other issues, such as prices, profit taxation, and personal income taxation. . . . The conflict of national wage bargaining with general economic and social consultation (or even co-determination concerning general social and economic issues) remains a fundamental issue for the NCRI's replacement body, the CRI" (Sziráczki, Szalai, and Ladó 1993, 127).

After 1990 the CRI underwent an extensive process of institutionalization. Initially this required the establishment of rules, boundaries, and a framework for control over government economic policy making. Organizationally, this involved the establishment within the CRI of several committees of government, business, and labor concerned with economic policy, labor market relations, social policies, information, training, and privatization.

It also involved the institutionalization of the tripartite status quo, which meant formalizing the organizations permitted to take part in CRI activities. The MSZOSZ (National Federation of Hungarian Trade Unions), ÉSZT (Rally of Trade Unions for Intellectual Workers), the Confederation of Autonomous Trade Unions, the LIGA (Democratic League of Independent Trade Unions), SWA (Solidarity Workers' Alliance), and the SZEF (Reconciliation Forum of Trade Unions) represented the trade unions. Participating from the business side were ÁFEOSZ (the National Federation of General Consumption Cooperatives), IPOSZ (the National Federation of Hungarian Industrial Associations–Hungarian Chamber of Artisans), KISOSZ (the National Organization of Petty Traders), MAOSZ (the National Federation of Employers), MGYOSZ (the National Alliance of Hungarian Industrialists), MOSZ (the National Alliance of Agricultural Producers and Cooperatives), the Hungarian Industrial Federation, and VOSZ (the National Federation of Entrepreneurs). The government was normally represented by the minister responsible for the issues under negotiation at the CRI.

While the MSZOSZ was the most powerful organization on the trade union side, its strongest counterpart on the business side was MAOSZ, whose membership included most of the large state-owned or partly privatized firms. In order to interpret the negotiations taking place at the CRI, it is important to point out that 80 percent of MSZOSZ members were employed in firms represented by MAOSZ. Some observers have noted that MAOSZ functioned at the CRI more like an industrial lobby instead of representing specific employers' interests against those of the employees (Kőhegyi 1994). This pattern of behavior was evident in the business side's peculiar passivity throughout the late November negotiations.

High-ranking government officials, such as the finance minister, repeatedly stressed the need to "maintain social peace," suggesting that the government felt forced to negotiate because of pressure from the various sources described above. It is doubtful, however, how much the Antall government really feared social conflict.

LAÉT, at the center of the most vigorous protest, should logically have been invited to the negotiating table. It is clear, however, that by the government's and the unions' decision to select the CRI as a forum for negotiations, it was automatically decided that except for the business associations and unions, no organization representing civil society would participate in resolving the conflict. (No civil organizations were members of the CRI.) Despite repeated claims, threats, and complaints, LAÉT could not manage to acquire even observer status at the negotiations on the social pact. The government may have thought that it was not hunger strikes but labor strikes that posed the greatest danger to its austerity program and to social peace. However, this explanation has many weaknesses too.

First, the government had to be aware of the unions' limited capacity to effectively paralyze the economy. From the press alone, the government would have known how contentious the issue of a strike was among the unions themselves. As a local LIGA leader in the Balinka coal mine put it, "We want to act through negotiations and agreements. I think after a strike call people today would only laugh loudly at us, because the country could easily import cheaper coal from the Ukraine or Slovakia for the time being" (*Magyar Hírlap*, November 3, 1992). Second, as I have already mentioned, by the time the talks on the social pact began, some of the strike threats had already been neutralized. Finally, if the government really wanted the pact in order to preempt all the remaining strike threats, it would soon be disappointed to learn that the tripartite agreement was not equally attractive to all unions. Indeed, the railway unions announced a two-hour warning strike on the very day of the negotiations. When Finance Minister Kupa, leading the government delegation, learned about the strike call, he asked the justifiable question, "Why should we come to an agreement if there is a war going on at the sectoral level and there is no social peace?" (*Magyar Hírlap*, November 23, 1992).

I think it was not literally "social peace" that was at risk beginning in early October 1992, but rather the overall balance of power between the government, the coalition, and the Parliament. What the government really may have feared was less the prospect of civil and labor protests than the fragmentation of the coalition in the face of the austerity program and the budget for 1993. Reformist technocrats and, more broadly, the government could be voted out by their own coalition parties. Most likely, the real interest of the government and financial technocracy was in using the pact to demonstrate social acceptance of their measures and to convince and discipline a shaky coalition. In this context it is easier to understand how and why the trade unions' symbolic threats, backed with only modest capacities for real pressure, were "upgraded," affording them a more solid bargaining position during the pact.

The Pact's Winners and Losers

The austerity and compensatory measures approved in the social pact of November 21 differed significantly from the original government plans, allowing the trade unions legitimately to claim victory. They stood to gain a great deal both in terms of compensatory financial relief for their constituencies and in political side payments for the organizations themselves. The former gains included the elimination of wage controls, which had been a central element in the Antall government's stabilization plan, as well as a substantial increase in the minimum wage, the retention of some tax incentives for home building and renovation, the reintroduction of a tax preference for white-collar employees, an increase in family allowances and tax preferences linked to the number of children in a family, the promise of wage increases in the health-care and education sector, and the elimination of taxes on medicines and household energy.

The withdrawal of a highly interventionist draft bill governing union elections and the division of union property can be seen as a political side payment in the bargaining process. According to some analyses, it was the latter that was the central issue for the unions (Héthy 1994). Indeed, one of the unions, the Solidarity Workers' Alliance, sufficiently dissatisfied to leave the CRI before the end of negotiations, strongly criticized its fellow federations for "trading economics for politics."[5] The Solidarity Workers' Alliance, was excluded from the CRI soon thereafter for its failure to cooperate and because its aims and methods were unacceptable to the six other unions.

The government, especially the reformists led by Kupa, might also have quietly celebrated victory. First, they had gained the unions' acceptance of modified tax reform and other tough measures, including a substantial increase in business and employee contributions to the unemployment benefit fund. Second, coalition dissent around the austerity package and the budget was diminished by the pact, allowing the government to win parliamentary support for the 1993 budget. Third, Kupa and the government demonstrated a form of strength or at least a capability for handling sociopolitical crisis. They also improved their image as policymakers by treating their societal partners seriously and negotiating instead of implementing government policies through coercion.

No wonder the winners more or less welcomed the pact with enthusiasm, while the aggrieved losers—the hunger strikers, civil organizations, and the popular groups backing them—realized that the pact was biased toward those who were somewhat better off: middle- and lower-middle-income groups that were politically more vocal and better represented in the negotiations. For example, the only demand specifically associated with the hunger-strike movement—a zero-rated VAT for basic food items—was somehow lost in the labyrinth of the tripartite negotiations. In fact, most elements in the agreement did little to help the poor (*Magyar Hírlap*, November 30, 1992).

The Aftermath of the Pact: Call for a Referendum

Aggrieved by its exclusion from the social pact and discontented with the government's economic policies and the design of the Hungarian democratic system in general, LAÉT soon initiated a new protest action. Aided by numerous other civil organizations, its activists began to collect citizens' signatures on December 15, 1992, in order to force a referendum on the dissolution of Parliament and a requirement for new general elections. They declared, "the Parliament in its recent structure proved to be impotent at solving the problems of the approximately 4.5 million Hungarians living below the subsistence minimum or very near to it" (*Magyar Hírlap*, December 8, 1992).

The action quickly became a remarkable success. It took only three weeks for LAÉT and its associates to collect the hundred thousand signatures required to call a referendum. The initiative enjoyed great popularity not only among impoverished social groups but among other Hungarians who were increasingly dissatisfied with the process of transformation in general. According to an opinion poll, in late 1992 about 25 percent of the supporters of coalition parties and 40 to 50 percent of opposition voters sympathized with the idea of holding general elections earlier than originally scheduled.

The political situation became even more roiled when LAÉT's new protest action coincided with a similar initiative by another civil organization. The rather vocal National Alliance of Political Prisoners

(POFOSZ) at its annual congress on December 5, 1992, proposed that Parliament amend the election law in three key areas. It suggested establishing a second parliamentary chamber for organizations outside the formal party system, reintroducing the rule to recall MPs, and a direct election of all MPs. The POFOSZ congress, threatened to collect citizens' signatures if the legislators did not consider their proposal (*Magyar Hírlap,* December 7, 1992).

The POFOSZ initiative reinforced the general picture reflecting the success of LAÉT's action. The actual political and institutional design of Hungarian democracy had yet to be legitimated and consolidated, but instead was disputed and challenged by broad societal groups from time to time. (See Kis 1992, on the legitimation deficiencies of the Hungarian regime.)

The unexpected success of LAÉT's action provoked a mixed reaction of guilt, uncertainty, and aversion to the referendum among the established parties and, more broadly, the Hungarian political and intellectual elite. Their sense of guilt may have been rooted in the fact that the elite who were overseeing the transformation had failed to specify the means and channels for civil control over state policies in the constitution. Uncertainty arose mainly from the questionable legal status of the referendum. The Constitutional Committee of the Parliament requested a Constitutional Court decision on the status of the referendum.

Most of the coalition and opposition parties shared an aversion to the referendum. They repeatedly pointed out the possible risks of civil action, including political chaos and anarchy and threats to Hungary's fragile democratic institutions in general. Without assessing the justifications for those fears, it will suffice here to stress that the formal political system strongly opted for the status quo and against popular claims on a new design for the political system. The defenders were joined by the MSZOSZ, which soon announced that it opposed the dissolution of the Parliament and preferred corporatist ways of overcoming social tensions (*Magyar Hírlap,* January 8, 1992). (In addition to their commitment to the existing democratic rules, most parties did not feel sufficiently prepared for elections in 1993.)

By mid-January 1993, when 172,000 citizens had already signed petitions supporting the referendum, the Constitutional Court decided that, while the referendum was legal, the referendum law itself violated the constitution. The court requested the Parliament to amend the law by the end of 1993. Parliamentary parties and other agents of the established political system learned about the decision with quiet satisfaction.

The movement to collect signatures lost momentum and stopped soon afterwards, and many civil organizations that had supported the protest actions subsequently dissolved. LAÉT itself attempted to found a political party, of which nothing was heard by the 1994 elections.

One way to learn from this case study is to reflect on some of the concepts and assumptions of the literature concerning social pacts, "negotiated," "consulted," or "interactive" policies, and on democratic types.

Government Strength, Union Strength

Analyses of neocorporatist arrangements (including social pacts) often stress that the preconditions for reaching agreement are government commitment and capacity, on one hand, and union and business organizational centralization and concentration and a monopoly on representation, on the other. A government's commitment and capacity is judged in terms of its willingness and ability to initiate, elaborate, and implement economic policies, and to monitor and enforce negotiated agreements. Unions' and businesses' centralization, concentration, and monopoly on representation, in turn, are instrumental in preventing the agreements reached at the macro level from being undermined by lower-ranking leaders, the rank and file, or other rival organizations (Valenzuela 1991, 19–20; O'Donnell and Schmitter 1986, 46).

Other analysts discuss the same qualities in terms of government, union, or business strength. In this more simple formulation it is the politically and organizationally strong governments and unions that have the best chance to succeed in negotiations and to conclude social pacts (Héthy 1994, 19).

The tendency to derive the notion of "capacity" or "strength" from the requirement of guarantees, which individual parties have to be able to provide if negotiation is to succeed, is common to the concepts mentioned. The implication is of a sort of absolute definition of the qualifications of the negotiating parties. But with or without negotiation, and essentially independent of a specific context, governments and unions may be characterized as strong or weak, and as capable or incapable of designing, implementing, or monitoring policies; they can also be centralized as monopolistic or decentralized and "fragmented." I wonder whether a definition of capacity or strength should not also incorporate contextual elements if it is about successful social interactions. After all, the negotiation and conclusion of agreements are cooperative activities, implying a multitude of exchanges among the partners and an ongoing, mutual assessment of each other's strengths and weaknesses.

The Hungarian case may reveal how important it is to pay attention to "relative" elements in the definition of strength and capacity as well as mutual perceptions of those capacities as conditions for successful pacts. Neither the government nor the trade unions in Hungary could perhaps have been characterized as either capable or strong by a narrow application of the terms contained in the above definition. This may have been even more true of the reformist, technocratic wing of the Antall government. Still, they were able to negotiate and sign a pact, a success in terms of peacefully resolving sociopolitical conflict and providing reformist initiatives with room to operate.

Certainly, the strength of the Antall government's financial technocrats was relative. That is, the reformist group may have been politically and organizationally weak, but it was still stronger and possessed greater vision, expertise, bureaucratic coherence, and capacity than any of its challengers. A similar assessment may also be true with regard to union strength. Although Hungarian unions were weak, they were still—especially the MSZOSZ—much stronger than their radical rivals in civil society or on the periphery of the trade union movement. It was their relative organizational and political strength that made them attractive partners in the resolution of conflict.

Government and union strength had to be assessed in terms of each other's capacities as well. The perceptions of the negotiating partners of their own as well as of each other's strength were important. A weak but relatively capable government and a weak but relatively well-organized trade union movement mutually reinforced and legitimated each other in their respective political and organizational contexts. The Antall government's financial technocracy and the MSZOSZ were the most important actors of the pact, and similarly it was they who profited most from it. Put another way, the government used its pact with the unions as a shield to insulate its economic policy making from the pressure both of political parties and of radical civil organizations. The unions, in turn, used their pact with the government to reinforce their efforts to monopolize constituencies, to solve conflicts within the union movement, and to crowd out rival civil associations.

Policy Style and the Development of Civil Society

According to a widespread view, based mainly on Third World experience but formulated in the East European context as well, there is a close relationship between the style of economic policy making and the prospects for sustainable democracy. The assumption is that an "insulated," "imperative" approach to economic reform can hamper democratic development by preventing civil organizations from emerging through a process of interaction with decision makers. Imperative policies are said to be inimical to the development of "strategic actors," while "consultative" or "negotiated" policies are assumed to facilitate democratization by encouraging civil organizations to develop, assisting the articulation and formulation of policy demands, and helping society to participate in elements of economic transformation (Hausner 1993, Ost 1995, Stark and Bruszt 1996).

This case study seems to offer an opportunity for critical reflection on these assumptions. I think that a simplistic, two-track comparison between "imperative" and "consultative" styles of economic policy making and their respective implications for the development of civil society may not be valid. Rather, it may be true that each policy style preselects certain civil organizations to succeed while causing others to fail. However, in different contexts both policy styles may support or constrain the development of civil society as a base for democratic institutionalization.

There is considerable evidence that certain neoliberal adjustment strategies, more or less associated with a humanitarian priority in targeting social support in favor of the very poor, may give rise to an organized sector of efficient and competent grassroots organizations (GROs) and nongovernmental organizations (NGOs) specialized in the allocation of social funds, mainly at the local level. This may have positive effects in terms of both economic needs and political development (C. Graham 1994, 60). There is little doubt, however, that neoliberal policies often discriminate against other civil organizations, especially labor unions, by generally limiting their influence over redistributive decisions.

Nevertheless, as in the Hungarian case, this is not entirely different from the interactive, "neocorporatist" style of economic decision making. The Hungarian Social Pact of 1992, representative of the consultative style of economic policy making, did not involve civil society as a whole. A few civil organizations were invited while others were excluded from influencing economic policy making. The former acquired legitimacy, encouragement for organizational development, and representation, while the latter were marginalized by the "consultative" style. Specifically, by including trade unions and business associations, the traditional social partners, in the negotiations, consultative policy approaches involved only a portion of an organized civil society in the policy discourse, while excluding numerous social groups with relatively little political weight.

This case study provides some empirical support to the second view outlined above. First, I have discussed how, despite dramatic organized protest, certain civil demands were disregarded and certain civil organizations were excluded from the economic policy discourse, even when the Antall government, which usually preferred to dictate economic policies, took steps toward policy consultation in the autumn of 1992.

Second, it was not the government alone that kept civil organizations and their demands at bay. Driven by their struggle for legitimacy, exclusivity, and attempts to monopolize constituencies, Hungary's trade unions did not welcome the participation of rival societal representatives in economic policy making. The unions maneuvered to crowd them out, then forgot about their demands. Third, similarly defensive and exclusive behavior was later observed on the part of the political parties.

Finally, these findings may confirm the importance of analyzing transitory, situation-bound political-institutional mechanisms through which styles of economic policy making affect civil society in particular, and democratization and the state-society relationship in general. The dynamics of conflict and its negotiated settlement may be differently interpreted as well.

"Learning by Doing" Democracy

If the question is raised whether the events I have described contributed to strengthening the prospects for democratic institutionalization and consolidation in Hungary, the answer would be positive. It is clear that from November 1992 to January 1993, dangerous threats to the consolidation process were neutralized.

The first result achieved in the process of conflict resolution was substantial progress in consolidating the CRI as a major institutional forum for rebuilding relations between government, labor, and business; for discussing and negotiating policy reforms with difficult distributional impacts; and also, if necessary, for solving countrywide political conflicts. The CRI's consolidation helped to stabilize the emerging democratic system because it created a temporary balance of power between interest organizations, the executive, and the legislature. However, the other political implication was the redistribution of political power from democratic institutions to a corporatist body.

Similarly, when the existing democratic institutions were challenged by means of direct democracy—the call for a referendum—the status quo could be defended by the enhanced decision-making power of the Constitutional Court, which is less usual in established democratic systems.

Both these phenomena fit the now traditional Hungarian pattern of democratic development "by undemocratic means" (O'Donnell and Schmitter 1986). Other milestones in the negotiated Hungarian transformation process have been the agreement between the Opposition Round Table and the Communist Party in the autumn of 1989 and the pact between the MDF, the main coalition party, and the Alliance of Free Democrats (SZDSZ), the major opposition party, after the 1990 elections. The coalition agreement between the Hungarian Socialist Party and the SZDSZ following the 1994 elections mitigated the outcome of the elections, which had given the socialists an absolute majority, and led to a consensual way of governing with veto rights for the smaller coalition member in all important issues. In addition, a new, general socioeconomic pact was a possibility in 1994, although it was abandoned.

Another result of the sociopolitical conflict of 1992–93 was that civil society learned that democracy constituted a balance between exclusion and inclusion, and it was the relative political power and organization, the concrete political and institutional context, and the overall economic situation that made the difference between those who were included and excluded. Citizens also had to learn that they could not punish the government for allegedly lacking social sensitivity whenever they wished.

Another important lesson concerned the importance of reinforcing and fine-tuning the functioning rules of democracy. LAÉT's referendum challenge provoked Hungarian politicians into renewing their commitment to the existing democratic institutional design, which provided only limited room for direct democracy. Similarly, the conflict reinforced the Constitutional Court in its specific, transformative role as an arbiter of last resort in consolidating democratic institutions in Hungary. Obviously, learning processes such as these are an integral part of democratic consolidation, and help to lead the society beyond the "nonsystem" disequilibrium and "fluid" state associated with systemic change (Bunce and Csanádi 1992).

While accepting these arguments about political consolidation, one may still ask what sort of system is supposedly consolidating in Hungary. More precisely, one may question whether the balance between exclusion and inclusion was too hastily and narrowly cemented, whether the preserved status quo did not unnecessarily exclude large social groups, and whether the system of consolidation would be sufficiently conducive for the "liberal elements of democracy" to unfold. These are questions formulated by O'Donnell (1992), Acuña and Smith (1994), and other theorists while conceptualizing new types of democracy in Third World countries.

Toward a "Dual Democratic" Regime?

Inclusion or exclusion—regarding societal control over economic decisions, direct or representative participation in democratic institutions, and the process of their creation—were the most hotly debated issues in the autumn of 1992. Undoubtedly, the mix of inclusionary and exclusionary traits of a democratic regime are important enough to be included as major constitutive elements in defining a typology.

In a recently elaborated typology Carlos H. Acuña and William C. Smith categorize democratic regimes essentially by their purpose, commitment, and capacity to include social actors. Acuña and Smith differentiate among democratic regime types according to the characteristic ways that democratic governments respond to worsening social tensions as a consequence of the *improvement* of economic performance. They describe three enduring scenarios: fragmented and exclusionary democracy with neoliberal economics; inclusionary democracy with strong actors and an activist state; and dual democratic regimes (Acuña and Smith 1994, 53). Rather than assess the relevance of the typology as a whole, I wish to consider the third element of the typology: dual democracy. Dual democracy is the most probable scenario, according to these authors, for most Latin American societies.

As Acuña and Smith put it, a dual democratic regime is based on an alliance between the governing elite and a strategic minority of the opposition. The purpose is to exclude "the majority of the remaining social actors by disarticulating and neutralizing their capacity for collective action." This dual logic of state power is complemented by an unequal distribution of resources; benefits are extended only to allied sectors of business and organized labor. The authors acknowledge that "all regimes manifest this dual character to some extent because every strategy of inclusion necessarily implies exclusion. The high ratio of exclusion to inclusion, the dependence of the regime's stability on this ratio, and the intention of the main political actors to maintain it are what differentiate dual democratic regimes from others" (Acuña and Smith 1994, 47).

This interpretation seems to fit rather well the Hungarian situation I have described here. Although a precise assessment of the real (economic and political) consequences of the 1992 social pact requires further in-depth research, the evidence seems to support the conclusion that the agreement included only a strategic minority while it excluded the majority of the social actors. Without trying to estimate the proportions of the population excluded and included, it suffices here to recall the elitist elements of the pact, the participants' organizational structures, their attitudes toward their rivals, and the large numbers of those who felt "crowded out."

The Antall government did not always pursue inclusionary policies, as it did in the autumn of 1992. In 1990 and 1991 the government was not significantly engaged in any social dialogue. On the contrary, it had sought to entirely disable and neutralize other social actors' capacities for collective action. After a long period, the MSZOSZ leader, Sándor Nagy, was "included" only through personal consultations with Prime Minister József Antall, when the largest labor federation threatened strikes (Bruszt 1994). In this context, the change in the government's attitude by late 1992 may be interpreted in Acuña and Smith's terms as a shift from a fragmented, exclusionary democracy toward a dual demo-cratic regime (Acuña and Smith 1994, 48). There are, however, several points at which the concept of dual democracy may be refined and mod-ified on the basis of the Hungarian experience. First, the muddling of the Hungarian government toward "dual democratic" (that is, selective) inclusion did not commence when the economic situation began to improve but instead began in the midst of a deep economic crisis. Second, although there was certainly a rise in social tensions, it is ques-tionable how much these contributed to changing the government's attitude. In particular, what were the specific elements of tension that pushed the government toward a more inclusionary political stance?

As we know, "crises" and "tensions" alone do not always explain the responses of those affected by them, and even less likely are they to pre-determine the outcome of a situation. According to the literature on the politics of economic stabilization and adjustment in LDCs, it is more the perception of (economic) crisis than the reality of the crisis itself that may influence the timing, content, and style of decisive government steps (Grindle and Thomas 1991). This is no different with regard to social tensions and sociopolitical crises. Incorporating perceptions of tension into the Acuña-Smith typology of democratic responses to increased sociopolitical tension may be helpful in fine-tuning it as an analytical instrument.

From a comparative perspective, the overall level of sociopolitical tension has been rather low over all of East Central Europe, including Hungary, during the entire period of transition to date. While tensions definitely increased during 1992 in Hungary, they certainly did not reach levels that the Antall government could not have neutralized. Still, the government's perception of high tension and its involvement in resolving it did not change. Why? As I suggested earlier, the government perception of the crisis was essentially political. Concerns about sporadic eruptions of social protest were tremendously boosted by fear of their coincidence with protest votes in Parliament, and splits in the coalition and the main coalition party.

While Acuña and Smith identify the attitudes of democratic governments and state elites as a principal factor explaining the inclusionary and exclusionary characteristics of a democratic regime, the Hungarian case suggests that it is not always or solely the government that decides who will be excluded and included, or how and to what degree this will happen.

In 1992 in Hungary, the government did not entirely oppose the incorporation of the hunger strikers' demands into the compensation package. Nor was it the government that selected the CRI as a locus of negotiation and thereby excluded LAÉT and its allies. It was rather the unions who performed the "dirty job" of exclusion, while in the case of the referendum the government did not even have much of a say in what would happen, and it was the political parties who excluded their rivals.

The case of the Hungarian Social Pact of 1992 may therefore offer a second aspect for further elaboration and fine-tuning of the concept of "dual democratic regimes." If the task is to understand the motives, mechanisms, and different combinations of exclusion and inclusion in dual democratic regimes, it may be essential to combine state-centered explanations with society-centered ones, the latter concentrating on relatively autonomous processes, conditions, and struggles and their outcomes in the development of civil society and the style of democracy. Throughout this book I have tried to show how society-centered views of the postcommunist reality may enrich its understanding.

If a regime is advancing toward democracy under economic stress, even if only a "dual democracy," this may imply that state elites will seek to share the detailed, selective decisions on the pattern, ratio, ways, and actions of exclusion of their ordinary citizens and potential challengers with those prospectively chosen for sharing part of the power with them.

Chapter 10
Crisis-proof, Poor Democracies

I began this book by positing the failure of the postcommunist break-down-of-democracy literature, which has elaborated various scenarios anticipating the destabilization and, indeed, the fall of the new democracies of Eastern Europe. My disagreement is based on three points of criticism.[1]

First, I concluded that the breakdown literature has made improper use of the Third World analogy. The East has not become the South. That is, the volatile and violent political conditions characteristic of Southern economic adjustment did not materialize during Europe's postcommunist transformations. And while expected similarities have turned out to be differences, actual similarities have gone unrecognized. Observers of the East European transition did not pay sufficient attention to the Latin American experience of a continentwide wave of democratization under economic stress. What East Europeanists have to learn from this experience is that economic crisis and the neoliberal strategy may affect the political dynamics of transformation in ways other than by precipitating systemic collapse. In the East, just as in the South, it is much less the mere existence or durability of democracy than a number of its crucial qualitative aspects—its representativeness, participatory features, and liberal elements—that may have been suffering from economic crisis and poverty.

Second, the breakdown literature, in both its socially biased leftist and radical neoliberal reformist versions, failed because its advocates were ideologically biased and preferred the activism of the policy adviser to the analytic approach of the social scientist. While they were engaged in ideological discourse over the proper economic transformation strategy, representatives of rival views of postcommunist market society frequently derived political forecasts directly from economics. They kept frightening each other and their audience with gloomy but invalid predictions about what would happen if their economic policy recommendations were rejected. However, the autonomy of politics and the possibility that the new postcommunist democracies might survive harsh economic times were barely considered by any of them. I criticized the breakdown theorists for their simplistic economic determinism, universalism, globalism, and teleology. One obvious negative consequence was that a number of terms that originally served the conceptualization of particular social phenomena became translated into mere catchwords of the political debate. For example, the terms "market socialism," "third way," or "populism" were widely used to indicate political pathology, at the cost of their empirical content and real meaning.

Third, and most importantly, the breakdown literature failed because its representatives were not well prepared to conceptualize the mechanisms and the nature of emerging new systems under postcommunism. The latter task implies an in-depth inquiry about the possible factors contributing to the durability and survival of new democracies.

The "Low-level Equilibrium" between the Economic and Political Spheres

Specifically, in this book I have made a comparative inquiry about the systemic, structural, institutional, and contextual features that might explain why the new democracies have proved to be crisis resistant, even more in the East than earlier in the South. Hence my questions were: Why was a low-level equilibrium between incomplete democracy and imperfect market economy possible? What politico-economic combination was entailed by this equilibrium? And what were its prospects for the future?

The summary of my answer is as follows. Supported by the atomizing impact of the transformation crisis, it was the very socioeconomic legacies of communism initially, and the structural and institutional consequences of the implemented neoliberal reforms later, that help in an understanding of why loyalty and exit (rather than voice, in Hirschman's [1970] terms) and stabilizing rather than disruptive forms of protest have emerged as dominant social responses to economic grievances. Structural, institutional, and cultural factors have inhibited politically destabilizing collective action and paved the way for the emergence of an enduring low-level equilibrium between incomplete democracy and imperfect market economy.

Communist Legacy and the Recession: Sources of Short-term Stability

Why is it that, despite pessimistic predictions, Eastern Europe's political life during the first seven transformation years exhibited less instability and violence than the politics of no more stressful economic reforms in the Third World in the 1980s? How is it that destabilizing socioeconomic threats to simultaneous reforms have rarely been activated and inherent tensions have so far only infrequently translated into disruptive political action? The comparison with Latin America helps to explain why changes have continued to advance in a nonviolent way from 1991 until 1996. Moreover, it provides us with the chance to enrich the broad picture with a couple of society-centered arguments.

My answer is that communism left behind societies characterized by a relative lack of the structural factors associated with violent collective action. This becomes especially clear in comparison with the more rebellious societies of the Third World. To put it differently, a number of the structural, institutional, and cultural legacies of communism have had a demobilizing and, consequently, politically stabilizing effect. It is the following legacies and effects that deserve particular attention.

Large popular sectors in the region had at their disposal relatively substantial reserves to survive hard times. The absence of extreme income inequality and of poverty of a Third World type—that is, concentrated in overpopulated and politically explosive informal urban settlements—may have contributed to weakening the threat of violent political mass actions. These circumstances may have been reinforced by such cultural factors as the region's substantially higher education standards or its lack of a living tradition of political violence.

Such structural legacies as the demographic characteristics of the postcommunist societies certainly mattered as well. Postcommunist societies are typically older and less urbanized than most of the rebellious Third World nations. Elderly people in general, and pensioners in particular, could not strike or riot, even if they felt aggrieved, and typically neither could members of the rural society, who lived dispersed in the countryside. Consequently, major social groups, like the poor, the pensioners, and the rural population have had to tolerate economic hardships. If they have associated their grievances with the strategy of economic transformation, their only avenue of protest has been to vote against the reformist governments.

Labor protest has not significantly shaped transformation politics either. At the beginning this could have been because the region's labor movements were suffering from credibility problems. It is also true that the few unions that were credible, like Poland's Solidarity, initially favored reform. Later, however, the transformational crisis—the decline in living standards, and the loss of job security associated with rapidly growing unemployment—may have curbed labor's collective protest. For example, labor's contentious tradition in Poland was weakened or

neutralized by the atomizing effect of the economic crisis. Three institutional factors, also originating partly in the communist past—the tradition of collusion between labor unions and management; the affinity
between the labor movement and the ruling political party; and government tactics—may have contributed to the cooperative rather than con-
frontational stance adopted by most unions.

In different forms and to differing degrees, all population groups,
including workers, the poor, the elderly, and the rural population, have
had an important alternative to protest. It is what I have called "going
informal" or shifting to the second economy. Noncriminal exit forms
may also have had a positive stabilizing effect, at least in the short term.

All in all, instead of protesting violently and directly, East Europeans
remained patient and either went informal or exploited their employers'
capacity to enforce protective state intervention. In politics they turned
to protest voting and channeled their demands through democratic
institutions, abjuring other tactics. Society's overwhelmingly patient and
democratic attitude has provided democratic reformist governments
with longer grace periods and longer time horizons in which to implement difficult reforms than governments in the South have generally
enjoyed.

Economic and Political Transformation: Their Interaction in the East

The foregoing observations allow me to challenge the claim that democratization necessarily threatens economic stabilization because it releases
claims on popular control over policy making from previously excluded
social groups. As I have argued, just the opposite has occurred in the
postcommunist East. The new political institutions may in fact have
acted as safety valves by channeling the expression of social discontent
into democratic processes, resulting in a delaying and balancing effect.
Instead of threatening economic stabilization and transformation,
democratization has turned out to be their political vehicle.

This latter statement requires qualification, however, in that the interaction between economic and political transformation has been more
complex in two respects. My point is that both the feasibility and the
shortcomings of simultaneous economic and political transformation in
the East are probably mutually interdependent. We have seen interaction, mutual concessions, and trade-offs between the economic and the
political sectors. First, while it is partly because of the simultaneous
democratization that economic reforms were not abandoned, as pes-

simists predicted, it is also due to democracy that they have advanced more slowly than the radical reformers initially expected. Second, belying the pessimistic prophecies, neither the economic crisis nor the neoliberal transformation resulted in the breakdown of democracy, and the new political system seems to have taken root throughout the East. However, it is partly due to the crisis and the reforms that some important ingredients of fully developed Western-type democracies continue to be in short supply.

To put it simply, democracy and a market economy could be simultaneously introduced only because neither has been fully implemented. Democracy could only stabilize at the cost of some of its qualitative aspects because of the crisis and economic transformation. Economic transformation, in turn, has remained feasible only at a cost of its speed and radicalism, and its many imperfections are due not least to the democratic framework of the change. The economic and political systems reached an equilibrium, but at a lower level than is typical, for example, of developed Western market democracies. With this in mind, I now briefly review the system and type of democracy taking root under postcommunism.

What Kind of Democracy?

If we take just the Hungarian case as an example, the postcommunist systemic change suggests a process of democracy building by "undemocratic means," with its resort to exclusive and elite negotiations, agreements, and pacts carried out behind closed doors. This is the pattern underlying Hungary's democratic development, but it also seems to correspond to other cases in the region.

All Eastern democracies are poor democracies. As a consequence of the dire economic situation left behind by their predecessors and aggravated by the transformation strategy, the new systems have proved incapable of meeting even some of the most justified demands of previously excluded or marginalized social groups or even of their middle strata, who have often experienced economic hardships in recent times. Related to this, the new democracies show exclusionary features, not only with respect to economic policy making but for many important political issues.

In this respect, the typology of democracy elaborated by Acuña and Smith seems relevant. As I have argued, the "qualitative adjustment" of democracies to poor economic conditions in the East reflects a preemptive attitude rather than a response to the relatively weak social protest.

However, keeping this difference in mind, I think that most new post-communist political systems fit in the continuum between "fragmented and exclusionary democracy with neoliberal economics" and "dual democratic regimes," as Acuña and Smith call them. The Eastern European style of economic policy making in many cases corresponds with features of the first type. Acuña and Smith comment further that "the democratic regime's capacity for political domination is based on the 'silence of civil society' resulting from the fragmentation of the social actors and the exclusionary design and implementation of social and economic policies" (1994, 43).

As I demonstrated earlier, in various periods and to varying degrees, Eastern reformist governments have more often than not followed an exclusionary style of strategic decision making characterized by a country-specific mix of the following elements: attempts at expanding the presidential powers; concentration of influential decision makers into strategic committees, advisory boards, and cabinets; secrecy; the weakening or elimination of opposing bureaucratic strongholds; failure to negotiate or even consult with the representatives of societal interests; and measures aimed at weakening the latter or profiting from their legitimation deficiencies.

However, according to a widespread view, there is a close relationship between the style of economic policy making and the prospects for sustainable democracy. The assumption is that the above "insulated" and "imperative" style of economic decision making in postcommunist countries may harm the development of democracy. While I do not think that this view is entirely false, based on the findings of this book I see the relationship between the style of economic decision making and democratic development as more complex.

Specifically, in this context we may ask to what extent the neoliberal reform project is unique in its elitist, autocratic, and exclusionary style of implementation. I pointed out earlier that other far-reaching reforms in the history of economic change, which were far from being neoliberal, have exhibited many or most of the latter's criticized characteristics. In general, I suggested that if wholesale social and economic structural change must be pushed through and enforced by the state because major societal groups have vested interests in maintaining the status quo, this very fact might quite naturally invoke the entire complex syndrome depicted above. The composition of the favored and disfavored groups seems to be the main element distinguishing neoliberal adjustment, import-substitution industrialization, export-oriented development, and economic populist episodes, rather than the general features of the bureaucratic pattern or political environment of their implementation.

Thus, we also have to ask whether there is any alternative to the autocratic political and economic policy style. Some scholars would strongly argue that there is. In contrast with the imperative style, "consulted" or "negotiated" policies are widely assumed to facilitate democratization by creating "strategic actors," encouraging civil organizations to develop, assisting the articulation and formulation of policy demands, and helping society to participate in elements of economic transformation.

However, my case study of the Hungarian Social Pact of 1992 suggests there are reasons to reconsider these assumptions. I found evidence in Hungary's postcommunist transformation to show that not only the neoliberal but also the social-democratic policy style preselects certain civil organizations to rise while others fall. However, in different contexts, both policy styles may support or constrain the development of civil society as a base for democratic institutionalization.

In the Hungarian case, to use Acuña and Smith's terms, it is "dual democracy" rather than "fragmented and exclusionary democracy with neoliberal economics" that is most in evidence. It has included the postcommunist labor union elites and the emerging nomenclature bourgeoisie, as well as many new civil actors, and also seems to be the characteristic politico-economic model in at least the Western rim of Eastern Europe.

The rest of the society, I have argued, has had little recourse other than protest voting to express their discontent with the economic losses associated with the crisis and transformation. The apparent lack of direct and synchronized protest actions, and the dramatic reshuffling of political support along various points of the political spectrum, are two sides of the same coin. The more Eastern societies seem to be "sentenced to patience" in the intervals between elections, the more pent-up demands are released during elections to punish those who have supposedly harmed the voters' interests. Thus the emerging new democracies under postcommunism exhibit a high degree of electoral instability and turnover—not only because they are at a relatively early stage of consolidation but also because the pattern of social response to economic stress is biased toward the use of the democratic procedures for the purpose of protest.

The above situation, however, facilitates a monopoly of representation that favors the political parties over labor unions and other social organizations and movements. A crucial question is to what extent the parties themselves are capable of interest representation rather than merely serving as safety valves for social discontent. If they do at least the latter effectively, as seems to be the case in much of the East, the prospects for democratic stabilization appear to be good. However, the picture is less bright as far as the representation of a broad range of societal interests is concerned. Due to the grave macroeconomic situation, as well as varying degrees of external influence and of commitments to join the European Community, policies implemented in different countries and under different governments have remained within fairly strict limits in Eastern Europe. The implication is that the most readily available way for broad groups in Eastern societies to respond to their economic losses, the democratic protest vote, may be only superficially effective. Citizens vote down economic policies injurious to their immediate interests, just to witness their stubborn recurrence under new regimes and new party banners.

The last question is how long it will continue to be like this. I cannot resist outlining some hypotheses regarding the foreseeable future in East Central Europe.

Medium-term Stability: Structural Effects of the Transformation Strategy

My hypothesis is that the low-level equilibrium between the economic and political spheres will prevail in the medium term. Even the more successful East European nations will continue to exhibit varied combinations of relatively low-performing, institutionally mixed market economies and incomplete, elitist, and exclusionary democracies with a weak citizenship component. Joan M. Nelson has reached a similar conclusion—that the politico-economic systems of Eastern Europe are likely to be "partial and distorted semi-democratic systems and poorly functioning versions of semi-market economies" (Nelson 1994, 3).

While it is reasonable to expect further slow advancement in the economic field, the probability of a dramatic breakthrough is low. Transforming countries reach a stage in which time-consuming, piecemeal improvements are called for in some areas, while challenging institutional innovations are still necessary in others. More effective enforcement of existing laws, improvements in tax collection, or smoother functioning in the infrastructure designed to support private initiative exemplify the first field, while restructuring the society's financial system and its social services denote the second. In these respects there is still far to go. According to one recent forecast, even in countries like the Czech

Republic, Poland, Hungary, and Slovenia, it will take no less than one to two more decades to "erase the economic connotations of the adjective *western* European" (Murrell 1996, 41).

It seems fair to predict that the agenda of economic policy elites will be further dominated by immediate concerns over macroeconomic stability, debt management, acquiring international finance for ambitious institutional innovations, and, in a few instances, fulfilling the requirements to join the European Union. Considering that such an agenda would place an additional burden on society, one should not expect them to make a priority of expanding representative social control over economic policy making. On the contrary, one cannot discount the possibility that the new tripartite institutions, created for the purpose of negotiating policy, may be weakened in the future, given that we can anticipate even more effective crowding out of the less politically vocal civil organizations from influence over the politics of party and union elites.

Is this bad news from the viewpoint of democracy under postcommunism? It depends. For, in turn, no obvious danger of authoritarianism is in sight. Reform elites need not be enticed by authoritarian temptations to defend their interests "at any cost, even at the cost of democracy" (Przeworski 1991, 187) because the transformation strategies they favor will not be effectively challenged by the rest of society. From the point of view of economic transformation, a turn to authoritarianism will continue to be unnecessary. (This, however, is not meant to deny the potential threat of other factors, such as nationalism, xenophobia, and ethnic tensions in some of the countries of the region.)

I base my hypothesis of medium-term political stability in transforming Eastern Europe on emerging evidence of the social structural impact of neoliberal transformation strategies in the East and the experience of some Latin American countries that are "more advanced" in this respect. In addition, I also consider socioeconomic structural trends that may lead to the decline of social democracy in Western Europe.

The argument in brief is that if the neoliberal transformation strategy continues to be more or less consistently implemented over the long run, its impact will reach to the roots of politics. Specifically, I argue that the structural changes induced by the chosen transformation path are *demobilizing*, in that they impair the capacities for collective action of the program's losers and opponents, particularly labor and lower-income groups.

I have in mind three major structural-adaptation processes. First, a dramatically increasing share of private nonindustrial employment and a rapid decrease of the average plant size can be observed throughout East Central Europe. According to analysts, the much longer and more gradual process by which corresponding structural changes occurred in Western Europe produced significant effects on both the civil and political spheres. It is not just that the process brought about a general decline in the level of unionization; much more important to my point is that, "the political implications of industrial restructuring hinge not so much on how it affects union membership, as on how it affects what unions do" (Pontusson 1995, 502). Unions facing the above structural changes in the U.K. and Sweden, for example, focused on a new set of issues introduced by industrial reorganization, "concerning technology and working conditions, that cannot be negotiated at the national level, and national politics appears to have become less relevant to union activities" (503).

Why would similar processes have different civil and political consequences in the East? Structural changes that evolved more gradually in the West are occurring at a magnified speed and intensity in the East. However, the labor unions facing them are entirely different in nature. Not only has union membership plunged rapidly from virtually 100 percent to a minority of the workforce but, more to the point, the remaining union organizations do not inspire confidence from the point of view of effective representation of labor interests. Soon, however, there may be a second and even more worrisome structural adjustment process underway in East Central Europe, for which a parallel can be found less in the West than in the South. Related to the expanding informalization mentioned earlier as one factor contributing to political stability, and also facilitated by the migration of labor from the poorer to the economically better-off East European countries, this process could include the rapid emergence of precarious forms of employment as a condition for competitiveness.

A closer look at the possible costs of neoliberal growth strategies, best exemplified by the Chilean case, may reveal some further implications for the future of labor in the East. According to a student of the process in Chile, "This precariousness is manifested in the low levels of job stability, dependence upon income from piecework, poor working conditions, rigid specialization at work (which comes close to a neo-Taylorist form of organization), little access to training, few possibilities for internal mobility in the company, impediments to collective negotiation, low levels of participation and, sometimes, subjection to authoritarian relations in the workplace" (Díaz 1993, 23). Again it is not difficult to see that a similar deterioration of the quality of employment, now well underway in the East, may have further unfavorable implications for the collective action capacities of labor and its representative organizations.

Finally, structural tendencies like the ones I have mentioned may further undermine the capacity of social democratic political forces to implement a social democratic strategy. In my view, and notwithstanding their rhetoric, postcommunist successor parties involved in implementing neoliberal economic strategies cannot be regarded as social democrats but rather as neoliberals. In this respect, my expectation is that left-oriented parties will be pushed to further realignment and adaptation to the harsh realities presented by structural change. Other signs of political adjustment, as I pointed out earlier, are the nonpopulist economic program and the societal base combining elite groups with low-income social strata by neopopulist movements and parties in the East just like in the South. As a consequence, I think East Europeanists have to seriously consider the newest body of Latin American transformation literature.

While I expect that the depicted type of democracy will continue in Eastern Europe into the foreseeable future, I cannot help repeating some of the reservations expressed by my Latin Americanist colleague: "Yet these regimes have been stable, in spite of the simultaneous implementation of potentially de-stabilizing economic reforms . . . we do not see much dispersion of power in the newly democratizing nations of the region. We witness a more active political involvement of business given its less formal but more transparent access to the state apparatus. . . . This is the new ruling coalition which has, paradoxically, provided support to democracy—to this type of democracy. This is the only game in Latin America today" (Schamis 1995, 36–37).

And what is in store in East Central Europe? Probably a somewhat similar "only game." It is admittedly a second-best option, certainly less "than one might have expected while watching the dancing at the Brandenburg gate" (Ost 1995, 178). But still, the best is unavailable.

Notes

Chapter 1
Introduction: Good-bye Breakdown Prophecies, Hello Poor Democracies

1. This chapter is partly based on my "Crisis-proof Democracy: On Failed Predictions and the Realities of Eastern Europe's Transformations," *International Politics* Vol. 34, no. 2 (June 1997): 193–211.

2. Many of my criticisms of this type of breakdown prophecy are in harmony with the views of László Bruszt (1993) and Alexander Smolar (1996).

3. Important contributions to the debate include Przeworski (1991), Bunce (1993, 1995), Nelson, ed. (1994), Walton and Seddon (1994), and Schmitter and Karl (1994).

4. For some of this advice see Offe (1993), Walton and Seddon (1994), Devatripont and Roland (1994), Roland (1991, 1992), Ost (1992), and Lomax (1993).

5. Even notions of economic determinism, however, can be adapted to the postcommunist transformation with much more conceptual openness and sensitivity than has been the case. For example, though the simplistic idea of an inverse relationship between economic performance and the intensity of social conflict or political protest has been repeatedly challenged by theorists, much of the postcommunist breakdown literature still stubbornly assumes that the worse the economic situation, the more severe the sociopolitical reaction will be, and vice versa. One point clearly missed by breakdown prophecies is that crises may limit people's collective capacities for action. I build on studies that rethink the relationship between economic conditions and collective action. See on this topic Hirschman (1981), Remmer (1991), and Acuña and Smith (1994).

Chapter 2
Crises and Neoliberal Transformations in the 1980s and 1990s

1. The expression is from Rodrik (1994). See Kahler (1990, 33–34) for the two views and their critical explication in the Third World context.

2. On ISI in East Europe and related development projects, see, for example, Csaba (1984), Greskovits (1988), Greskovits and Máté (1988), Bauer et al. (1980), Botos and Papanek (1984), and Tardos, ed. (1980).

3. This political, intellectual, and moral climate is very well highlighted by János Mátyás Kovács: "In their view, by touching upon the taboos of real socialism, the former *socialist* 'liberals' can become genuine liberals who will complete the theoretical work started by the reformers back in the 1950s. Accordingly, there is no need for cathartic changes: the original premises of reform thinking should not be essentially revised but only supplemented with the missing elements of privatization and political democracy" (Kovács 1994, 22).

4. For the first type of reactions see "A Világbank Magyarországi Irodája" (1995) and for the second type Kopácsy, (1995). Excellent critical studies by prominent reform economists include Lányi (1994 and 1995) and Köves (1995). For critical views of sociologists see Szalai (1995) and Ladányi and Szelényi (1995). Sociologists blamed the neoliberal strategy for lacking social sensitivity.

5. Two puzzling rumors might be interpreted as signaling the possibility that by 1989 Polish reform communists had been ready for such a transformation. Robert Norton tells the anecdote that Jeffrey Sachs received an invitation to visit Poland before the Solidarity times, from the communist government (Norton 1994, 233). The other interesting rumor is that allegedly during the debate of the Balcerowicz program on December 17, 1989, in the Sejm, which was dominated by the communist coalition, "the Communist Party adopted the slogan 'Your Government, Our Program,' suggesting that the new program had been prepared by the Rakowski government and thus rationalising its support" (Johnson and Kowalska 1994, 197–98). However, my interviews in Poland in 1997 did not confirm the above accounts.

Chapter 3
The Loneliness of the Economic Reformer

1. The old agencies were relegated to less crucial functions. "Sometimes key economic policymakers were appointed to head the agencies. . . . They held the positions in order to be part of the economic team and, in effect if not by design, to stop any etatist initiatives from being launched by traditional elements in their agencies" (Önis and Webb 1994, 148–49).

2. "Without foreign financial backing, Gaidar began to search for domestic political support through compromises with 'centrist' forces that were pushing for huge subsidies. . . . The decisive blow came when Gaidar acquiesced to centrist demands that Victor Gerashchenko, Gorbachev's Soviet Central Bank chief, take over control of the Russian Central Bank" (Sachs 1994, 16).

3. In the Philippines, "Ironically, the first acts of Aquino's presidency resembled closely Marcos' actions on declaring martial law: the dissolution of the National Assembly; a deep purge of regional and local governments, the judiciary, and, to a lesser extent, the armed forces; the replacement of ousted officials by Aquino loyalists; and a sequestration of the assets of political opponents" (Haggard 1990, 250). In 1984 in Ecuador, President Febres-Cordero and his team "did not enjoy a 'honeymoon' period after assuming office. In fact, the first six months of the new administration were marked by violence and confrontation with the congress, including the use of riot police and tear gas within the legislative chamber, repeated general strikes by the labour unions and street protests by students, and executive actions to curtail such activities" (Grindle and Thoumi 1993, 146). On Peru's experience with "fujimorismo" see Roberts 1995.

4. "The refusal to accept input from business groups derived from the economists' view that the majority of Chilean firms were not good capitalists and therefore could not be counted on to build a "new" capitalist system in Chile. The businesses were only out to protect their individual interests through access to protection and favours of various types from the state" (Stallings and Brock 1993, 98–99).

5. Moreover, when Miguel Roig, the newly appointed economic minister, died only six days after the government took office, "Menem took pains to publicize his consultations with Jorge Born, the head of the Bunge and Born group, in the search for a successor to Roig. Thus, the legitimacy of the incoming minister of economy, Néstor Rapanelli, like that of Roig, rested on his representing the policies that Bunge and Born considered appropriate for Argentina" (Acuña 1994, 38).

6. However, we have examples where anti-neoliberal statist and protectionist businessmen from communist big business acquired top policy-making and political positions and blocked neoliberal reforms. Essentially this is what happened in Russia after the cooptation of Georgi Khiza, a former defense enterprise manager and the head of St. Petersburg Enterprises' Association, who became both minister of industry and deputy prime minister, and of two other deputy prime min-

isters: Vladimir Shumeiko, a former enterprise manager in heavy industry and the former president of the Russian Confederation of Entrepreneurs' Unions, and the eventual prime minister, Victor Chernomyrdin, the former head of Gasprom, the Soviet gas monopoly (Jeffries 1993, 104).

7. As a group of prominent economists put it, "When Argentina and Peru embark on their next stabilization programs, they will get roughly similar recommendations from their economic advisers on how to proceed. But how much of what we had learned is relevant for Eastern Europe? . . . Aren't the initial conditions so different as to require a drastically different approach? We do not think so. Most of the logic behind the standard stabilization package applies to Eastern Europe as well" (Blanchard et al. 1991, 1).

8. As Stallings found, in her analysis of more than a dozen Third World instances of structural adjustment in the 1980s, "The new interest in structural reform did not come from efforts by domestic interest groups. While there were groups favouring such policies (probably strongest in Mexico), they were weak and had never had much success in advocating these policies before" (Stallings 1992, 76).

9. "[I]t may in fact be preferable for the governments of the late-late industrializing countries to be run by *tecnicos,* by groups of planner-technicians, rather than by the new industrialists themselves. It has been in fact due to the regulations issued by the *tecnicos* of the Kubitschek administration that backward linkage was *enforced* rapidly in the Brazilian automotive industry in the late fifties" (Hirschman 1968, 19).

Chapter 4
Local Reformers and Foreign Advisers

1. After all, one can argue, like Balcerowicz, that what happened to be most important in this respect was not country-specific but "therapy-specific" knowledge (Balcerowicz 1995, 247–48).

2. As to the relationship with the international financial organizations, Klaus liked to represent himself as a pioneer of stabilizing reforms and stability, independent from any external influence. "Fiscal policy, my fiscal policy in 1990 and in 1991, is based on something unique in this part of the world, on a surplus state budget, on no-deficit financing. And in this respect, ironically, we are probably the only country in the world which has no problems with the International Monetary Fund, because

our own policy prescriptions are probably harsher than the medicine the IMF is trying to prescribe to us" (Klaus 1992, 20).

3. For a list of Polish and foreign advisers see Balcerowicz (1995, 304, n. 13). Jeffrey Sachs is mentioned as one of them.

4. This corresponds to Stallings's findings on international influence on Third World economic policy making and also represents an attempt to apply Drake's findings on postcommunist cases (Stallings 1992, Drake 1994).

5. This section is based on Meaney (1995).

Chapter 5
Legacies of Communism and the Social Response to Economic Hardship

1. This chapter is partly based on my "Social Response to Neo-liberal Reforms in Eastern Europe in the 1990s," in *Inequality, Democracy and Economic Development,* ed. Manus Midlarsky (Cambridge and New York: Cambridge University Press, 1997).

2. There were IMF riots in Peru in almost every year between 1976 and 1985; in Jamaica in 1979 and 1985; in Argentina for each year between 1982 and 1985 (and sometimes several times a year) and in 1989; in Ecuador in 1982, 1983, 1985, and 1987; in Bolivia yearly between 1983 and 1987; in Chile in 1983 and 1985; in Brazil in 1983, 1985, 1986, and 1987; in Panama in 1983 and 1985; in Dominica in 1984, 1985, and 1987; in Haiti in 1985 and 1991; in Guatemala in 1985; in El Salvador in 1985 and 1986; in Mexico in 1986, 1989, and 1990; and in Venezuela in 1989.

The IMF riots were not restricted to Latin America. Similarly passionate mass anti-austerity protests were reported from Senegal in 1987, 1988, and 1989; Ghana in 1986 and 1987; Zambia in 1986 and 1987; Nigeria in 1986, 1987, and 1988; Egypt in 1977; Tunisia in 1984; Morocco in 1981; Algeria in 1988; the Philippines in 1985; Cameroon in 1990; the Ivory Coast in 1990; Gabon in 1990; Jordan in 1989; Kenya in 1990; Mali in 1991; Niger in 1990; and Trinidad and Tobago in 1990. For more details see also Walton and Seddon (1994), George (1992), Nelson (1990), Bates and Krueger (1993), Haggard and Webb (1994), and Drake (1994).

3. "In Russia, for example, total inward investment flows from 1989 to 1995 amounted to only one-third of Russian capital flight during reforms" (Plan Econ Report 1995, 1, quoted by Murrell 1996, 40).

4. See for the term and concept of hybridization accompanying privatization in the U.K., Abromeit (1986). See Stark (1996) for the most recent conceptualization of the hybridization of the East European economies.

5. The term "the political economy of patience" is used by Offe (1991, 887–88), based on Hirschman (1981, 39–58).

6. Important works conceptualizing the three realms include Stepan (1988) and Cohen and Arato (1992).

Chapter 6
Rethinking Populism under Postcommunism

1. The second part of this chapter is based on my "Demagogic Populism in Eastern Europe?" *Telos* no. 102: 91–106 (Winter 1995).

2. This part is based mainly on Dornbusch and Edwards (1989), Kaufman and Stallings (1991), Sturzenegger (1991), Bazdresch and Levy (1991), and Lago (1991).

3. Salvador Allende's Unidad Popular (UP) in Chile saw its share of the vote climb from the 36 percent it won in the presidential election of 1970 to about 50 percent in the 1971 municipal elections. Even in 1973, six months before the coup, the UP share stood at 44 percent. Similarly, Alán García, whose APRA party took 46 percent of the votes in the 1985 elections in Peru, won considerable support even from the business class for the success of his recovery strategy a year after his program started (Dornbusch and Edwards 1989). In Brazil, trust in José Sarney's government increased from 40 percent in September 1985 to 72 percent one year later, along with an impressive growth in Sarney's personal popularity. This may have been due to the initial results of the expansionary policies followed since early 1985, which were further enhanced by the Cruzado program, a heterodox stabilization plan (Kaufman 1990, 79).

4. Figures for Poland are from 1990, for Romania from 1992, for other countries from 1991 (United Nations Economic Survey on Europe 1994, 68).

5. The same effect can be studied in the Southern European political and economic transformations. Strong ties with the international financial community and especially with the EC definitely oriented both politics and economic policy making in Spain and Portugal after the democratic transition.

6. For the distinction between right-wing and left-wing populism in Hungary see Kis (1992).

7. For the opposite view see Stark and Bruszt (1996).

Chapter 7
Populist Transformation Strategies: The Hungarian Case in Comparative Perspective

1. Translations of quoted material in this chapter have been made by the author.

2. I am indebted to Kamilla Lányi for the point that not only István Csurka's but also József Torgyán's economic vision is close to the mainstream ideas on economic transformation.

3. See Gábor Tóka's excellent study, which gives empirical support to the idea that if, "in the transition period there is hardly any space left for ideologically motivated differences between their economic policies," competing politicians will attempt to differentiate themselves through their positions on noneconomic issues, such as abortion, nationalism, religious matters, or anticommunism (Tóka 1996, 1–2).

4. In Hungary, similar to earlier "bourgeois revolutions" that were spearheaded in the West by Ronald Reagan, Margaret Thatcher, and Helmut Kohl, "Issues that were once regarded as subjects of political choice have been effectively relegated to the constrained realm of technocratic, marginal tinkering. If there has been something like a 'bourgeois revolution'. . . it can be seen most clearly in these cases of politically induced convergence" (Pierson and Smith 1993, 509).

Chapter 8
Compensation as a Government Tactic

1. See Nelson (1989b). A careful and enlightening analysis on various kinds of pro-poor policies in different countries is offered by Carol Graham (1994).

2. For a recent approach to the problem of winners and losers in the context of East European transformations, see Rychard (1996).

3. In a very similar sense Andrzej Rychard, in the context of the postcommunist transformation, differentiated between "rule knowledgeable losers"—that is, those who understand the rules of transforming resources into capital, but do not have the resources with which to do it—and "rule ignorant winners," who, in turn, do not know the rules

that would enable them to transform their resources into capital. Under certain conditions both groups may finally end up either as winners or as losers (Rychard 1996). Which of these possibilities actually occurs is an important political question and, I believe, depends partly upon the pattern of compensation.

4. Positive examples of government assistance to help extricate short-term losers from their losers' position are described by Haggard, Cooper, and Moon (1993) about Korea; Önis and Webb (1994) about Turkey; and Doner and Laothamatas (1994) about Thailand.

Chapter 9
Conflict, Social Pact, and Democratic Development in Transforming Hungary

1. This chapter builds on my "Hunger Strikers, the Unions, the Government and the Parties. A Case-Study of Hungarian Transformation: Conflict, the Social Pact, and Democratic Development," Occasional Papers in European Studies 6 (Colchester: Centre for European Studies, Essex University, 1995). The case study is based mainly on the extensive coverage of events from October 1992 to January 1993 by the influential daily newspapers *Magyar Hírlap* and *Népszabadság,* and on private communication with the architects and participants in the pact.

2. The Hungarian VAT system, introduced in 1988, consisted of three tax rates: 0, 15, and 25 percent, affecting about 44, 5, and 46 percent of consumption expenditures respectively, while certain goods and services (connected mainly to health care, culture, education, and social care) were free of taxes.

3. The folklore of the movement includes the scandal of a journalist who was sent by her editor to spy on the movement's headquarters and try to discover whether the protest leaders were secretly eating at night. The suspicious hunger strikers soon asked the police to remove the journalist, who lost her job immediately thereafter (*Magyar Hírlap,* November 27, 1992). Other newspapers tried to ruin the credibility of protest leader Ferenc Valencsik by circulating rumors of his alleged thefts at his earlier jobs.

4. The portrait of the CRI is based mainly on Sziráczki, Szalai, and Ladó (1993), Herczog (1993), Bruszt (1994), and Héthy (1994).

5. As Sándor Bátonyi, chairman of the Solidarity Workers' Alliance put it, "The recent CRI negotiations were based on an attempt to black-

mail the government to accommodate the union agreement. That is why unions were so keen on keeping all problems together in an indivisible package" (*Magyar Hírlap,* November 23, 1992).

Chapter 10
Crisis-proof, Poor Democracies

1. Some of my conclusions and hypotheses are published in my "Crisis-proof Democracy: On Failed Predictions and the Realities of Eastern Europe's Transformations," *International Politics (Coexistence)* no. 34 (June 1997): 1–19.

Bibliography

A liberális megoldás. 1991. (The liberal solution.) Budapest: Szabad Demokraták Szövetsége.

"A Magyar Út Körök Mozgalom Programja (tervezet)." 1993. (The program of the Hungarian Way Circles movement [draft].) *Magyar Fórum,* June 24, 15–21.

"A Világbank Magyarországi Irodája, James D. Wolfensohn elnök úr részére." 1995. (To the Hungarian Bureau of the World Bank, and Mr. Chairman James D. Wolfensohn.) Advertisement, *Magyar Nemzet,* October 28.

Abromeit, Heidrun. 1986. "Privatisation in Great Britain." *Annales de l'Economie Publique, Sociale et Coopérative* no. 74: 153–80.

Acuña, Carlos H. 1994. "Politics and Economics in the Argentina of the Nineties (Or, Why the Future No Longer Is What It Used to Be)." In Smith, Acuña, and Gamarra, eds., *Democracy, Markets, and Structural Reform in Latin America,* 31–74.

Acuña, Carlos H., and William C. Smith. 1994. "The Political Economy of Structural Adjustment: The Logic of Support and Opposition to Neoliberal Reform." In Smith, Acuña, and Gamarra, eds., *Latin American Political Economy in the Age of Neoliberal Reform,* 17–67.

Ágh, Attila. 1991. "Transition to Democracy in East Central Europe: A Comparative View." In Szoboszlai, ed., *Democracy and Political Transformation,* 103–22.

———. 1994. "The Revival of Mixed Traditions: Democracy and Authoritarian Renewal in East-Central Europe." Paper presented at the Essex Conference on Democratic Modernisation in the Countries of East Central Europe." University of Essex in Colchester: May 11–14.

Alesina, Alberto. 1994. "Political Models of Macroeconomic Policy and Fiscal Reforms." In Haggard and Webb, eds., *Voting for Reform,* 37–60.

Anderson, Ronald W., Erik Berglöf, and Kálmán Mizsei. 1996. "Banking Sector Development in Central and Eastern Europe." *Summary of the Forum Report of the Economic Policy Initiative* No. 1. Warsaw, Prague, Budapest, Kosice, New York: Centre for

Economic Policy Research (CEPR), Institute for East-West Studies.

Aslund, Anders. 1991. "Principles of Privatisation." In Csaba, ed., *Systemic Change and Stabilization in Eastern Europe,* 17–31.

Balassa, Béla, et al. 1971. *The Structure of Protection in Developing Countries.* Baltimore: Johns Hopkins University Press.

Balcerowicz, Leszek, ed. 1995. *Socialism, Capitalism, Transformation.* Budapest, London, New York: Central European University Press.

Balcerowicz, Leszek, and Alan Gelb. 1995. "Macropolicies in Transition to a Market Economy: A Three-Year Perspective." In Balcerowicz, *Socialism, Capitalism, Transformation,* 202–31.

Barnes, Samuel, Max Kaase, et al. 1979. *Political Action: Mass Participation in Five Western Democracies.* Beverly Hills: Sage.

Bates, Robert H., and Paul Collier. 1993. "The Politics and Economics of Policy Reform in Zambia." In Bates and Krueger, eds., *Political and Economic Interactions in Economic Policy Reform,* 387–443.

Bates, Robert H., and A. O. Krueger, eds. 1993. *Political and Economic Interactions in Economic Policy Reform: Evidence from Eight Countries.* Oxford, U.K., and Cambridge, Mass.: Blackwell.

Bauer, Tamás, Anna Patkós, Károly Attila Soós, Éva Tárnok, and Péter Vince. 1980. *Járműprogram és gazdaságirányítás.* (The vehicle program and economic policy making.) Budapest: Magyar Tudományos Akadémia Közgazdaságtudományi Intézete.

Bazdresch, Carlos, and Santiago Levy. 1991. "Populism and Economic Policy in Mexico, 1970–1982." In Dornbusch and Edwards, eds., *The Macroeconomics of Populism in Latin America,* 223–62.

Betz, Hans-George. 1993. "The New Politics of Resentment: Radical Right-Wing Populist Parties in Western Europe." *Comparative Politics* 25, no. 4: 413–28.

Bhagwati, Jagdish. 1994. "Shock Treatments." *The New Republic,* March 28, 39–43.

Bibó, István. 1986. "Eltorzult magyar alkat, zsákutcás magyar történelem." (Distorted Hungarian build, deadlocked Hungarian history.) In *Válogatott tanulmányok. Második Kötet. 1945–1949.* (Selected works. Volume two. 1945–1949), 569–621. Budapest: Magvető Könyvkiadó.

Blanchard, Olivier, Rüdiger Dornbusch, Paul Krugman, Richard Layard, and Lawrence Summers. 1991. *Reform in Eastern Europe.* Cambridge, Mass., and London: MIT Press.

Boeckh, Andreas. 1993. "Populism in Latin America: Economic Crises and the Rise of New Development Coalitions." *Working Paper Series* 2. Budapest: Central European University, Political Science Department.

Borbándi, Gyula 1989. *A magyar népi mozgalom.* (The Hungarian populist movement) Budapest: Püski.

Botos, Balázs, and Gábor Papanek. 1984. *Kérdőjelek iparunk fejlesztésében.* (Question marks in our industrial development.) Budapest: Közgazdasági és Jogi Könyvkiadó.

Bozóki, András. 1994. "Vázlat három populizmusról: Egyesült Államok, Argentína és Magyarország." (An outline of three populisms: The United States, Argentina, and Hungary.) *Politikatudományi Szemle* 3, no. 3: 33–69.

Bozóki, András, and Miklós Sükösd. 1993. "Civil Society and Populism in the Eastern European Democratic Transitions." *Praxis International* 13, no. 3: 224–41.

Brada, Josef. 1996. "Privatization Is Transition—or Is It?" *Journal of Economic Perspectives* 10, no. 2: 67–88.

Brady, Henry E., and Cynthia S. Kaplan. 1994. "Eastern Europe and the Soviet Union." In *Referendums around the World: The Growing Use of Direct Democracy,* ed. David Butler and Austin Ranney, 174–217. Washington, D.C.: AEI Press.

Bresser Pereira, Luis Carlos. 1993. "Economic Reforms and Economic Growth: Efficiency and Politics in Latin America." In *Economic Reforms in New Democracies: A Social Democratic Approach,* ed. Luis Carlos Bresser Pereira, José María Maravall, and Adam Przeworski, 15–76. Cambridge: Cambridge University Press.

Bruszt, László. 1992. "Transformative Politics: Social Costs and Social Peace in East Central Europe." *East European Politics and Societies* 6, no. 1: 55–72.

———. 1993. "Why on Earth Would Eastern Europeans Support Capitalism? Democracy, Capitalism, and Public Opinion." Budapest: Central European University, Political Science Department. Photocopied.

———. 1994. "Az Antall-kormány és a gazdasági érdekképviseletek." (The Antall government and the economic interest associations.) In *Kormány a mérlegen, 1990–1994,* ed. Csaba Gombár, Elemér Hankiss, László Lengyel, and Györgyi Várnai, 208–30. Budapest: Korridor Politikai Kutatások Központja.

Bunce, Valerie. 1993. "Leaving Socialism: A 'Transition to Democracy'?" *Contention* 3, no. 1: 36–47.

———. 1994. "Sequencing of Political and Economic Reforms." *East-Central Europe in Transition*. Washington, D.C.: Joint Economic Committee, U.S. Congress.

———. 1995. "Should Transitologists Be Grounded?" *Slavic Review* 54, no. 1: 111–27.

Bunce, Valerie, and Mária Csanádi. 1992. "A Systematic Analysis of a Non-System: Post-Communism in Eastern Europe." In Szoboszlai, ed., *Flying Blind*, 204–26.

Callaghy, Thomas. 1989. "Toward State Capability and Embedded Liberalism in the Third World: Lessons for Adjustment." In Nelson, ed., *Fragile Coalitions*, 115–38.

———. 1990. "Lost between State and Market: The Politics of Economic Adjustment in Ghana, Zambia, and Nigeria." In Nelson, ed., *Economic Crisis and Policy Choice*, 257–320.

Cardoso, F. H., and Enzo Faletto. 1979. *Dependency and Development in Latin America*. Berkeley, Los Angeles, London: University of California Press.

Cohen, Jean, and Andrew Arato, 1992. *Civil Society and Political Theory*. Cambridge, Mass.: MIT Press.

Collins, Joseph, and John Lear. 1995. *Chile's Free-Market Miracle: A Second Look*. Oakland, Calif.: Institute for Food and Development Policy.

Commisso, Ellen. 1991. "Political Coalitions, Economic Choices." In Szoboszlai, ed., *Democracy and Political Transformation*, 122–37.

Commisso, Ellen, Steven Dubb, and Judy McTigue. 1992. "The Illusion of Populism in Latin America and East Central Europe." In Szoboszlai, ed., *Flying Blind*, 27–58.

Conaghan, Catherine M. 1989. "Loose Parties, Floating Politicians, and Institutional Stress: Presidentialism in Ecuador, 1979–1988." Paper prepared for the research symposium "Presidential or Parliamentary Democracy: Does It Make a Difference?" Georgetown University, Washington, D.C., May 14–16.

———. 1994. "Reconsidering Jeffrey Sachs and the Bolivian Economic Experiment." In Drake, ed., *Money Doctors*, 236–66.

Constable, Pamela, and Arturo Valenzuela. 1991. *A Nation of Enemies*. New York: Norton.

Cornea, Giovanni A., Richard Jolly, and Frances Stewart, eds. 1987. *Adjustment with a Human Face: Protecting the Vulnerable and Promoting Growth.* Oxford: Clarendon Press.

Crawford, Beverly, and Arend Lijphart. 1995. "Explaining Political and Economic Change in Post-Communist Eastern Europe: Old Legacies, New Institutions, Hegemonic Norms, and International Pressures." *Comparative Political Studies* 28, no. 2: 171–99.

Crowley, Stephen. 1994. "Barriers to Collective Action: Steelworkers and Mutual Dependence in the Former Soviet Union." *World Politics* no. 46: 589–615.

Csaba, László. 1984. *Kelet-Európa a világgazdaságban: Alkalmazkodás és gazdasági mechanizmus.* (Eastern Europe in the world economy. Adaptation and economic mechanism.) Budapest: Közgazdasági és Jogi Könyvkiadó.

———, ed. 1991. *Systemic Change and Stabilization in Eastern Europe.* Aldershot, Brookfield, U.S.A., Hong Kong, Singapore, Sydney: Dartmouth.

Csurka, István. 1992a. "Néhány gondolat a rendszerváltozás két esztendeje és az MDF új programja kapcsán." (Some thoughts on the first two years of the systemic change and the new program of the MDF.) *Magyar Fórum,* August 20.

———. 1992b. "Keserű Hátország." (Bitter hinterland.) *Magyar Fórum,* December 31.

———. 1993. "Gondolatok a Magyar Út Körök Mozgalom készülő programjához." (Thoughts on the new program of the movement of Hungarian Way Circles.) *Magyar Fórum,* June 3.

De Melo, Martha, Cevdet Denizer, and Alan Gelb. 1995. *From Plan to Market: Patterns of Transition.* Washington, D.C.: The World Bank.

Devatripont, Mathias, and Gerard Roland. 1994. "Eastern Europe: Less Haste, More Speed." *European Economic Perspectives* no. 3.

Díaz, Alvaro. 1993. "Restructuring and the New Working Classes in Chile: Trends in Waged Employment, Informality and Poverty, 1973–1990." Discussion Paper 47. United Nations Research Institute for Social Development. Geneva, Switzerland.

Dobry, Michel. 1992. "Problems and Illusions in the Study of Transition to Democracy." *Sisyphus Social Studies* 2, no. 8: 29–34.

Doner, Richard F., and Anek Laothamatas. 1994. "Thailand: Economic and Political Gradualism." In Haggard and Webb eds., *Voting for Reform,* 411–52.

Dornbusch, Rudiger. 1993. *Stabilization, Debt, and Reform: Policy Analysis for Developing Countries.* New York, London, Toronto, Sydney, Tokyo, Singapore: Harvester Wheatsheaf.

Dornbusch, Rudiger, and Sebastian Edwards. 1989. "The Macroeconomics of Populism in Latin America." World Bank Policy, Planning, and Research Working Papers 316. Washington, D.C.: The World Bank.

———, eds. 1991. *The Macroeconomics of Populism in Latin America.* Chicago: University of Chicago Press.

Drake, Paul W. 1982. "Conclusion: Requiem for Populism?" In *Latin American Populism in a Comparative Perspective,* ed. M. L. Conniff. Albuquerque: University of New Mexico Press.

———. 1989. "Debt and Democracy in Latin America, 1920s–1980s." In *Debt and Democracy in Latin America,* ed. Barbara Stallings and Robert Kaufman, 39–58. Boulder, San Francisco, and London: Westview Press.

———. 1991. "Comment." In Dornbusch and Edwards, eds., *The Macroeconomics of Populism in Latin America.*

———. 1994. "Introduction: The Political Economy of Foreign Advisers and Lenders in Latin America." In *Money Doctors, Foreign Debts, and Economic Reforms in Latin America from the 1890s to the Present,* ed. Paul W. Drake, a Scholarly Resources Inc. Imprint. Wilmington, Delaware, xi–xxxiii.

Eckstein, Susan. 1989. "Power and Popular Protest in Latin America." In *Power and Popular Protest: Latin American Social Movements,* ed. Susan Eckstein, 1–60. Berkeley: University of California Press.

Economist Book of World Vital Statistics, The. 1993. New York: Times Books, Random House.

Ekiert, Grzegorz. 1993. "Public Participation and Politics of Discontent in Post-Communist Poland, 1989–1992." Working Paper Series 30. Harvard University, Minda de Gunzburg Center for European Studies, Program on Central and Eastern Europe.

Ekiert, Grzegorz, and Jan Kubik. 1995. "Rebellious Civil Society and the Consolidation of Democracy in Poland, 1989–1993." Paper presented at the Fifth World Congress of Central and Eastern European Studies. International Council for Central and East European Studies, Warsaw, August 6–11.

———. 1996. "Strategies of Collective Protest in Democratizing Societies: Hungary, Poland and Slovakia since 1989." Paper prepared for the Tenth International Conference of Europeanists, Chicago, March 14–16.

Elster, Jon. 1993. "The Necessity and Impossibility of Simultaneous Economic and Political Reform." In *Constitutionalism and Democracy,* ed. Douglas Greenberg et al., 267–74. New York and Oxford: Oxford University Press.

Epstein, Edward C. 1989. "Austerity and Trade Unions in Latin America." In *Lost Promises: Debt, Austerity and Development in Latin America,* ed. William L. Canak, 169–89. Boulder and London: Westview Press.

Evans, Peter B. 1979. *Dependent Development.* Princeton, N. J.: Princeton University Press.

———.1992. "The State as Problem and Solution: Predation, Embedded Autonomy, and Structural Change." In Haggard and Kaufman, eds., *The Politics of Economic Adjustment,* 139–181.

Fischer, Stanley. 1990. "Comments." In Williamson, ed., *Latin American Adjustment.*

Fischer, Stanley, Ratna Sahay, and Carlos Végh. 1996. "Stabilisation and Growth in Transition Economies: The Early Experience." *Journal of Economic Perspectives* 10, no. 2: 45–66.

Fishlow, Albert. 1986. "The East European Debt Crisis in the Latin American Mirror." In *Power, Purpose, and Collective Choice: Economic Strategy in Socialist States,* ed. Ellen Commisso and Laura D'Andrea Tyson, 391–99. Ithaca and London: Cornell University Press.

Fordulat, biztonság, felemelkedés: Szabad Demokraták Szövetsége, választási program. 1994. (Turnabout, safety, rise: Alliance of Free Democrats, campaign program.) Budapest: Szabad Demokraták Szövetsége.

Foxley, Alejandro. 1983. *Latin American Experiments in Neoconservative Economics.* Berkeley: University of California Press.

Frenkel, Roberto, and Guillermo O'Donnell. 1979. "The 'Stabilization Programs' of the International Monetary Fund and Their Internal Impact." In *Capitalism and the State in U.S.–Latin American Relations,* ed. Richard R. Fagen, 171–203. Stanford, Calif.: Stanford University Press.

Frieden, Jeff. 1988. "Classes, Sectors, and Foreign Debt in Latin America." *Comparative Politics* (October): 1–20.

Gács, János. 1993. "A külkereskedelem liberalizálása Indonéziában." (Liberalization of foreign trade in Indonesia.) In *A nyitás gaz-*

daságpolitikája. Importliberalizálási tapasztalatok (Experiences with import liberalization), ed. Kamilla Lányi and Judit Szabó, 153–75. Budapest: A Magyar Tudományos Akadémia Közgazdaságtudományi Intézete, és KOPINT-DATORG Konjunktúrakutatási Alapítvány.

Galbraith, John Kenneth. 1991. "Political Change, Military Power: The Failed Economic Response." Paper presented at the IAREP/SASE Conference, Stockholm, June 16–19.

Geddes, Barbara. 1991. "The Effect of Political Institutions on the Feasibility of Structural Adjustment." Report prepared for the World Bank Project on the Political Economy of Adjustment in New Democracies: October. Photocopied.

George, Susan. 1992. *The Debt Boomerang: How Third World Debt Harms Us All.* Boulder and San Francisco: Westview Press.

———. 1993. "Debt as Warfare: An Overview of the Debt Crisis." *Third World Resurgence* no. 28: 14–19.

Gergely, Jenő, Ferenc Glatz, and Ferenc Pölöskei, eds. 1991. *Magyarországi Pártprogramok 1919–1944.* (Party programs in Hungary 1919–1944.) Budapest: Kossuth Könyvkiadó.

Gerschenkron, A. 1962. *Economic Backwardness in Historical Perspective.* Cambridge, Mass.: Belknap Press of Harvard University Press.

Gibson, Edward. 1995. "Populism across Developmental Eras: Rural and Urban in the Transformation of the PRI in Mexico and Perónism in Argentina." Paper presented at the Ninety-first Annual Meeting of the American Political Science Association, Chicago, August 31–September 3.

Gourevitch, Peter A. 1989. "Keynesian Politics: The Political Sources of Economic Policy Choices." In *The Political Power of Economic Ideas: Keynesianism across Nations,* ed. Peter A. Hall, 87–106. Princeton, N.J.: Princeton University Press.

Graham, Carol. 1994. *Safety Nets, Politics, and the Poor: Transitions to Market Economies.* Washington, D.C.: Brookings Institution.

Graham, Lawrence S. 1992. "Points of Commonality." *Problems of Communism* (May–June): 51–54.

Greskovits, Béla. 1986. "Fejlesztés és szelekció." (Development and selection.) *Tervgazdasági Fórum* no. 2.

———. 1987. "The Hungarian Credit Programme to Stimulate Exports." In *Investment System and Foreign Trade Implications in*

Hungary, ed. András Rába and Karl-Ernst Schenk, 189–229. Stuttgart and New York: Gustav Fischer Verlag.

———. 1988. "Western Technology Policies and the Approach of the Hungarian Industrial Policy." In *Acta Oeconomica: Special Supplement,* ed. Tamás Földi, 95–110.

Greskovits, Béla, and Katalin Máté. 1988. "A magyar-lengyel kooperáció két esete." (Two cases of Hungarian–Polish cooperation.) *Külgazdaság* no. 7, 21–31.

Grindle, M. S., and J. W. Thomas. 1991. *Public Choices and Policy Change: The Political Economy of Reform in Developing Countries.* Baltimore and London: Johns Hopkins University Press.

Grindle, Merilee S., and Francisco E. Thoumi. 1993. "Muddling toward Adjustment: The Political Economy of Economic Policy Change in Ecuador." In Bates and Krueger, eds., *Political and Economic Interactions in Economic Policy Reform,* 123–78.

Haggard, Stephan. 1989. *Pathways from the Periphery: The Politics of Growth in the Newly Industrializing Countries.* Ithaca and London: Cornell University Press.

———. 1990. "The Political Economy of the Philippine Debt Crisis." In Nelson, ed., *Economic Crisis and Policy Choice,* 3–32.

Haggard, Stephan, Richard N. Cooper, and Chung-in Moon. 1993. "Policy Reform in Korea." In Bates and Krueger, eds., *Political and Economic Interactions in Economic Policy Reform,* 294–332.

Haggard, Stephan, and Robert R. Kaufman. 1992. "The Political Economy of Inflation and Stabilization in Middle-Income Countries." In *The Politics of Economic Adjustment: International Constraints, Distributive Conflicts, and the State,* ed. Stephan Haggard and Robert R. Kaufman, 270–318. Princeton, N.J.: Princeton University Press.

———. 1995. *The Political Economy of Democratic Transitions.* Princeton, N.J.: Princeton University Press.

Haggard, Stephan, and Steven B. Webb. 1990. "Executive Summary: Political Economy of Structural Adjustment." Prepared for the World Bank Project on the Political Economy of Adjustment in New Democracies. Photocopied. Washington, D.C.

———. 1991. "What Do We Know about the Political Economy of Policy Reform?" Prepared for the World Bank Project on the Political Economy of Adjustment in New Democracies. Harvard University Center for International Affairs, The World Bank. Country Economics Department. Photocopied. Washington, D.C.

————, eds. 1994. *Voting for Reform: Democracy, Political Liberalization, and Economic Development.* Published for the World Bank. Oxford University Press.

Hausner, Jerzy. 1992. *Populist Threat in Transformation of Socialist Society.* Warsaw: Friedrich Ebert Foundation, Warsaw Office.

————. 1993. "Imperative vs. Interactive Strategy of Systemic Change in Central and Eastern Europe." Paper presented at the workshop "Institutionalising Democratic Transition," Radziejowice, Poland, November 16–17. Photocopied.

Herbst, Jeffrey, and Adebayo Olukoshi. 1994. "Nigeria: Economic and Political Reforms at Cross Purposes." In Haggard and Webb, eds., *Voting for Reform,* 453–502.

Herczog, László. 1993. "Az érdekegyeztetés tapasztalatai, továbbfejlesztése." (Experiences with interest reconciliation and its development.) Budapest. Photocopied.

Heredia, Blanca. 1994. "Making Economic Reform Politically Viable: The Mexican Experience." In Smith, Acuña, and Gamarra, eds., *Democracy, Markets, and Structural Reform in Latin America,* 265–97.

————. 1995. "Capital Emboldened: State–Business Relations in Post-Reform Mexico." Paper presented at the Ninety-first Annual Meeting of the American Political Science Association, Chicago, August 31–September 3. Photocopied.

Héthy, Lajos. 1994. "Tripartizmus és politikaformálás Magyarországon. Az 1992. novemberi ÉT megállapodás és összefüggései." (Tripartism and the formation of politics in Hungary. The CRI agreement of November 1992 and its context.) Munkaügyi Kutatóintézet és Magyar Munkaügyi Kapcsolatok Társaság—a Nemzetközi Munkaügyi Hivatal Támogatásával. Tripartizmus Közép és Keleteurópában. Nemzetközi Szakértői Kerekasztal Tanácskozás. Budapest, May 26–27. Photocopied.

Hirschman, Albert O. 1968. "The Political Economy of Import-Substituting Industrialization in Latin America." *Quarterly Journal of Economics* 82, no. 1: 1–32.

————. 1970. *Exit, Voice, and Loyalty: Responses to Decline in Firms, Organizations, and States.* Cambridge, Mass., and London: Harvard University Press.

————. 1981. *Essays in Trespassing: Economics to Politics and Beyond.* Cambridge and New York: Cambridge University Press.

Jameson, K. P. 1985. "Latin American Structuralism: A Methodological Perspective." Working Paper 43. Helen Kellogg Institute for International Studies, University of Notre Dame, Notre Dame, Indiana.

Jeffries, Ian. 1993. *Socialist Economies and the Transition to the Market.* London and New York: Routledge.

Johnson, Simon, and Marzena Kowalska. 1994. "Poland: The Political Economy of Shock Therapy." In Haggard and Webb, eds., *Voting for Reform*, 185–241.

Jowitt, Ken. 1992. "The Leninist Legacy." In *Eastern Europe in Revolution,* ed. Ivo Banac, 207–24. Ithaca and London: Cornell University Press.

Juberías, Carlos F. 1992. "The Breakdown of the Czecho-Slovak Party System." In Szoboszlai, *Flying Blind,* 147–76.

Juhász, Gyula. 1983. *Uralkodó eszmék Magyarországon 1939–1944.* (Regnant ideas in Hungary 1939–1944.) Budapest: Kossuth Könyvkiadó.

Ka, Samba, and Nicholas Van de Walle. 1994. "Senegal: Stalled Reform in a Dominant Party System." In Haggard and Webb, eds., *Voting for Reform,* 290–359.

Kahler, Miles. 1989. "International Financial Institutions and the Politics of Adjustment." In Nelson, ed., *Fragile Coalitions,* 139–60.

———. 1990. "Orthodoxy and Its Alternatives: Explaining Approaches to Stabilization and Adjustment." In Nelson, ed., *Economic Crisis and Policy Choice,* 33–63.

———. 1992. "External Influence, Conditionality, and the Politics of Adjustment." In Haggard and Kaufman, eds., *The Politics of Economic Adjustment,* 89–138.

Kaufman, Robert R. 1990. "Stabilisation and Adjustment in Argentina, Brazil and Mexico." In Nelson, ed., *Economic Crisis and Policy Choice,* 63–112.

Kaufman, Robert R., Carlos Bazdresch, and Blanca Heredia. 1994. "Mexico: Radical Reform in a Dominant Party System." In Haggard and Webb, eds., *Voting for Reform,* 369–410.

Kaufman, Robert R., and Barbara Stallings. 1991. "The Political Economy of Latin American Populism." In Dornbusch and Edwards, eds., *The Macroeconomics of Populism in Latin America,* 15–33.

Kis, János. 1992. "Gondolatok a közeljövőről." (Thoughts about the near future.) *Magyar Hírlap*, December 24.

Klaus, V. 1992. *Dismantling Socialism: A Preliminary Report (A Road to Market Economy II)*. Prague: Top Agency.

Klaus, Václav, and Tomás Jezek. 1991. "Social Criticism, False Liberalism, and Recent Changes in Czechoslovakia." *East European Politics and Societies* 5, no. 1: 26–40.

Kőhegyi, Kálmán. 1994. "A szociális paktum politikai veszélyeiről." (On the dangers of the social pact.) Budapest: Pénzügykutató Rt. Photocopied.

Kopácsy, S. 1995. *Van kiút!* (There is a way out.) Budapest: Belvárosi Könyvkiadó.

Kornai, János. 1980. *Economics of Shortage*. Amsterdam: North-Holland.

———. 1990. *The Road to a Free Economy*. New York: Norton.

———. 1992a. *The Socialist System: The Political Economy of Communism*. Princeton, N. J.: Princeton University Press, and Oxford: Oxford University Press.

———. 1992b. "Visszaesés, veszteglés vagy fellendülés." (Recession, stagnation, or recovery?) *Magyar Hírlap*, December 24.

———. 1993. "Transzformációs visszaesés: Egy általános jelenség vizsgálata a magyar fejlődés példáján" (Transformational recession: A general phenomenon examined through the example of Hungary's development.) *Közgazdasági Szemle* 40, nos 7–8: 569–599.

———. 1995. "Négy jellegzetesség: A magyar fejlődés politikai gazdaságtani megközelítésben." (Four characteristics: Hungarian development in a political economy approach.) Discussion Papers 19. Budapest: Collegium Budapest/Institute for Advanced Study.

———. 1996. "Kiigazítás recesszió nélkül: Esettanulmány a magyar stabilizációról." (Correction without recession: Case study about the Hungarian stabilization.) *Közgazdasági Szemle* 43, nos. 7–8: 585–613.

Kovács, János M. 1994. "Planning the Transformation? (Notes about the Legacy of the Reform Economists)." In *Transition to Capitalism? The Communist Legacy in Eastern Europe*, ed. János M. Kovács, 21–46. New Brunswick, N.J., and London: Transaction Publishers.

Köves, András. 1995. "A stabilizáció gazdaságpolitikájáról." (On the economic policy of stabilization.) *Népszabadság*, April 1.

Krueger, Anne O., and Ilter Kuran. 1993. "The Politics and Economics of Turkish Policy Reforms in the 1980s." In Bates and Krueger, eds., *Political and Economic Interactions in Economic Policy Reform*, 333–86.

Lackó, M. 1975. *Válságok—választások.* (Crises—choices.) Budapest: Gondolat.

Ladányi, János, and Iván Szelényi. 1995. "Posztkommunista New Deal?" (Postcommunist New Deal?) *Népszabadság*, November 11.

Lago, Ricardo. 1991. "The Illusion of Pursuing Redistribution through Macropolicy: Peru's Heterodox Experience, 1985–1990." In Dornbusch and Edwards, eds., *The Macroeconomics of Populism in Latin America*, 263–323.

Laki, Mihály. 1993. "Chances for the Acceleration of Transition: The Case of Hungarian Privatization." Budapest: *East European Politics and Societies 7*, no. 3: 440–451.

Lal, Deepak, and Sylvia Maxfield. 1993. "The Political Economy of Stabilization in Brazil." In Bates and Krueger, eds., *Political and Economic Interactions in Economic Policy Reform*, 27–77.

Lányi, Kamilla. 1994. "Alkalmazkodás és gazdasági visszaesés Magyarországon és más országokban. I. Tények és magyarázatok." (Adjustment and economic recession in Hungary and other countries. Part 1: Facts and explanations.) *Társadalmi Szemle* 49, no. 12: 13–25.

———. 1995. "Alkalmazkodás és gazdasági visszaesés Magyarországon és más országokban. II. Gazdaságpolitika és szelekció." (Adjustment and economic recession in Hungary and other countries. Part 2: Economic policy and selection.) *Társadalmi Szemle* 50, no. 1: 3–20.

Leith, J. Clark, and Michael F. Lofchie. 1993. "The Political Economy of Structural Adjustment in Ghana." In Bates and Krueger, eds., *Political and Economic Interactions in Economic Policy Reform*, 225–93.

Lipton, David, and Jeffrey Sachs. 1990. "Creating a Market Economy in Eastern Europe: The Case of Poland." Paper presented at the Brookings Institution Panel on Economic Activity, Washington, D.C., April 5–6. Photocopied.

Little, I., T. Scitovsky, and M. Scott. 1970. *Trade and Industry in Some Developing Countries*. Oxford: Oxford University Press.

Lomax, Bill. 1993. "From Death to Resurrection: The Metamorphosis of Power in Eastern Europe." Budapest. Photocopied.

Londregan, John, and Kenneth Poole. 1990. "Poverty, the Coup Trap, and the Seizure of Executive Power." *World Politics* 42: 151–83.

Major, Iván. 1992. "Privatisation in Eastern Europe: An Alternative Approach." Discussion Papers 2. Budapest: Institute of Economics, Hungarian Academy of Sciences.

Meaney, Constance S. 1995. "Foreign Experts, Capitalists, and Competing Agendas: Privatization in Poland, the Czech Republic, and Hungary." In "Post-Communist Transformation in Eastern Europe," special issue, ed. Beverly Crawford and Arend Lijphart, *Comparative Political Studies* 28, no. 2: 275–305.

Meszleny, László. 1995. "A magyar adósságkezelés a rendszerváltozáskor." (Hungarian debt management during systemic change.) *Magyar Nemzet,* December 23.

Morales, Juan A. 1988. "The End of the Bolivian Hyperinflation." *Vierteljahresberichte* no. 114. Forschungsinstitut der Friedrich Ebert Stiftung, Bonn.

Murrell, Peter. 1992. "Conservative Political Philosophy and the Strategy of Economic Transition." *East European Politics and Societies:* 6, no. 1: 3–6.

———. 1996. "How Far Has the Transition Progressed?" *Journal of Economic Perspectives* 10, no. 2: 25–44.

Nagy, András. 1989. "Külkereskedelmi orientációváltást." (Let's change the orientation of foreign trade.) *Közgazdasági Szemle* 29, no. 9: 18–32.

Nelson, Joan M. 1989a. "Overview: The Politics of Long-Haul Economic Reform." In *Fragile Coalitions: The Politics of Economic Adjustment,* ed. Joan M. Nelson, 3–26. New Brunswick, N.J., and Oxford: Transaction Publishers.

———. 1989b. "The Politics of Pro-Poor Adjustment." In Nelson, ed., *Fragile Coalitions,* 95–114.

———, ed. 1990. *Economic Crisis and Policy Choice: The Politics of Adjustment in the Third World.* Princeton, N.J.: Princeton University Press.

———. 1990. "Introduction: The Politics of Economic Adjustment in Developing Nations." In Nelson, ed., *Economic Crisis and Policy Choice,* 3–32.

———. 1991. "Organized Labor, Politics, and Labor Market Flexibility in Developing Countries." *World Bank Research Observer* 6, no. 1: 37–56.

———. 1992. "Poverty, Equity, and the Politics of Adjustment." In Haggard and Kaufman, eds., *The Politics of Economic Adjustment,* 221–69.

———, ed. 1994. *Intricate Links: Democratization and Market Reforms in Latin America and Eastern Europe.* New Brunswick, N.J., and Oxford: Transaction Publishers.

———. 1994. "Overview: How Market Reforms and Democratic Consolidation Affect Each Other." In Nelson, ed., *Intricate Links,* 1–36.

Norton, Robert E. 1994. "Jeff Sachs—Doctor Debt." In Drake, ed., *Money Doctors,* 231–35.

O'Donnell, Guillermo. 1992. "Delegative Democracy?" Working Paper 172. Helen Kellogg Institute for International Studies, University of Notre Dame, Notre Dame, Indiana.

———. 1993. "On the State, Democratisation, and Some Conceptual Problems: A Latin American View with Glances at Some Post-communist Countries." *World Development* 21, no. 8: 1355–1369.

O'Donnell, Guillermo, and Philippe C. Schmitter. 1986. *Transitions from Authoritarian Rule: Tentative Conclusions about Uncertain Democracies.* Baltimore and London: Johns Hopkins University Press.

Offe, Claus. 1991. "Capitalism by Democratic Design? Democratic Theory Facing the Triple Transition in East Central Europe." *Social Research* 58, no. 4: 865–92.

———. 1993. "The Politics of Social Policy in East European Transitions: Antecedents, Agents, and Agenda of Reform." *Social Research* 60, no. 4: 649–84.

Önis, Ziya, and Steven B. Webb. 1994. "Turkey: Democratisation and Adjustment from Above." In Haggard and Webb, eds., *Voting for Reform,* 128–84.

Ost, David. 1992. "Labour and Societal Transition." *Problems of Communism* 33 *nos* 5–6: 48–51.

———. 1995. "Labor, Class, and Democracy: Shaping Political Antagonisms in Post-Communist Society." In *Markets, States, and Democracy: The Political Economy of Post-Communist Transformation,* ed. Beverly Crawford, 177–203. Boulder, San Francisco, and London: Westview Press.

Pfeffermann, Guy, P. 1991. "Poverty Alleviation." In *Politics and Policy Making in Developing Countries,* ed. Gerald M. Meier, 179–199. San Francisco: ICS Press.

Pierson, Paul, and Miriam Smith. 1993. "Bourgeois Revolutions? The Policy Consequences of Resurgent Conservatism." *Comparative Political Studies* 25, no. 4: 487–520.

Plan Econ Report. 1995. "The Scale and Significance of Foreign Investment in Russia." Supplement. 11: 30–31.

Pontusson, Jonas. 1995. "Explaining the Decline of European Social Democracy: The Role of Structural Economic Change." *World Politics* no. 47: 495–533.

Przeworski, A. 1991. *Democracy and the Market: Political and Economic Reforms in Eastern Europe and Latin America.* Cambridge and New York: Cambridge University Press.

Remmer, Karen. 1991. "The Political Impact of Economic Crisis in Latin America in the 1980s." *American Political Science Review* 85, no. 3: 777–800.

Roberts, Kenneth M. 1995. "Neoliberalism and the Transformation of Populism in Latin America: The Peruvian Case." *World Politics* no. 48: 82–116.

Rodrik, Dani. 1994. "The Rush to Free Trade in the Developing World: Why So Late? Why Now? Will It Last?" In Haggard and Webb, eds., *Voting for Reform,* 61–88.

Roland, Gerard. 1991. "Political Economy of Sequencing Tactics in the Transition Period." In Csaba, ed., *Systemic Change and Stabilisation in Eastern Europe,* 47–63.

———. 1992. "Issues in the Political Economy of Transition." Paper presented at the conference "The Economic Consequences of the East." Frankfurt am Main, March 22–23. Photocopied.

Roxborough, Ian. 1992. "Inflation and Social Pacts in Brazil and Mexico." *Journal of Latin American Studies* 24, no. 3: 639–64.

Rueschemeyer, Dietrich. 1992. "The Development of Civil Society after Authoritarian Rule." Brown University and Swedish Collegium for Advanced Study in the Social Sciences, November. Photocopied.

Rychard, Andrzej. 1996. "Beyond Gains and Losses: In Search of 'Winning Losers'." *Social Research* 63, no. 2: 465–85.

Sachs, Jeffrey D. 1989. "Social Conflict and Populist Policies in Latin America." Working Paper 2897. National Bureau of Economic Research.

———. 1990. "Eastern Europe's Economies: What Is to Be Done?" *The Economist,* January 12, 19–24.

———. 1994. "Betrayal." *The New Republic,* January 31, 14–18.

Sachs, Jeffrey, and David Lipton. 1990. "Poland's Economic Reform." *Foreign Affairs* 69, no. 3: 47–65.

Schamis, Hector. 1995. "Collective Action, Institution Building, and the State: The Politics of Economic Reform in Latin America."

Paper presented at the Ninety-first Annual Meeting of the American Political Science Association, Chicago, August 31–September 3.

Schmitter, Philippe C., and Terry L. Karl. 1994. "The Conceptual Travels of Transitologists and Consolidologists: How Far to the East Should They Attempt to Go?" *Slavic Review* 53, no. 1: 173–85.

Sík, Endre. 1994. "From the Multicoloured to the Black and White Economy: The Hungarian Second Economy and the Transformation." *International Journal of Urban and Regional Research* 18: 46–70.

Silva, Patricio. 1994. "Technocrats and Politics in Chile: From the Chicago Boys to the CIEPLAN Monks." In Drake, ed., *Money Doctors*, 205–30.

Smith, William C., Carlos H. Acuña, and Eduardo A. Gamarra, eds. 1994a. *Democracy, Markets, and Structural Reform in Latin America*. New Brunswick, N.J., and London: Transaction Publishers.

———. 1994b. *Latin American Political Economy in the Age of Neoliberal Reform: Theoretical and Comparative Perspectives for the 1990s*. New Brunswick, N.J., and London: Transaction Publishers.

Smolar, Alexander. 1996. "From Party State to Liberal Democratic State in Central and Eastern Europe." Photocopied.

Stallings, Barbara. 1992. "International Influence on Economic Policy: Debt, Stabilisation and Structural Reform." In Haggard and Kaufman, eds., *The Politics of Economic Adjustment*, 41–88.

Stallings, Barbara, and Philip Brock. 1993. "The Political Economy of Economic Adjustment: Chile, 1973–90." In Bates and Krueger, eds., *Political and Economic Interactions in Economic Policy Reform*, 78–122.

Stark, David. 1996. "Recombinant Property in East European Capitalism." *American Journal of Sociology* 101, no. 4: 993–1027.

Stark, David, and László Bruszt. 1996. "Postsocialist Pathways: Transforming Politics and Property in East Central Europe." Cambridge University Press. In press.

Stenzel, Konrad. 1988. "Markets against Politics in the Chilean Dictatorship—The Role of Professional Economists." *Vierteljahresberichte* no. 113: 325–34. Forschungsinstitut der Friedrich Ebert Stiftung, Bonn.

Stepan, A. 1988. *Rethinking Military Politics.* Princeton, N.J.: Princeton University Press.

Sturzenegger, Federico A. 1991. "Description of a Populist Experience: Argentina, 1973–1976." In Dornbusch and Edwards, eds., *The Macroeconomics of Populism in Latin America,* 77–118.

Szalai, Erzsébet. 1995. "Feljegyzések a cethal gyomrából." (Notes from the stomach of the whale.) *Kritika* no. 11. Budapest.

Szárszó 1943: Dokumentumok. (Szárszó 1943: Documents.) Eds Győrffy, Sándor, Pintér, István, Sebestyén, László, and Sipos, Attila. 1983. Budapest: Kossuth Könyvkiadó.

Sziráczki, György, Júlia Szalai, and Mária Ladó. 1993. "Labour Market Trends and Policies: Hungary." In *Structural Change in Central and Eastern Europe: Labour Market and Social Policy Implications,* ed. Georg Fischer and Guy Standing, 95–132. Paris: OECD.

Szoboszlai, György, ed. 1991. *Democracy and Political Transformation: Theories and East-Central European Realities.* Budapest: Hungarian Political Science Association.

——, ed. 1992. *Flying Blind: Emerging Democracies in East-Central Europe,* Budapest: Hungarian Political Science Association.

Tardos, Márton, ed. 1980. *Vállalati magatartás—vállalati környezet.* (Enterprise behavior—Enterprise Environment.) Budapest: Közgazdasági és Jogi Könyvkiadó.

Tarrow, Sidney. 1991. "Understanding Political Change in Eastern Europe." *PS: Political Science and Politics* no. 3: 12–20.

——. 1994. *Power in Movement: Social Movements, Collective Action, and Politics.* Cambridge and New York: Cambridge University Press.

Tények könyve '93. (Book of facts '93.) 1993. Budapest: Gregor Média Kft.

Tilly, C. 1978. *From Mobilization to Revolution: Readings.* Massachusetts: Addison-Wesley.

——. 1986. *The Contentious French.* Cambridge: Harvard University Press.

Tóka, Gábor. 1995. "Political Parties and the Bases of Party Support in East Central Europe." Paper prepared for the conference "Consolidating the Third Wave Democracies: Trends and Challenges," organized by the Institute for National Policy Research, Taipei, and the International Forum for Democratic Studies—National Endowment for Democracy, Washington: in Taipei, August 27–30. Photocopied.

————. 1996. "The Impact of Various Policy Domains on Politicians' Coalition Preferences in East Central Europe." Paper presented at the workshop "Transition and Power" organized by the European Science Foundation, Cambridge, April 19–21. Photocopied.

Torgyán, József. 1995a. *Hazánk Holnap, Kisgazda Program I.* (Our country, tomorrow.) Supplement. *Független Magyar Újság.* Budapest: October.

————. 1995b. *Kisgazda Program II. Az Alternatív Gazdaságpolitika: Célok és Lehetőségek.* (Alternative economic policy: Goals and possibilities.) Supplement. *Független Magyar Újság.* Budapest: October.

Tóth, István J. 1992. "Gazdasági szervezetek és érdekérvényesítési módszerek (első megközelítés)." (Economic organizations, chances for interest representation.) Budapest. Photocopied.

Ungvárszki, Á. 1989. *Gazdaság-Politikai ciklusok Magyarországon, 1948–1988.* (Economic and political cycles in Hungary, 1948–1988.) Budapest: Közgazdasági és Jogi Könyvkiadó.

United Nations Economic Survey on Europe. 1994. New York and Geneva: United Nations.

Urbán, László. 1991. "Why Was the Hungarian Transition Exceptionally Peaceful?" In Szoboszlai, ed., *Democracy and Political Transformation,* 303–9.

Valenzuela, Samuel J. 1991. "Labor Movements and Political Systems: A Conceptual and Typological Analysis." Working Paper 185. Helen Kellogg Institute for International Studies, University of Notre Dame, Notre Dame, Indiana.

Voszka, Éva. 1992. "Not Even the Contrary Is True: The Transfigurations of Centralisation and Decentralisation." *Acta Oeconomica* 44, no. 1–2: 77–94.

Walters, Alan. 1992. "The Transition to a Market Economy." In *The Emergence of Market Economies in Eastern Europe,* ed. Christopher Clague and Gordon C. Rausser, 99–108. Cambridge, Mass., and Oxford: Blackwell.

Walton, John. 1989. "Debt, Protest, and the State in Latin America." In Eckstein, ed., *Power and Popular Protest,* 299–328.

Walton, John, and D. Seddon. 1994. *Free Markets and Food Riots: The Politics of Global Adjustment.* Oxford, and Cambridge, Mass.: Blackwell.

Waterbury, John. 1989. "The Political Management of Economic Adjustment and Reform." In Nelson, ed., *Fragile Coalitions,* 39–57.

Williamson, John. 1990. "What Washington Means by Policy Reform." In *Latin American Adjustment: How Much Has Happened?* ed. John Williamson, 7–20. Institute for International Economics, Washington, D.C.

———. 1993. "Democracy and the 'Washington Consensus'." *World Development* 21, no. 8: 1329–36.

Wojtyna, Andrzej. 1992. "In Search of a New Economic Role for the State in the Post-Socialist Countries." In *Mixed Economies in Europe,* ed. Wolfgang Blaas and John Foster, 158–77.: Aldershot, Vermont and Edward Elgar Publishing Limited.

World Bank. 1988. *Adjustment Lending: An Evaluation of Ten Years Experience.* Policy and Research Series 1. Washington, D.C.: The World Bank.

World Development Report 1991: The Challenge of Development. 1991. Published for the World Bank. Oxford University Press.

Index